THE BRINY SOUTH

THE BRINY SOUTH

A THEORY IN FORMS BOOK
A series edited by   Nancy Rose Hunt and Achille Mbembe

DISPLACEMENT AND SENTIMENT

IN THE INDIAN OCEAN WORLD

Nienke Boer

Duke University Press   *Durham and London*   2023

© 2023 DUKE UNIVERSITY PRESS
All rights reserved
Designed by Matthew Tauch
Typeset in Minion Pro and Trade Gothic LT Std
by Westchester Publishing Services

Library of Congress Cataloging-in-Publication Data
Names: Boer, Nienke, [date] author.
Title: The briny South : displacement and sentiment in the Indian Ocean world / Nienke Boer.
Other titles: Theory in forms.
Description: Durham : Duke University Press, 2023. | Series: A Theory in forms book | Includes bibliographical references and index.
Identifiers: LCCN 2022039964 (print)
LCCN 2022039965 (ebook)
ISBN 9781478019558 (paperback)
ISBN 9781478016915 (hardcover)
ISBN 9781478024200 (ebook)
Subjects: LCSH: Forced labor—Indian Ocean Region—History. | Labor in literature. | Indian Ocean Region—Biography—Sources. | Netherlands—Colonies—Africa. | Netherlands—Colonies—Asia. | Great Britain—Colonies—Africa. | Great Britain—Colonies—Asia. | BISAC: HISTORY / Africa / East | HISTORY / Asia / South / General
Classification: LCC HD4875.I55 B64 2023 (print) | LCC HD4875.I55 (ebook) | DDC 325.492—dc23/eng/20221117
LC record available at https://lccn.loc.gov/2022039964
LC ebook record available at https://lccn.loc.gov/2022039965

COVER ART:
"Cape Town: Number of Males/Number of Females" (detail). In "Various Slave Returns, 1816–1834," Slave Office (SO) 7/36, p. 183, Western Cape Archives and Records Service, Cape Town, South Africa.

Kerst & Marieta Boer

CONTENTS

Acknowledgments · ix

Introduction · 1
Enslaved, Indentured, Interned

1 Representing Speech in Bondage in the Court Records of the Dutch Cabo de Goede Hoop, 1652–1795 · 17

2 Silencing the Enslaved: The Aesthetics of Abolitionism in the British Cape Colony, 1795–1834 · 48

3 "Grievances More Sentimental than Material": Representing Indentured Labor in Natal, 1860–1915 · 82

4 A Sentimental Education in Boer War Imprisonment Camps in South Asia, 1899–1902 · 109

5 Sentiment and the Law in Early South African Indian Writing, 1893–1960 · 132

Coda · 154
No Human Footprints

Notes · 161
Bibliography · 187
Index · 205

ACKNOWLEDGMENTS

This book has taken both far too long and the exact amount of time it needed, and I am grateful to the various institutions that made it possible for me to write it. The book was supported by funding from New York University and generous grants and invaluable sabbatical time provided by Yale-NUS College in Singapore. I am grateful for all the individuals and institutions who still believe in the humanities.

Written in New York, London, Cape Town, and Singapore, I'd like to think that this book has absorbed some of the spirit of these port cities. I remain deeply thankful for the support and feedback from my earliest readers—Mark Sanders, Isabel Hofmeyr, Kristin Ross, Manu Goswami, and Jay Garcia. Other important navigators on this journey have been Gaurav Desai, Meg Samuelson, and Pallavi Rastogi. I have benefited from various workshops here in Singapore and would like to thank Chitra Venkataramani, Tapsi Mathur, Anne Thell, Christine Walker, Gretchen Head, Robin Zheng, Gabriele Koch, Geoff Baker, Rajeev Patke, Christopher Trigg, and Kate Wakely-Mulroney for their suggestions and encouragement. My other colleagues in Singapore, including Shaoling Ma, Mira Seo, Andrew Hui, Steven Green, Carissa Foo, Ila Tyagi, Laurel Fantauzzo, Rohan Mukherjee, Anju Mary Paul, Clay Eaton, Jessica Hanser, Nurfadzilah Yahaya, Stuart Strange, and Joanne Roberts, have been immensely helpful in this process. I cannot overstate how wonderful, brilliant, supportive, and insightful the students at Yale-NUS have been—teaching them has enriched my writing tremendously. I hope this book acts as a testament to the extraordinary intellectual endeavor that briefly was Yale-NUS College.

I am also indebted to the organizers and attendees of various panels and conferences where I have been able to present on this work and to Magalí Armillas-Tiseyra, Anne Garland Mahler, and Laura T. Murphy for helping me think through some of the central ideas in the book by inviting me to contribute to various publications: *Global South Studies: A Collective Publication* with *The Global South*; a special issue of *Comparative Literature Studies* (vol. 58, no. 3, 2021) on "New Directions in Global South Studies" (which debuted the concept of the *briny South*); and the *Cambridge Companion to Global Literature and Slavery*. I am also grateful to readers and editors at the *Journal of Commonwealth Literature* (vol. 54, no. 3, 2019) and *Research in African Literatures* (vol. 47, no. 4, 2016), in which portions of chapters four and five appeared.

Behind the scenes, the team at Duke University Press, especially Elizabeth Ault and Benjamin Kossak, have been supportive, positive, and reassuring. The comments by the reviewers have improved this book immensely. I gratefully acknowledge the archivists at the British Library, the National Archives in Kew, the War Museum of the Boer Republics, the Free State Archives Repository, the National Archives Repository in Pretoria, the Western Cape Archives, and the Gandhi-Luthuli Centre at the University of KwaZulu-Natal, who are all performing heroic tasks. I would like to thank Erika le Roux, Vicky Heunis, and Etna Labuschagne particularly, and I acknowledge the Western Cape Archives and Records Services and the War Museum of the Boer Republics for their permission to reproduce items from their holdings. Tara Mendola capably provided developmental editing for some of these pages.

My friends and family have also been living with this book in different ways. Beth, Kav, Sanhita, Sam, Helmae, Scott, Chan, Amity, Jina, Nick, Carlos, Peter, Magalí, Agata, Elizabeth, Amy, Amanda, Ozen, Sonia, Emma, Bilal, Angela, Shailey, Rohan, Chitra, Tapsi, Christine, Clay, Ila: you have variously proofread, listened to me complain, bought me coffee and drinks, stayed up late, written next to me, lent me clothes, made me laugh, and otherwise carried me during the hard times, and I am thankful. My in-laws are far more amazing than anyone deserves. Elliot, Kathy, Ian, Adina, Erin, Germán, Aran, Karolina, Lauren, Luciano, and all my nieces and nephews—thank you for taking this only child into your busy, wonderful, warm embrace. My adopted US family—Heather, John, and Elaine—helped me survive the cold winters and supported this project in myriad ways. I also can't neglect the very important emotional support provided by various dogs over the years—the three generations of Boxer clowns—Zella, Emma, and Lucy—as well as Bubbles, Foxy, Petite, and, of course, the sagest Diogenes. Thanks to the extended Boer and Groeneveld families who have loved and encouraged me always. Nienke and Johan Esterhuizen have been constants in my peripatetic life: your house is home.

It is impossible to list the ways in which my parents, Kerst and Marieta Boer, have supported me: you are the pointy bit of my heart, the little ears of the hippopotamus, the mountain keeping the monsters away. Words clearly cannot convey what you mean to me, but please accept this book, full of words, dedicated to you.

And finally, my beloved, Kevin, whose wedding vows included a lifetime of proofreading (all errors remain mine): you remain my perfect gentleman, my safe space, and my favorite travel companion. Wherever we go, we go together.

INTRODUCTION

Enslaved, Indentured, Interned

Upon receiving these blows the prisoner expressed himself, without equivocating, as such: I do not want to be silent, and must retain my right to speak; adding: Sir must stop hitting me like that.—CAESAR VAN MADAGASCAR (1793)

The Council of Justice at the Cape of Good Hope tried Caesar van Madagascar in 1793 for grabbing and slicing in two the *sjambok* (a kind of rawhide whip) that the slaveholder, Daniel Malan, had been using to whip him.[1] Caesar was sentenced to twenty-five years of hard labor, in chains, on Robben Island. His words underscore what seem to be self-evident truths: that the right to speak is a necessary precondition for resistance and speech a form of expressing the internal self. In the absence of autobiographical narratives by the enslaved from the Indian Ocean world, it is tempting to turn to the detailed legal records from the Dutch and later British courts in these regions to find the voices of the enslaved.

These represented voices, however, cannot be taken at face value, as they are always mediated through documents of imperial power. *The Briny South: Displacement and Sentiment in the Indian Ocean World* examines the supposed sentiments of the disempowered as they appear in various genres: court records, political pamphlets, memoir, and fiction. From the seventeenth-century Dutch colonial occupation at the Cape of Good Hope to the twentieth-century segregationist apartheid state, this book examines the danger of sentiment when recorded in archives—both legal and literary—of imperial violence. Throughout, I chart a path between analyzing the imperial context of subaltern sentiment and attending to breaks in the archive of imperial control, through which a glimpse of "subjectivity in bondage" can be seen.[2] Between these two forms of analysis lies a history of sentiment as violence in the development of a racialized order in the Indian Ocean.

Caesar van Madagascar's example, supposedly a direct quote, reads like a political claim to the right to speech, particularly when coupled with his action of destroying the weapon with which the man had beaten him. The phrase with which his manner of speech is described, *without equivocating* (*zonder bewimpeling*), even seems to express a kind of admiration for the directness of the utterance. But the court officials recorded it as part of a narrative about insubordination, in which the exact details (such as Caesar's recorded statement that "I was awake early, but because the weather was bad, I did not want to get up") evince "excessive and inappropriate remarks," and thus justify his cruel punishment.[3] The proximity of speech to violence in Caesar's recorded remarks, in which he seems to couple his right to speak to his demand that the slaveholder stop hitting him, is mirrored by the proximity of the act of recording speech and the violence of the courtroom. This reflects the complex relationship between the representation of subaltern speech and the exercise of symbolic violence in the naming and creation of identities. Whether or not Caesar uttered these exact words, once they enter the archival record, they are framed by the prosecutor in a way that exceeds the moment of utterance. At the same time, these words linger on the page, becoming legible to future researchers in a different way from how they were received at the time, creating a small rift through which it becomes possible to imagine the subjectivity of the enslaved.

If increased mobility, in the form of voyages of exploration, territorial conquest, and settlement, marks the advent of European modernity, the other, or obverse, side of that coin is the forced or coerced mobility of millions of enslaved persons, penal deportees, soldiers, indentured laborers, and war prisoners. These individuals are set in motion by the twin demands of imperial expansion: war and labor. Such forced displacement remains the side of empire experienced by most of the world. *The Briny South* deals in this obverse empire. In this book I discuss accounts of enslaved persons transported to the Cape of Good Hope by the Dutch East India Company (Vereenigde Oostindische Compagnie, or VOC) from their Indian Ocean outposts in South and Southeast Asia and East Africa in the seventeenth and eighteenth centuries; narratives by and about South Asian indentured laborers sent to the British colony of Natal between 1860 and 1911; and the writings of South African war prisoners shipped to camps in British India and Ceylon during the second South African War (1899–1902). These three groups comprise the majority of unfree migrants crossing the Indian Ocean under European imperialism. While individual systems of forced or coerced displacements in the Indian Ocean have been the subject of several excellent studies, *The Briny South* juxtaposes these three forms of displacement, using the depiction of speech and silence as a locus to examine how sentiment functions in the formation of displaced identities.[4]

The term *sentiment* in this book denotes the depiction or representation of emotions. I start from the premise that we have no access to the immediate experience of emotion, particularly in historical subjects: all we can analyze is how emotion is conveyed. The somewhat stilted term, *sentiment*, stresses that there is nothing unmediated about these depictions. *Sentiment* also differs from *affect*, which was first used in psychoanalysis to distinguish the feelings discerned by the analyst, considered nonnarrative, from the emotions explicitly expressed by the analysand.[5] *Affect* thus describes the realm of nonverbal expressions of emotion: facial expressions, tone of voice, and so forth. *Sentiment* here refers to how emotion and affect are described and recorded, in legal, political, and personal writing. Sentiment, then, is particularly vulnerable to manipulation. The use and misuse of sentiment works to both silence and racialize the subaltern transnational subjects I study. Sentiment informs how individuals are imagined, as slaves or indentured laborers—and, eventually, how they can imagine and represent themselves. As Lisa Lowe explains, "Elaborations of racial difference were not universal or transhistorical; they did not occur all at once but were local, regional, and differential, articulated in dynamic, interlocking ways with other attributes of social difference within various spaces in an emerging world system."[6] This book focuses on the forms of racialization that emerge out of the displacement of individuals across the Indian Ocean and the role played in this process by the representation of sentiment in documents of imperial control.[7]

When speaking particularly about the most marginalized subjects of this book, the enslaved and indentured, the truth is that the sentiments ascribed to them by others are the only aspect of their inner lives we can access. Whether in court records, as described by witnesses or accusers, or in the political pamphlets written by abolitionists or anti-indenture activists, we can only read what is recorded. Even Caesar van Madagascar's voice, expressing anger and rebellion, is mediated by the legal archive. Hence my focus specifically on sentiment, as a mediated representation of emotion. In the cases where we have access to individuals representing their own emotions as sentiments, in autobiographical writings, these are relatively privileged subjects as compared with the enslaved and indentured: an abolitionist writing about the British Cape Colony, for example, or a Boer war prisoner publishing a memoir after the war. The term *sentiment* still applies though, as even in fashioning their own narratives, these individuals are responding to historical pressures to frame their emotions, and the emotions of others, in a certain way.

Take, for example, a pamphlet written by Mohandas K. Gandhi during his time in South Africa, titled *The Grievances of the British Indians in South Africa: An Appeal to the Indian Public* (1896). In this pamphlet, he indicates that his previous complaints to the British authorities had been dismissed as "grievances... more sentimental than material."[8] Partly because of the sentiment-laden appeals of earlier abolitionists, British officials, Gandhi suggests, were no longer responsive to appeals foregrounding the sentiments of the powerless. Gandhi's response is to foreground the material consequences of anti-Indian rhetoric and policy. When Gandhi thus describes one particular case involving an indentured laborer, he is careful to balance his description of the suffering of the man with concrete evidence of bodily harm, while showing the man as capable of writing out his own complaint. Gandhi's pamphlet can be directly contrasted to an 1826 pamphlet by Scottish abolitionist Thomas Pringle on the enslaved at the Cape Colony, in which they are depicted as dismal, silent victims, while the abolitionist speaks on their behalf.[9] In the seventy years between these two texts, the strategy regarding the representation of the emotions of the marginalized as sentiment has shifted, reflecting both historical changes and the relative positions of privilege occupied by Pringle and Gandhi, respectively. The use of sentiment is thus always contingent upon the conditions of its legibility, which are set by the powerful.

The ability to control the depiction of sentiment is dangerous. It is dangerous because of the ease with which these sentiments can be manipulated, controlled, and rewritten by the keepers of the documents of power. This danger plays out slightly differently throughout this book, as I move from the Dutch Cape of Good Hope to apartheid-era South Africa. Initially, it may be surprising that the sentiments of the enslaved did not require suppression or censorship in eighteenth-century court records, but the texts I examine in the first chapter begin to demonstrate how sentiments can be manipulated, both in the court records and in literary discourse more broadly, to ascribe specific characteristics to the enslaved. In the nineteenth century, sentiment-filled writing by both pro- and antislavery activists is used to render the enslaved as inarticulately suffering: an insidious form of racialization that infantilizes the enslaved while centering the authority of the abolitionist or slaveholder. Turning to writing about indenture, we see Gandhi acknowledging the dangers of sentiment in his suggestion that the political use of sentiment by the oppressed is easily dismissed by those in power.

The dangers of sentiment become particularly visible in the twentieth century. While sentiment is initially subject to vigorous censorship in the British prisoner-of-war camps where captured Boer fighters find themselves, something disturbing happens when sentiment is seized upon by later Afrikaner nationalists: sentiment becomes a justification for the oppression of others, including the descendants of indentured laborers and the enslaved. Apartheid theorists and lawmakers explicitly deploy sentiment to perpetuate the precarity of South Asians in South Africa, whereas Afrikaners are, partly because of the now-enshrined suffering of the Boer war, seen as rooted in the soil. Sentiment, while sometimes treated as a form of resistance that needs to be suppressed by those in power, never successfully becomes a weapon of the subaltern, suggesting that the language of sentiment is always biased toward the powerful.

For those displaced across the Indian Ocean during the period under consideration, the ocean forms the backdrop against which their new lives must play out. The ocean is the start (and sometimes the end) of their journey, and even though they may never cross the ocean again, this oceanic displacement can never be completely forgotten. These are oceanic stories, even as they are not all stories about the ocean. Many of the sources I examine document the desire, on the part of these individuals, to turn away from the ocean—to establish a life outside of slavery or indenture; but these acts of escape still take place against the backdrop of the oceanic journeys that lead to these individuals' appearance in the archives. These journeys thus suggest a productive intersection between two contemporary approaches within the humanities: Global South studies and ocean studies. Both fields emerge as ways of investigating an increasingly global, transnational literary terrain that is no longer tied to nation-states or continental area studies.[10]

This intersection between Global South and ocean studies, which I term the *briny South*, mobilizes the strengths of these two approaches to map an imagined cartography that combines the historical depth of ocean studies with the political and ethical drive toward understanding the subaltern experience of globalization that marks Global South studies. *Briny* here, of course, refers to the ocean ("of or pertaining to brine or the sea; saturated with salt," an adjective used in this context since 1618), to reflect the saltwater that continues to mark the lives of these oceanic migrants.[11] It also refers to the more colloquial use of the term as a noun to refer to the ocean—the briny—to indicate the vernacular nature of the kinds of networks studied under this heading. Drawing on the increasing geographic fluidity of both fields, the *South* in *briny South* does not refer to the geographic South but acknowledges that all oceans have histories in which global Souths and global Norths are entangled: voyages of conquest and exploration involved the labor of innumerable sailors, ship's cooks, indigenous navigators, and so forth, who have been largely rendered anonymous in historical memory, while the same ships that transported captive Africans to the "New World" also carried settlers, adventurers, and merchants profiting from the trade in human lives.[12] The briny South paradigm focuses on the role of the world's oceans in perpetuating forms of oppression and exploitation throughout history, but it also draws attention to the emergence of oceanic lines of subaltern connection, solidarity, and shared resistance to globalized networks of power. This book imagines the Indian Ocean as a specifically briny South site: a site of subalternization and solidarity, of violence and care, with a long history of transnational exploitation and connection.[13]

The transatlantic slave trade has dominated understandings of modern slavery. Shifting focus to the Indian Ocean, however, allows for a change in perspective on involuntary displacement and bonded labor, emerging out of the differences in legal systems, local histories, languages, and imperial documentation styles prevalent in these two oceanic worlds. The Dutch East India Company adapted and expanded various forms of preexisting slave trading networks in the Indian Ocean world from the seventeenth century onward.[14] Whereas the Atlantic slave trade was unidirectional (the enslaved were transported from Africa to various regions of the Americas), the enslaved in the Indian Ocean were transported in multiple directions, between Southeast Asia, South Asia, the Mascarenes, Madagascar, and Africa.[15] The Cape of Good Hope, for example, served only as a destination for the enslaved, as the African indigenous inhabitants of the Cape could not be captured or sold into slavery.

As the enslaved came from South and Southeast Asia, as well as Madagascar and the eastern coast of Africa, the racial dynamics of enslavement were different than in the Atlantic. The types of sources available to us from the Indian Ocean also differ: Dutch, French, and eventually British courts in Ceylon, Batavia, the Malabar and Coromandel coasts, the Mascarenes, and the Cape of Good Hope tried both enslaved and free inhabitants in the same courts, thereby producing volumes of historical records in which details about the everyday lives of the enslaved are documented. The story of Indian Ocean involuntary displacement is one of recorded legal speech and autobiographical silence, as opposed to the anglophone Atlantic world, which produced autobiographical narratives but legal silence. The glimpses of

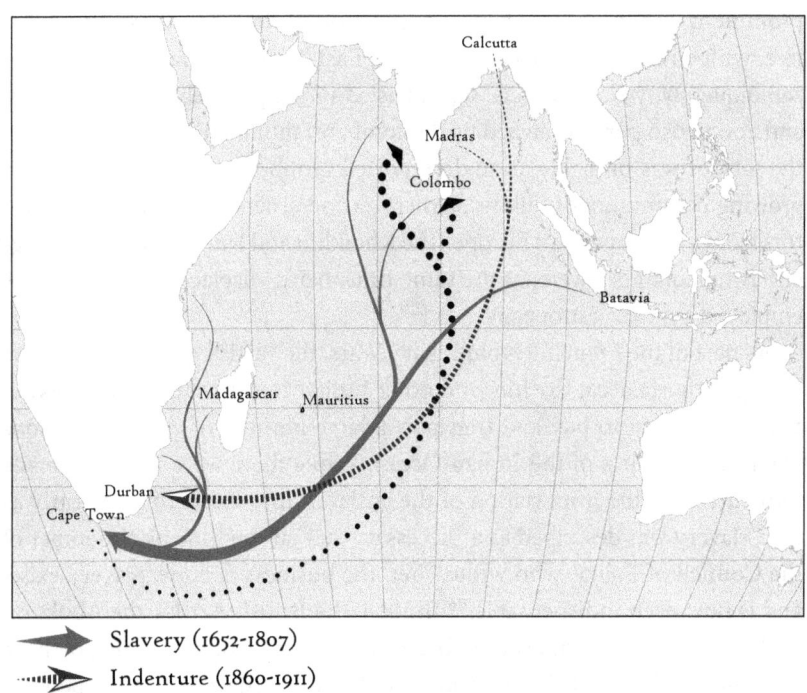

→ Slavery (1652–1807)
⇢ Indenture (1860–1911)
•••▶ War Imprisonment (1899–1902)

MAP I.1. Map of the Indian Ocean, showing the routes taken by the enslaved, indentured laborers, and war prisoners between South and Southeast Asia and Southern Africa. Map by Areet Roychowdhury with revisions by Geoffrey Wallace (G. Wallace Cartography & GIS).

"subjectivity in bondage" from these oceanic worlds complement each other, even as the Indian Ocean narrative of unfree labor has, until now, only been told in parts.

This story of unfree labor begins in 1653, one year after the first Dutch settler ships arrive at the Cabo de Goede Hoop, at the southwestern tip of the African continent. This is when the first enslaved man, Abraham van Batavia, landed at the Cape on the VOC ship, the *Malacca*. Following this, other ships from South Asia, Southeast Asia, East Africa, and Madagascar would transport the enslaved to the Cape. In the early years of the settlement, the most important source of forced labor was the Indian subcontinent (Arakan/Bengal, Malabar, and Coromandel) and Ceylon. Though persons continued to be traded from South Asia well into the eighteenth century, after 1731 more individuals came from Southeast Asia (Sulawesi, Java, Dutch Timor, and Malacca). A further source of forced labor, which became increasingly

Enslaved, Indentured, Interned · 7

prominent under the later British occupation of the Cape, was eastern Africa, with enslaved persons coming from East Africa, Madagascar, and Mozambique. By 1795, the official figures listed 16,789 privately owned persons, and 400 to 650 persons owned by the company, though historians agree that the former was probably an underreported number. The enslaved joined a growing community of sailors, soldiers, farmers, servants, and administrators from various parts of Europe. The Khoikhoi and San people—the indigenous inhabitants—were, at the same time, being displaced and coercively employed by these Europeans.

As part of the French Revolutionary Wars, the British occupied the Cape (along with Malacca, Cochin, and other Indian Ocean VOC settlements) in 1795, continuing to buy and transport a large number of enslaved persons from various parts of the Indian Ocean. While there were inquiries made into curtailing the importation of the enslaved into Cape Town as early as 1797, slavery was described as a "necessary evil" at the time by a member of the Council of Policy, who wrote, "Yet, the business is done. Slavery exists and is now even indispensable."[16] In 1808, the British Act for the Abolition of the Slave Trade (1807) was enforced in the Cape Colony (as the, by now, far larger settlement is known), and in 1834, the enslaved at the Cape were emancipated.

The next chapter of this story takes place on the southeastern coast of Africa, in Natal, colonized by the British in 1818 after the end of the slave trade. Following the emancipation of the enslaved in the British Empire, British and other colonies turned to indenture—a system whereby workers signed indenture contracts to labor for a specific period of time in another part of the world in return for passage (usually return passage) and wages—as a source of labor. Under this system of indenture in the nineteenth century, 1.5 million laborers traveled from South Asia to British and Dutch Guiana, Trinidad, the French Caribbean, Fiji, British East Africa, Natal, and the Mascarenes.[17]

The substantial sugar plantations cultivated by British settlers in Natal starting in the late 1840s required cheap labor—and in 1860, the *Truro* landed at Durban carrying 342 indentured laborers from British India. Over the next fifty years, 151,842 more indentured laborers traveled to South Africa, under contracts ranging from three to five years. The transport of indentured laborers to Natal continued (with some modifications and occasional suspensions) until 1911. While some of these laborers returned to India, many chose to stay and settle in South Africa.

Tensions between Dutch settlers and their descendants, who became known as the Boere (farmers), and English-speaking British settlers, were simmering at the Cape even before the British occupation of 1795 and resulted in the so-called Great Trek that began in 1835, when many Dutch-speaking settlers moved to occupy the interior of South Africa, beyond the territory occupied by the British. By the end of the nineteenth century, this conflict between the British and the so-called Boer Republics, the South African Republic (Zuid-Afrikaansche Republiek) and the Orange Free State (Oranje Vrijstaat), had escalated into two wars, the first South African War (1880–1881) and the deadlier second South African War (1899–1902).[18] During the course of the war, the British military authorities shipped around twenty-four thousand war prisoners to islands within the empire (Bermuda, St. Helena, and Ceylon) and eventually to the mainland of British India. Between August 1900 and May 1901, 5,127 war internees were transported to Ceylon, and from April 1901, 9,131 prisoners were transported to India, where they were kept in a number of different camps in the Punjab, Bengal, Madras, and Bombay Commands.[19] Prisoners were allowed to return to South Africa at the conclusion of the war on May 31, 1902, if they agreed to take an oath of allegiance to the British Crown.

The juxtaposition of these three groups in one study should not suggest equivalence. Reading the narratives by and about these groups next to each other, however, allows me to highlight unexpected connections. As a methodology, connected histories is particularly productive for a space like the Indian Ocean, where historical connections between different oceanic rim communities predate European interventions in this arena.[20] On one level, this project follows the trajectory of those who crossed the Indian Ocean at the whim of empire, traveling between Southeast Asia, South Asia, and southern Africa. But I also trace the less obvious textual connections between forms of displacement through the figurative deployment of speech and sentiment.

The censored sentiments of Boer war prisoners, for example, resurface as the sentimental claims of belonging to the land that animate the racial thinking of an early-apartheid legal theorist against South Asian would-be settlers. Or, take the affective connection with Ceylon expressed by Boer war prisoner J. N. Brink, engendered by his childhood memories of songs about the island. To fully grasp the depth of that connection, the modern reader must understand the lines of continuity between the Dutch and British Indian Ocean empires. Gandhi's efforts to highlight the material, rather than sentimental, grievances of indentured laborers stem from earlier abolitionist use of sentiment in advocating for the enslaved—a strategy that, Gandhi suggests, no longer worked in the late nineteenth century.

Such lines of connection are often invisible, not only in traditional area studies approaches, where the history of South Africa is treated as separate from that of Asia, but also in studies of South Asian diasporas (which focus only on journeys outward from South Asia), or empire studies (in which Dutch, British, and French empires are usually studied as separate systems). These displacements are forms of "minor transnationalism," as described by Françoise Lionnet and Shu-mei Shih. Dutch Indian Ocean slavery, indenture in South Africa, and the internment and transportation of Boer prisoners of war have all been overshadowed by other narratives: enslavement and indenture in the Atlantic Ocean world and Boer war concentration camps for women and children. As Lionnet and Shih point out, rather than placing the minor in juxtaposition to the major, there is value in examining the unexpected connections that emerge when putting the minor in conversation with other minors.[21]

Taking a *longue durée* view of each of these systems of coerced displacement allows me to demonstrate the interplay of different empires and their afterlives, showing how, for example, the Dutch imperial footprint at the Cape influenced the British legal system and how, in turn, British systems of displacement and control influenced later apartheid lawmakers and theorists (the indenture contract providing a model for apartheid theorist Geoffrey Cronjé, for example). This is a form of what Laura Doyle refers to as *inter-imperiality*: the understanding that empires, and those at the mercy of empires, exist not independently but in a web of relations, which include the realms of language and aesthetics. As Doyle suggests, labor and the control of labor power lie at the heart of the imperial project, but, as my project also shows, hegemonic control includes the "near monopoly of the power to name relations and 'identities'—a wish to control the terms of relationality."[22] It is this relationship between the control of labor and the control of naming that I locate at the intersection of law and sentiment.

Legal genres are continually entangled with sentimental expressions: from the early court records to Gandhi's legal pamphlets, sentiment is deployed as a weapon to silence, rather than reveal, the inner lives of the powerless. Over the course of the book, I examine court cases, laws, ledgers, complaint books, correspondence, pamphlets, censors' reports, public commissions, articles, newsletters, and folk songs, as well as South African and South Asian works of fiction and autobiography such as Gandhi's autobiography, Ansuyah R. Singh's novel *Behold the Earth Mourns*, Pringle's poetry, and memoirs by Boer war prisoners. These texts were selected because of their relationship to the archive of imperial dominance and control, circling outward: from court records and legal complaints, laws, imperial ledgers and complaint books, public commissions and censors' reports, where the words and voices of the oppressed appear only in strict constraints, to the pamphlets, articles, and newsletters that represent the official response to those imperial documents, to works of autobiography and fiction increasingly distanced in time from the original acts of displacement and violence, these documents allow me to investigate the strategic use of sentiment as a silencing force.

My approach in each chapter is twofold. First, I describe and analyze the conditions of possibility for speech to both be recorded and understood. These conditions are both formal and legal—the rules that govern the recording and legibility of speech depend both on the form in which it is recorded and the actual laws governing the circumstances under which it can be recorded or understood. This is a historical project, in which I engage with the texts and narratives within the context of the period in which they were written.

Second, then, once the limits governing the recording and legibility of speech have been established, I attempt a more utopian project of attending to the unspoken, or barely spoken, or unheard, along the margins of the recorded and archived. Here, I engage in what Ann Laura Stoler calls reading "along the grain" of the archives, or Stephanie E. Smallwood theorizes as "the counterfact, by which I mean the fact the archive is seeking to ignore, marginalize and disavow—the detail it does not want to animate and make narratable," or Stephen Best calls attending to "impossible speech" or "gossamer writing" ("a writing predicated on knowing what withholds itself from the possibility of being known, one that sought to acknowledge without actually knowing").[23] As this list suggests, my methodology builds upon the work of scholars of colonialism and slavery in other contexts—historians and literary theorists who have also grappled with the question of how to engage with archives of power, acknowledging the distorting effect of that power without giving up the possibility that an alternative viewpoint can be wrested from the discourse of absolute control. By attending to the modes of expression adopted by the powerless within the limits established for their possibility of speech, I offer a glimpse, not of the voice of the oppressed or their inner lives, but of an opaque, counterfactual, impossible, or gossamer form of subjectivity that can be conjectured but not fully grasped.

The chapters in this book are organized chronologically to tell the story of unfree transnational displacement, sentiment, and law in the Indian Ocean from the eighteenth to the twentieth century.

Chapter one, "Representing Speech in Bondage in the Court Records of the Dutch Cabo de Goede Hoop, 1652–1795," examines the witness statements, interrogations, sentences, and confessions in eighteenth-century Cape court cases, asking why lawmen of the time chose to include supposed direct speech, and specifically speech expressing strong emotion, by the enslaved in these documents. I argue that the inclusion of these fragments of direct speech forms part of a larger system of legal verisimilitude that creates plausible narratives through the inclusion of actions, speech, untranslated exclamations, and visual description, rather than exposition or summary. In the final part of the chapter, I suggest that portraying enslaved voices in the archives also allows for textual friction—heteroglossia, ambiguity, and untranslatability—to infiltrate these records, such that contemporary readers can glimpse an alternative to the slave archive as purely crypt or tomb.

In chapter two, "Silencing the Enslaved: The Aesthetics of Abolitionism in the British Cape Colony, 1795–1834," I analyze discourse by abolitionist Thomas Pringle, slaveholder S. E. Hudson, and the civil servants working at the Office of the Registrar and Guardian of Slaves to show that the enslaved are silenced in similar ways by abolitionists, slaveholders, and civil servants alike, through the erasure of their imagined direct speech in all these writings. Though the disappearance of direct speech by enslaved persons may seem like a minor change, I contend that it is part of a larger process by which the enslaved are increasingly spoken for, or ventriloquized, by pro- and antislavery activists alike. Abolitionist discourse produces the figure of the slave that will persist in the public, and administrative, imagination: inarticulate, suffering, and lacking in moral complexity or depth. Turning briefly from Pringle's Romantic poetry to the question of visual representation, the final part of the chapter asks about different ways of imagining the enslaved, suggesting that slave ledgers offer an unsettling alternative aesthetic compared to Romantic depictions of the enslaved circulating at the time. These ledger pages, I propose, invite an ethically engaged contemporary artistic encounter with the archive of enslavement.

Chapter three, "'Grievances More Sentimental than Material': Representing Indentured Labor in Natal, 1860–1915," examines the distinction drawn by Gandhi in an 1896 pamphlet on British Indians in South Africa between "material" and "sentimental" grievances, demonstrating how the indentured community at large increasingly reframed their legal complaints as the former. These texts by and about indentured laborers show that, in contrast to the effectiveness of sentimental descriptions in abolitionist discourse, appeals to the sentiments of contemporaneous readers are seen as less effective than concrete demonstrations of material harm. This chapter concludes by briefly turning to contemporary debates about indenture as either a new system of slavery or a form of free labor migration to demonstrate the enduring impact of equating indentured laborers with the enslaved. Examining sources from the indentured diaspora beyond Natal, I suggest more nuanced frameworks for thinking about indenture and its legacies today.

The first three body chapters of this book respond to the lack of conventional autobiographical material produced by the enslaved and indentured in the Indian Ocean. Focusing mainly on legal documents, I ask whether these imagine and depict the subaltern displaced subjects as speaking, or silent. I thus take literally Gayatri C. Spivak's famous question about subaltern speech and adapt it slightly to ask under which circumstances the subaltern *can be depicted as* speaking.[24] The first two chapters reveal an evolution in the conventions governing court records, which mirrors public discourse on slavery more broadly. While expressions of sentiment on the part of the enslaved are intelligible, and valid, in earlier Dutch court records, legal documents are increasingly scrubbed of sentiment at the same time as abolitionist authors weaponize the expression of sentiment in writing. Later in the nineteenth century, when indentured laborers are transported to Natal, the illegibility of sentiment as a valid form of official complaint can be seen when Gandhi stresses that material grievances are more effective in law. These two centuries thus see a solidification of the conventions of legal complaints, court cases, and public discourse such that expressions of sentiment become invalid, or at least illegible, in these forms.

The final two body chapters ask, then, what happens to sentimental utterances in the writings of private individuals. In which forms can sentiment be expressed, and how is this affected by genre? These chapters demonstrate that the dichotomy of speech and silence is never clear-cut: even in writing memoir and fiction, genre shapes and constrains the forms in which experiences can be described, and the sentiments that can be expressed. In Lauren Berlant's useful working definition, genre is "a loose affectual contract that predicts the form that an aesthetic transaction will take."[25] Genre conventions and sentiment are closely linked: certain genres demand specific sentiments and govern the way in which those sentiments are expressed.

Titled "A Sentimental Education in Boer War Imprisonment Camps in South Asia, 1899–1902," chapter four examines how expressions of sentiment regarding both the Boer Republics and the British Empire change over time: from letters and newssheets written in Diyatalawa to memoirs published immediately following the war to memoirs published in the 1930s and 1940s as Afrikaner nationalists were consolidating power. The British attempted a sentimental education in the prisoner-of-war camps, using the censorship of news from South Africa, among other strategies, to turn unruly Boer rebels into pacified British subjects. This sets the scene for understanding newssheets circulating in the camps during the war and memoirs written by former war prisoners immediately afterward. Both memoirs and newssheets read not, as one would expect, as prison or war writing, but as travel literature. The descriptions of landscapes and sightseeing excursions in these texts suggest a cultural imaginary built on travel and cultural exchange, as opposed to the insular Afrikaner nationalism that would follow empire. By inscribing their work in the narrative tradition of European explorers and travelers, these writers both occupy and satirize the position of the British subject. However, comparing these immediate postwar memoirs with ones edited and published in South Africa in the 1930s and 1940s demonstrates how, in these later texts, sentiments of nostalgia for the South African landscape begin to dominate the narrative, reflecting a growing national myth of Boer war suffering and ties to the land.

The final chapter turns to the writings of South Asians living in South Africa as apartheid gains ideological ground, to see how these authors mobilize the sentiments associated with the settler narrative to combat the lawfare of the segregationist state. Chapter five, "Sentiment and the Law in Early South African Indian Writing, 1893–1960," traces the afterlife of the indenture contract in fictional and autobiographical texts by South African Indians, including Ansuyah R. Singh's *Behold the Earth Mourns* and Gandhi's *Autobiography: The Story of My Experiments with Truth*. Placing Gandhi's autobiography in conversation with lesser-known narratives written by South African Indians allows me to reinterpret it as typical of a certain kind of "settler" narrative in which both the descendants of indentured laborers and traders who traveled to South Africa imagine themselves as settlers. However, the specter of the indenture contract introduces the rhetoric of law into their work, at odds with the sentimental language associated with settler narratives. The turn to the settler novel as a form of resistance in apartheid-era South Africa makes sense when read alongside apartheid legal theorist Geoffrey Cronjé. Cronjé deploys specific sentimental tropes we begin to see emerging in the previous chapter about the relationship between the Afrikaner and the land to argue for the perpetual outsider status and permanent exclusion of so-called Asiatics.

The conclusion, or coda, "No Human Footprints," collapses the time between the imperial Indian Ocean world and the present moment. In this short coda, I turn to the invocation of Robinson Crusoe—both as a character in the eighteenth-century novel but also as the fictional incarnation of Robert Knox, a seventeenth-century captive on the island of Ceylon—in recent legal documents about the Chagos Archipelago, a series of islands in the middle of the Indian Ocean. References to "man Fridays" and "human footprints" in British claims justifying the deportation of the descendants of the enslaved and indentured laborers from these islands exemplify the invocation of literary expressions of sentiment in shaping legal narratives about displacement even today.

Increasingly, works on enslavement and its afterlives in the Atlantic context have been reckoning with the violence of research on slavery itself: in the now-famous formulation posed by Saidiya Hartman, "How does one revisit the scene of subjection without replicating the grammar of violence?"[26] Scholars like Stephen Best and Christopher Freeburg have traced the development of scholarly approaches on slavery, from works that saw enslaved Africans as rendered childlike and powerless by the fact of enslavement, to social histories concerned predominantly with identifying moments of resistance and agency, to what Best calls a current thread of "melancholic historicism" concerned with the "taking possession of . . . grievous experience and archival loss."[27] This latter kind of work, Best contends, sees in the horrors of enslavement both the origin and the mirror of contemporary experiences of Blackness.[28] In this work, I avoid both simply diagnosing the agency, or lack thereof, of the subaltern and collapsing the distance between the present and the past. Shuttling between different historical moments, I see the relationship between them (borrowing again from Best) as one of neither pure causality nor pure analogy.[29] The past does not lead inevitably to the present, but neither is the present simply a repetition of the past. During apartheid, slavery in South African history became, for many writers, simply an allegory for apartheid.[30] In the postapartheid years, slave memory has, as Pumla Dineo Gqola describes, played a prominent part in reconstructing or rememorying postapartheid identities.[31] Rather than attempting to locate the genealogy of the present in the past, however, each of the chapters in this book aims to immerse the reader in the archival materials from that period. While I remain thoroughly aware of the dangers of working with the imperial archive, and the inability of texts—even memoir and fiction—to fully escape its mediation, I also try not to succumb to the melancholy that Best diagnoses. In each chapter, I point to strategies (whether historiographic, artistic, literary, or political) through which we can attend to speculative glimpses of subjectivity in bondage—flashes of a world in which someone like Caesar of Madagascar would have a "right to speak," and have his words heard, more than 220 years later. What emerges from this methodology is, on one level, a transnational history of apartheid, tracing the centrality of different forms of forced imperial displacement, and the legal frameworks that accompanied them, to apartheid ideology. However, forced displacement is also one of the key features of imperialism as it played out across the globe in the eighteenth and nineteenth centuries. At a broader level, then, this book is a study of the effect of displacement in the formation of racialized identities across the imperial world, the consequences of which still reverberate today.

1. REPRESENTING SPEECH IN BONDAGE IN THE COURT RECORDS OF THE DUTCH CABO DE GOEDE HOOP, 1652–1795

Cupido van Mallebaar, 1739

"What do you want now, that I kill you or myself?" Taking the knife out of his pocket and setting the same with its back against his throat, he asked if his mistress wanted to see him cut his own throat, whereupon the mistress questioned him as to why he would do such a thing, and if something was the matter with him, to which the prisoner replied: "So much." Then, after taking off his shirt and vest and throwing them on the ground, he pointed to his leather trousers, saying: "In my country we do not wear trousers like these, I have already worked here for two or three years, and I do not see the *baas* [master] buying more *jongens* [boys] or *nonje* [mistress] buying a *meijd* [girl] for me, *baas* and *nonje* can laugh and talk all you like."[1]

Cupido van Mallebaar (Malabar), an enslaved man at the Dutch Cabo de Goede Hoop, or Cape of Good Hope, stood trial in 1739 for attempted murder and arson. After using a knife to slash at the hands of the slaveholder, Maria Klaasz, he first tried unsuccessfully to set the Klaasz's farmhouse on fire and then to kill himself with the same knife. The above extract is taken from the verdict or sentence (*sententie*) pronounced on his case by the Council of Justice (Raad van Justitie). The reasons for Cupido's act of rebellion—his distaste for the clothing he has to wear and nostalgia for his own country, his loneliness, and his shame at the slaveholders' mockery—are not paraphrased but stated in his own words. Quoted direct speech conveys Cupido's presumed emotions much more strongly than a paraphrase could have. These words came from Klaasz's statement, which Cupido had been required to confirm under interrogation. The details were then directly transcribed into the final sentence. This chapter focuses on instances like this, when eighteenth-century lawmen chose to represent direct speech by the enslaved in the written sentences and claims of the Council of Justice at the Cape of Good Hope, in order to ask what effect this formal choice has, both on the way these documents were used at the time and the way we read them today.

There is no Olaudah Equiano, Quobna Cugoano, Ignatius Sancho, or Phillis Wheatley to speak for the Indian Ocean slaves transported by the functionaries of the Dutch East India Company (Vereenigde Oostindische Compagnie, or voc) to the Cape of Good Hope. No example of slave autobiography from this region exists. Even in the Atlantic world, slave narratives should not be read as unmediated expressions of the experience of enslavement: Simon Gikandi points out that, although the abovementioned autobiographical accounts exist, they are retrospective documents written from the perspective of a former slave, now free person and self-imagined modern subject. Gikandi thus suggests that one challenge to scholars of the Black Atlantic is to "recover black subjectivity *in bondage*."[2] In Saidiya Hartman's essay "Venus in Two Acts," she famously asks, "How does one rewrite the chronicle of a death foretold and anticipated, as a collective biography of dead subjects, as a counter-history of the human, as the practice of freedom?"[3] The historical materials available to scholars of slavery in the Dutch Indian Ocean world may differ from those available in the Black Atlantic, but these questions remain relevant. The Indian Ocean has produced a legal archive of enslavement that is far more abundant than that of the British Black Atlantic, as the enslaved were tried, and allowed to testify, in the same court as the free inhabitants of the colonies: in Dutch Ceylon, Batavia, Malabar, the Cape of Good Hope, and French Mauritius, for example.[4] These legal archives contain numerous depictions of direct speech by enslaved subjects. The formal choice of representing slaves as speaking is noteworthy: in the next chapter, I will show how both pro- and antislavery activists at the Cape most frequently represented slaves as silent, or inarticulately suffering. What happens, then, when slaves are depicted as speaking, and specifically, as expressing their sentiments, in the legal archives of enslavement? In this chapter, I discuss, first, how the imagined sentiments of enslaved persons at the Dutch Cape of Good Hope are mediated by the form of the legal record: specifically, the claims made by fiscals, summarizing the case, and the sentences pronounced by the Council of Justice. Later, I pivot to speculate on the afterlife of this imagined enslaved speech effect for contemporary scholars of enslavement, suggesting that it may offer an outside to discussions of agency/damage or resistance/complicity that still frequently shape academic discourse on the archives of enslavement.[5]

Cupido's sentence continues: "The prisoner stated that he had at a certain time gone into the bedroom while her husband was sleeping, with the intention of killing him, but, looking at him, he had a change of heart, because he felt sorry for the wife and her child. After this, the prisoner took his mistress outside and showed her five bullets, which he took out of his pocket, saying: 'These bullets I have made for myself' [*Die koogels hebbe ik voor mij selfs gemaak*]" (Cupido van Mallebaar 1739).[6]

This section of the sentence demonstrates the difference between paraphrasing (the prisoner stated that . . . he felt sorry for the wife and child) and quotation (saying: "These bullets I have made for myself"). The image of Cupido saying "*Die koogels hebbe ik voor mij selfs gemaak*" while showing the woman the actual bullets is a far more vivid way of conveying Cupido's suicidal desperation. The emotional intensity of this moment is conveyed directly to the readers of the sentence—and listeners, as these sentences were read out loud on De Kat, one of the balconies of the Castle of Good Hope, before the prisoner was led out to be punished. The enslaved, though certainly constrained by the circumstances of the courtroom, not to mention their status as property, are still allowed a full inner life in these court documents. For example, while marriage between slaves was illegal, and enslaved families frequently separated, direct speech by enslaved people that expresses the strength of the emotional attachment between couples, and between parents and children, appears frequently in the records. In the sentence above, Cupido's loneliness is a direct result of his enslavement: we hear his longing for his homeland, and his resentment of the fact that companionship can only be procured for him by the slaveholders. His words, however, are not seen as a challenge to the institution of slavery.

Including these words describing his emotional state in Cupido's sentence could, perhaps, have served to create sympathy for him, and distaste for the institution that causes his suffering. For theorists of eighteenth-century literature and society, narratives including many expressions of sentiment are closely associated with the sensation of sympathy, both as a desirable characteristic in protagonists, but also as the intended effect on the reader. Toward the end of the eighteenth century, the language of sentiment and feeling becomes particularly associated with abolitionist writing in English, where its aim is specifically to put the reader in a place where they feel identification with the suffering of the slave.[7] This, however, is not what happens in Cupido's case. Turning to the end of his sentence, we read his prescribed punishment: "To be brought to the place where criminal punishment is usually executed, there to be handed to the executioner to be bound on a cross, to be broken alive from the bottom up, without the blow of mercy [*slag van gratie*], to stay bound on the cross until he has given up the spirit [*den geest sal hebben gegeeven*]; and after death, the body to be dragged outside to be set on a wheel, remaining there until the air and birds of heaven have devoured it" (Cupido van Mallebaar 1739).[8]

We can presume that the intention of the council's sentence was not to create sympathy for the prisoner, as being broken on the cross while alive, and displayed on the wheel, is perhaps the cruelest of the many spectacular punishments handed out by the court at the time. The speaking slave in these legal documents is thus not the "sentimental figure of empire" we find in abolitionist texts, and who we will encounter again in the next chapter.[9] Rather, these enslaved individuals are shown as speaking, and speaking of their feelings, but elicit no sympathy—they are punished in a myriad of spectacularly cruel ways that, while not uncommon across European polities at the time, were largely reserved for the enslaved at the Cape of Good Hope.[10] Death sentences involving dismemberment and torture such as this one are handed out disproportionately to slaves.[11] Why, then, include the supposed direct speech by Cupido at all in the sentence, if the purpose is not to elicit sympathy for him?

Researchers working on slavery in territories under the control of the Dutch East India Company have access to an abundance of records from the eighteenth century—the high level of documentation that exists for legal cases especially is unheard of in British colonies from the same period, which had separate slave courts. This is an archive that is not available in the eighteenth-century British Atlantic world, since British slave courts were far more informal, and, if records of proceedings were kept, they have not survived.[12] Similar legal records do exist from other Dutch imperial possessions, such as Suriname (Dutch West India Company) and Ceylon (VOC), while Spanish and French imperial territories also kept extensive legal documentation.[13] The records from the Council of Justice at the Cape of Good Hope encompass more than six hundred volumes in the archives in Cape Town and The Hague, including depositions, confessions, records of interrogations, witness statements, supporting pieces of evidence, claims (*eijschen*), and verdicts/sentences.[14] Slaves appear as witnesses, defendants, and accusers in these files, since slaves could testify against slaveholders, other free persons, or fellow slaves. According to the law in place at the time, "Crimes committed by slaves are amenable the same as those committed by free persons, to the judgment of the Court of Justice, and are punished with the same punishments. Crimes against the life or safety of their master's persons are however more severely punished than those against others, whence it comes that slaves, in case they proceed so far as to assail their master, although without weapons, they must suffer death without mercy, agreeably to the express commands of the law."[15] Slaves had the right to lodge complaints with the fiscal or *landdrost* (magistrate) if they were "being ill-treated by their master or representatives or not being properly provided with the necessaries of life."[16]

While the glimpses we get of the enslaved through these records are necessarily distorted, the narratives that emerge from the records are fascinating, providing evidence not only for detailed works of social history, but for creative writers.[17] These records provide a detailed view of the everyday operation of law in an eighteenth-century slave society. In reading these cases, however, I am not reading them to uncover the lived experience of enslaved people in this period. I am, rather, sensitive to the *form* of these sentences and claims: how they juxtapose different discourses, from high legal rhetoric to everyday language, how they construct a logical tale, and how they transform the dialogue of the interrogation or combine different witness statements into a single authoritative legal narrative. I am primarily interested, then, not in what these cases tell us about the institution of slavery, but in how they are written.[18] The inclusion of represented slave speech in court documents, I argue, forms part of a larger system of legal verisimilitude that works to create plausible narratives through the inclusion of actions, direct speech, and visual descriptions, rather than exposition or summary. The "inner lives" of the enslaved as represented through their expressions of sentiment are, in this reading, a function of this legal verisimilitude, where the enslaved are imagined as plausibly experiencing the same emotions as those who are not enslaved.

This book examines the form taken by expressions of sentiment in the records resulting from the forced or coerced migration of slaves, indentured laborers, and war prisoners across the Indian Ocean by imperial powers. In this context, this chapter establishes that, at least initially, expressions of sentiment by the enslaved were not seen as requiring legal silencing. Slaves are depicted as expressing sentiments of love, self-pity, or nostalgia for their country of origin in legal records, without this being seen as a threat to the institution of slavery itself. This changes when the British take control of the Cape Colony at the height of the abolitionist movement, in 1795. As discussed in the following chapter, what Lynn Festa brilliantly calls the "redundant humanizing of the already human" performed by abolitionist discourse serves to call into question something that is taken for granted in these early court records: the humanity of the enslaved person.[19] Rather than the sentimental discourse about the enslaved that, I will show, animates both pro- and antislavery writings in the nineteenth-century Cape Colony, here the sentiments—verbal expressions of inner emotions—are imagined as being spoken by the enslaved themselves, but not registered as critiques of the system of slavery itself. The larger part of this chapter, then, analyzes the system of legal verisimilitude that cultivated the representation of direct speech by the enslaved, alongside the other inhabitants of the Cabo de Goede Hoop, in legal claims and sentences, while the conclusion suggests that the incorporation of quoted direct speech, alongside other formal features unique to these records, can be viewed as a form of textual friction that, to the contemporary reader, unsettles the hegemonic power of the archive of enslavement.

Before we turn to other depictions of enslaved speech in the Council of Justice records, I briefly locate these records in the context of the larger social and political organization of the Cabo de Goede Hoop in the eighteenth century. The linguistically and ethnically diverse slave population living there embodies what I call the *briny South*, a reimagining of the Global South that explicitly includes earlier forms of subaltern solidarity predating the Cold War and emerging not only from willed alliances, but also more contingent solidarities among people thrust together involuntarily by imperial powers. The VOC established a refreshment station at the Cape of Good Hope in 1652, and soon thereafter began bringing over enslaved people from its other outposts in South and Southeast Asia, and later from Madagascar and eastern Africa. Initially, the most important source of forced labor at the Cape was the South Asian subcontinent, but, though slaves continued to be traded from South Asia into the eighteenth century, after 1731 the majority of slaves came from Southeast Asia. A further source of forced labor was eastern Africa, with slaves coming from East Africa, Madagascar, and Mozambique. In the final years of Dutch control at the Cape and under the first British occupation (1795–1803), most slaves came from eastern Africa, especially Mozambique.[20] During the very early years of the settlement, some enslaved persons were also transported to the Cape from West and Central Africa, but, while the Dutch West India Company (WIC) held slave-trading posts in West Africa, these slaves were transported across the Atlantic, and, due to intense competition with the VOC, were not sold in the

VOC-held settlement of the Cape of Good Hope.[21] Slave society at the Cape was thus comprised of a mix of South Asian, Southeast Asian, and East African slaves, speaking various languages. Creole Portuguese and Melayu were two commonly spoken *lingua francas*, as was a simplified kind of "kitchen Dutch" that would eventually evolve into Afrikaans.[22] The Council of Justice allowed witnesses to testify in their language of choice, and the languages listed in the records include Bugis, Arabic, Chinese, Javanese, Malagasy, Portuguese, Melayu, German, Dutch, and English (although the records are all transcripts of the Dutch translations).

Aside from the legal records, scholars have used wills, inventories, and records of the Council of Policy to study the lives of early Cape slaves. While no slave narratives or creative works by slaves have survived, two other interesting sources are the diary of a slave schoolmaster, Jan Smiesing, and a collection of thirty-two letters addressed to two former slaves who had returned to Batavia, written between 1728 and 1733. This latter collection reveals an intricate subaltern network connecting the Cape, Amsterdam, Colombo, and Batavia. Jan Smiesing's diary, unfortunately, records few

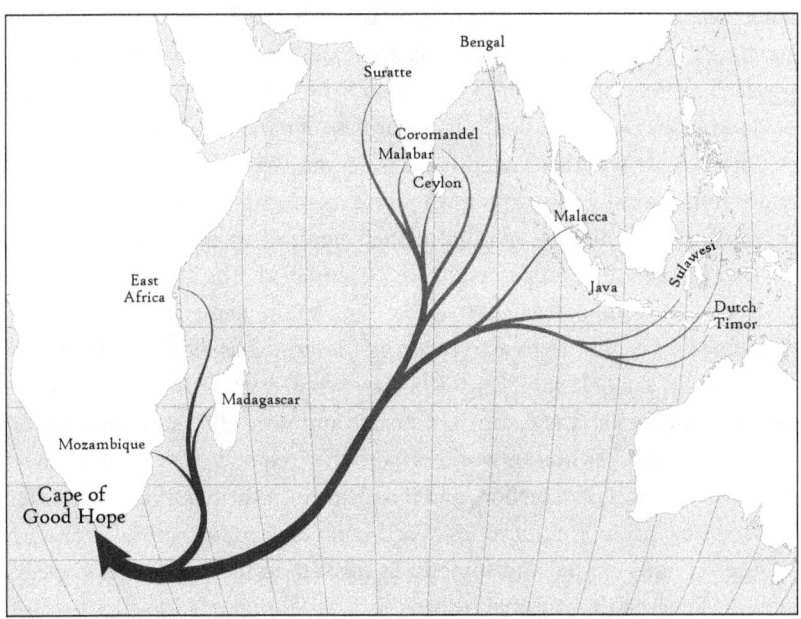

MAP 1.1. Map showing the regional origins of the enslaved at the Cape of Good Hope. Map by Areet Roychowdhury with revisions by Geoffrey Wallace (G. Wallace Cartography & GIS).

personal details or reflections: he lists the dates of birth for his own children and relatives, examples of arithmetic, the alphabet in upper and lower case, a hymn, and a list of medical cures in Tamil. Both these sources also make it clear that slaves at the Cape were not all illiterate (Smiesing in fact taught reading and writing at the Slave Lodge), and many might have been engaged in writing letters or other forms of personal documentation that simply did not survive. Other contemporaneous sources include diaries and letters written by European visitors, the daybooks kept by the VOC governors at the Cape, and the expedition records for various explorers at the Cape.[23]

All enslaved people at the Cape were referred to as *slaven* or *lijfeigenen* (bondsmen). The term *zwarten* (Blacks) was used for all people of African, Malagasy, South Asian, or Southeast Asian origin, and the term *vrijzwart* (free Black) referred both to former slaves and to former convicts from Southeast Asia.[24] The VOC also used the Cape of Good Hope as a destination to deport political exiles, often very high-ranking figures of authority, from their territories in South and Southeast Asia.[25] The names of the enslaved (Tromp van Madagascar, Aaron van Bengalen, Jan van de Caab, etc.) often, though not always, tell of their origin. In some cases, this suffix identifies only the slave's most recent point of embarkation, so that slaves could be named for the place where they were sold (this is particularly likely for slaves named for significant entrepôts, such as Batavia and Colombo).[26] One can thus not always tell a slave's ethnicity from their moniker (and all slaves born at the Cape of Good Hope were "van de Caab," regardless of parentage). A further feature of Cape society was that the enslaved lived and worked alongside the indigenous inhabitants of this region, who were increasingly recruited or coerced, through the colonial occupation of their land, to work on settler farms.[27] By law, indigenous groups could not be enslaved. The Khoikhoi and Sān people—both groups referred to at the time by the name Hottentots—were the subject of typical European othering (described as either monstrous or, occasionally, as noble savages).[28] Khoisan people were tried by, or could appear as witnesses at, the Council of Justice and were allocated direct speech in these records.[29] Khoisan workers were the frequent coaccused of slaves, especially in cases of desertion, and it is clear from various trials of deserters that heterogeneous communities of self-emancipated former slaves and unwilling servants existed and sometimes thrived on the margins of Cape society.[30] However, the criminal records also clarify that relationships between slaves and servants were certainly not always cordial, with Khoisan servants turning in runaway slaves, for example, or slaves and servants getting into violent altercations.[31] Court records from the period also contain many instances of reported direct speech by enslaved women, and their testimony does not seem to be subject to different standards or expectations than that of enslaved men, or servants.[32]

Initially, the Council of Policy and the Council of Justice at the Cape were the same body, combining legislative and judicial powers. The first case recorded in the Council of Justice documents is the trial of VOC employee Jan Plancx (or Blanck) for insubordination on July 8, 1652. The early cases are mostly those of sailors, accused of insubordination, fighting, desertions, petty theft, and the like. The first time an enslaved person appears in the records is in a transcription of a sentence handed out in Dutch Batavia: that of Catharina van Palliacatte (Pulicat]), whose death sentence for the murder of her lover is commuted to lifelong exile at the Cape in 1656.[33] Slaves are first tried for crimes at the Cape in 1660, when Willem and Claes are tried for desertion and stealing and killing a pig. The Council of Justice, at this point consisting of the three senior VOC officials at the Cape and two burghers, sentenced them to be scourged and branded. In the early years of the settlement, a number of people were also tried for excessive punishment of slaves, having sexual relations with slaves, and even, in one case, winning too much money off an enslaved person.[34] In 1685, the Council of Policy and the Council of Justice were officially separated (though the same people could serve on both). Subsequently the Council of Justice consisted of the governor, his second, the two military officials with the highest rank, four other VOC officials, three burghers, and a secretary without voting rights (who recorded the verdicts). The fiscal served as the state prosecutor.[35] The laws in force at the Cape of Good Hope were an amalgamation derived from various sources, including Roman law, Dutch maritime law, laws prescribed by the Council of Batavia (the imperial headquarters of the VOC outside the Netherlands), and local ordinances (*plakkaaten*) issued at the Cape of Good Hope.[36] In compiling the various regulations and laws related to slavery in response to the British taking over the legal system at the Cape in the nineteenth century, the fiscal at the time cites laws passed at the Cape of Good Hope, the Statutes of India (issued in Batavia), Roman law, and Dutch authorities on Roman law such as Hugo Grotius.[37]

Legal Verisimilitude

In *Talking Voices: Repetition, Dialogue, and Imagery in Conversational Discourse*, linguist Deborah Tannen writes, "The representation of speech in dialogue is a narrative act, not the inevitable result of the occurrence of speech in the episode. By setting up a little play, a speaker portrays motivations and other subtle evaluations internally—from within the play—rather than externally, by stepping outside the frame of the narrative to make evaluation explicit."[38] Implicit in this description is Tannen's larger claim: that quoted direct speech, except in the most exceptional of circumstances, is always at least slightly fictionalized. It is unrealistic to expect anyone to recall the exact words that someone uttered, and, in the case of the Council of Justice records, the translators and recorders of these reported words, deliberately or inadvertently, introduce further distortions. However, in the "play" Tannen describes above, the very fact that the enslaved are given a speaking role, that their words are considered important enough to record, is significant.

This documentation of the speech of the enslaved in the court records differs markedly from their depiction in wider discourse at the time. The following example will clearly distinguish between contemporaneous European depictions of slaves, and the court records' depiction of a similar incident: that of a slave running "amok." The term *amok* derives from the Melayu word *mengamuk* and is seen, starting in the early eighteenth century, as being a culturally specific syndrome prevalent in Southeast Asian societies, affecting predominantly men, manifesting as sudden incidents of excessive violence, usually involving homicide, and often ending in the suicide of the affected person.[39] The phenomenon of *amok* becomes part of the racialization of Southeast Asian subjects of European colonial rule, as discussion of these instances easily leads to generalizations about the psyche and behavior of a racialized group.

Here is how Jemima Kindersley, a British travel writer whose correspondence was published as *Letters from the Island of Teneriffe, Brazil, the Cape of Good Hope and the East Indies by Mrs. Kindersley* (1777), describes one such incident:

> This cast of people [the Malays] are remarkable for the violence of their passions, and are to the utmost degree revengeful; a melancholy instance of their violence has happened lately. One of them being offended with his master, gave himself up to the fury of his passion, and as the term is, *run a muck*, a thing which is not unusual. The first step he took was to intoxicate himself with opium, then letting his long hair loose about him, he sallied out with a knife in his hand, running straight forward, to stab every man, woman, child or animal which he met with.[40]

Here, discussion of sentiment, or "passions," clearly forms part of a broader cultural discourse on race and constructing race. "This cast of people" have violent passions and are "revengeful." This extract is from a letter in which Kindersley is discussing other characteristics of the "Malays," a term that referred then to all persons from Dutch Southeast Asia (the islands of Java, Sulawesi, and Timor, as well as Malacca). The event of an individual's running "a muck" thus becomes simply corroborating evidence for an emergent racialized stereotype. This observation holds true even of more sympathetic portrayals of the enslaved. The Swedish traveler Anders Sparrman, who penned some of the earliest antislavery writings about the Cape Colony after his travels in 1772–1776, had this to say about acts of running amok: "In consequence of this [unfair punishment], the unhappy slaves, who are frequently endued with finer feelings and nobler sentiments of humanity, though for the most part actuated by stronger passions than their masters, often give themselves up totally to despondency, and commit various acts of desperation and violence."[41] Sparrman, even when speaking of the "finer feelings and nobler sentiments of humanity," cannot help adding that the enslaved are "actuated by stronger passions than their masters," stressing their "despondency" and "violence."

In contrast, here is an excerpt from Baatjoe van Mandhaar's (Mandar, Sulawesi) sentence (1757):

> [The slaveholder, Broderick, enters the kitchen after hearing noise]: "Who does that?" to which the prisoner replied: "Me, Baas!" to which Broderick responded by ordering him to come down [from the attic], to which the prisoner also said "Soon," without actually doing so. The aforementioned Broderick, after repeating his order several times, said that if the prisoner did not come down, he would come up. Upon which the prisoner gave his assurances in Dutch to come on up as it was the prisoner's birthday, while adding in Portuguese that he the prisoner would murder him the slaveholder, during which the abovementioned Broderick, understanding no Portuguese, started climbing up the ladder only to have the latter translated to him by other slaves, and was held back by them to prevent his climbing the ladder (Baatjoe van Mandhaar 1757).[42]

In this sentence, the term *amok* is not used for Baatjoe van Mandhaar's behavior, but in the testimony of one of the witnesses, he stated that he had been called out because one of the slaves "amok maakte" (was making amok) (Baatjoe van Mandhaar 1757, 337 footnote 3). Baatjoe had barricaded himself in the attic of the house where he was enslaved and attacked the members of the colonial police force who attempted to extract him, finally attempting suicide by injuring himself in the neck. Here we can see the difference between narrating an alleged case of amok as an exemplar of a type of slave behavior and narrating similar events as part of a legal case. In the latter narration, the specifics of the individual case matter, whereas in Kindersley's letter, even though she describes one specific case, she erases all personal details about the man. In her description, the Malay slave is a type; in the court's, Baatjoe is individuated.

Baatjoe's sentence also demonstrates the effect of direct speech in the legal context: Baatjoe's exact words, his strategic deployment of different languages, matter, both in determining his guilt, but also in telling his story as vividly and plausibly as possible. Baatjoe refused to descend, calling out "I am a Mandhaar, you come up to me!" (Baatjoe van Mandhaar 1757, 338). The council responds to Baatjoe's act of defiance by sentencing him to the same gruesome death as Cupido van Mallebaar, his stated refusal of slavery ("I am a Mandhaar!") punished by the symbolic display of his body on the wheel "until consumed by the air and the birds of heaven" (Baatjoe van Mandhaar 1757, 338). The details of what, exactly, Baatjoe said form part of the overall narrative strategy to add as many specific details as possible: the strange fact regarding Baatjoe's invocation of his own birthday, the role of the other slaves in translating Baatjoe's sentence, and a very long and detailed description of how, exactly, the police officers and their assistants tried to get Baatjoe out of the attic.

One can trace an evolution of the use of direct speech in the Cape legal archives from 1652 onward. While cases from the seventeenth and early eighteenth centuries include direct speech, the quotations are quite factual: "[Anthonij asked Ari:] 'What are you doing here?,' to which Ari replied: 'What are you doing here?,' to which Ari was answered 'We are looking for food here, we have already run away, we think you have too,' whereupon they all formed an alliance" (Ari 1706, 8). While interesting to a linguist (Ari's speech contains some grammatical oddities that foreshadow the emergence of Afrikaans as a separate language), these quotations are bland in content. This begins to change in the 1720s, where we find the following lively account of the attack on a farm by a group of self-liberated former slaves:

> He did hear a person standing at the outside saying: "You damned fool, why do you not break open the door" . . . and thereupon the aforenamed *knecht* [servant] said to the slaves in the house: "Jongens, I must flee, let

them take what they want" whereupon this *knecht*, wearing only a blue nightshirt, fled through the broken door past several slaves ... who were fugitives, being immediately followed by all these slaves calling "*Pege, pege*"[43] or in other words "seize him, seize him" (Scipio van de Cust 1726, 104).

One cannot miss the drama in this description or the urgency expressed by the speech instances included. Even the fact that the rebellious slaves called out in Portuguese is recorded. In subsequent cases, it becomes increasingly common to include direct speech at key dramatic moments.[44]

Often, expressions of sentiment make it into the record in this way: for example, Andries van Bengalen's words to his straying lover, "Poeta [Puta]! Why do you do this to me?" (Andries van Bengalen 1741) or Jacomijn's plaintive, "At Sieur De Waal's I at least always had somebody to look after my child, but now there is nobody; she will scream herself to death" (Francois de Wet 1792).[45] Were these instances of speech perhaps included to testify to slaves' supposed lack of rationality, in the same way as we see Kindersley invoking the "violence of their passions"? Could one read these court documents as implicit justifications for slavery through depicting the passions of slaves: jealousy, for example? I believe not. While the impulse to depict the enslaved as driven by baser passions forms part of some strategies of racialization, that explanation is unsatisfactory in accounting for the examples of direct speech in these court records. Even the examples I cite above suggest that the emotions that the enslaved are allowed to testify to in their own words are not limited to base passions—Jacomijn's complaint that her child will cry herself to death in the absence of someone to look after her seems to bespeak not only maternal concern for the child but also a rational argument about the necessity of childcare.

I suggest, rather, that the inclusion of direct speech, rather than testifying to either the passions of the enslaved or to their humanity, is part of a complex system of legal verisimilitude. These details, included to attest to the plausibility of the testimony, partly work in a similar way as such details do in realist novels. Speaking of Daniel Defoe's 1719 novel *The Life and Strange Surprising Adventures of Robinson Crusoe, of York, Mariner, as Related by Himself*, J. M. Coetzee provides an eloquent description of "moderate realism": "Supply the particulars, allow the significations to emerge of themselves. A procedure pioneered by Daniel Defoe. Robinson Crusoe, cast up on the beach, looks around for his shipmates. But there are none. 'I never saw them afterwards, or any sign of them,' says he, 'except three of their hats, one cap, and two shoes that were not fellows.' Two shoes, not fellows: by not being fellows, the shoes have ceased to be footwear and become proofs of death, torn by the foaming seas off the feet of drowning men and tossed ashore."[46]

The same principle is at work in the court records as in Defoe's novel. A servant running away dressed only in a blue shirt, slaves calling out *"pege, pege"* (seize him, seize him) in Portuguese—these are the details that convince the judges of the truth of this account, which create the narrative of believable testimony, in the same way the two unmatched shoes create the narrative of a believable castaway. Roland Barthes famously describes such "useless details" or "insignificant notation" as part of a reality effect, in which these details "denote what is ordinarily called 'concrete reality.'"[47] Norman Page, in *Speech in the English Novel*, discusses the "delicate balance between the use of some of the observed features of actual speech and the interposing of a more or less elaborate code of stylistic conventions" that goes into creating what is considered to be realistic dialogue in the novel.[48] Page's analysis of novelistic speech reminds us that, as Tannen also pointed out, the kinds of direct speech that are accepted and read as "realistic" resemble "a very limited and selective observance of the features of actual speech," again cautioning us against taking these fragments of supposed direct speech in the court records as representing actual speech by the enslaved.[49]

Another example, from a 1739 case, involved the enslaved man Alexander van Maccasser (Makassar, Sulawesi), who is accused of insurrection. In the sentence, the following scene is described: "When he (the prisoner) returned home, his owner was immediately warned by the female slave Dorinde that he was drunk, saying 'Sir, Alexander is drunk again, he is hitting me and throwing fire at my body,' whereupon the master went into the kitchen and said to the prisoner, 'Are you drunk again and causing trouble?,' to which he replied 'I am not drunk'" (Alexander van Maccasser 1739).[50] The narrative continues by including details such as that the prisoner, looking for a knife he had allegedly hidden before, said "I hid it here, who took it away," and then picked up "a knife with a white handle, being a table-knife he had shortly before laid on the table" and, putting the knife in his pocket, went "through the foyer to the door of the room where his owner and mistress sat eating at a small table" (Alexander van Maccasser 1739, 170). The sentence thus both says that Dorinde told the man that Alexander was drunk and then repeats her supposed direct words, for example—a kind of narrative duplication that the dialogue between Alexander and the slaveholder echoes. Their reported direct speech here is part of the same net of detail as the fact that the knife had a white handle, or that the two slaveholders sat at a small table, while Alexander addressed them from the door: details that exceed the purpose of simply establishing guilt or innocence. If, as Page claims, the "history of the novel is partly the history of the adoption and development of these conventions" of realism, this chapter is in part dedicated to studying the adoption and development of the conventions of legal verisimilitude in Dutch eighteenth-century court records.[51]

J. Paul Hunter, who examines the cultural contexts leading to the rise of the novel as a form in England, identifies the proliferation of journalistic accounts in periodicals and pamphlets beginning in England in the 1690s as a crucial prefiguration of novelistic elements. Specifically, the greater interest in "private life, the personal, and the subjective" that marks journalism in this era produces novelistic features: "the way they blend contemporaneity, subjectivity, concentration on detail, [and] emphasis on the usual that happens even to the most ordinary of mortals."[52] Hunter also points to a corresponding rise in interest in the individual as eyewitness, "the validation of individuals, not necessarily trained individuals, as observers and interpreters" as a cultural movement influencing both journalism and the novel, stating that "it manifested itself everywhere, it is the essence of Protestantism."[53] We can speculate that, while the novel as genre appears later in Dutch literature, these developments in journalism, which also take place on the other side of the English Channel, may have influenced the conventions of legal verisimilitude in the VOC empire as much as it influenced the novel as a form in England.[54] The exclamations by slaves included in the court records are part of a kind of storytelling that relies on the inclusion of seemingly inconsequential details and eyewitness testimony in order to convey an impression of immediacy and accuracy. Barthes concludes that, while apparently denoting nothing except concrete reality, these "useless details" in novels in fact "[become] the very signifier of realism."[55] In the genre of the legal record, these details have a different function, denoting the accuracy of the account (including the exact words uttered at crucial junctures during the incident under investigation) and thus connoting the justness of the legal sentence pronounced. The precise and correct detailing of the facts will lead to the precise and correct sentence. As I will demonstrate in the reading of Jephta van Batavia's case below, however, this does not always mean that the writers of these legal records are accurately transcribing evidence: rather, what is plausible can supersede other accounts that make for a less believable narrative.

Scholars working on French slave societies have drawn attention to the importance of quoted direct speech by the enslaved, or the records of interrogations of the enslaved in which their exact responses are recorded, in allowing for different kinds of analysis of these societies than are possible in anglophone Atlantic colonies, where the enslaved could only testify in special slave courts that did not keep detailed records. The French legal system, both in the metropole and the colonies, "hinged on testimony as central to judicial procedure. In particular, it privileged confession as the 'queen of proofs,'" explains Sophie White, working on trial records from French Louisiana.[56] "Although trials were not devoid of biases both implicit and explicit, the trial record purported to be a truthful rendering of what had taken place and had been said in court," she adds.[57] Megan Vaughan, working on eighteenth-century Isle de France (Mauritius), also stresses the importance of testimony to the French legal system, writing that "ancien régime criminal procedure (unlike English law of the time) required an extremely detailed written record to be produced, from the first investigation into a crime to the last deliberations of the judge, including verbatim (or supposedly verbatim) records of the interrogations of suspects and witnesses."[58] Vaughan, though interested in mining these recordings of speech for their insight specifically into the development of language, admits that they are "deceptively immediate. They are in fact renditions, reordered written versions of speech in an unstable linguistic situation, with multiple opportunities for incomprehension and mistranslation."[59] This is closer to my own approach to the "deceptively immediate" snippets of recorded direct speech in the Dutch legal archives.

Both White and Vaughan suggest that the purpose of recording enslaved speech in the French legal archives is to satisfy an understanding of the law as thorough, invested in the spoken word, and, above all, invested in documentation. In criminal cases, the Cape Council of Justice also relied on the inquisitory procedure, which was prevalent in Europe (including France), whereby the accused had to confess their crime before they could be found guilty. Thus part of what is at work in these records is also a privileging of confession, and thus speech, as the most valuable form of testimony. If the accused did not initially confess, they were interrogated by delegates from the Council of Justice, based on a list of questions drawn up by the fiscal based on evidence he had collected. The interrogation format takes the form of leading questions, often simply requiring a yes/no answer. There is a kind of ritualistic element to these performances, which clearly stage the power imbalance between the questioner, who is in charge of steering the conversation, and the accused.[60] If a confession could not be extracted through interrogation, court officials could and did resort to torture. The summary narrative, called an *eijsch ende conclusie* (claim with conclusion), produced at the end of this interrogation by the fiscal, demonstrates how this story gets written: any discord or faltering within the performance is erased, and a plausible narrative, conforming to the expectations of the legal authorities in charge of the case, results.

The interrogation records, listing on the right half of the page the questions asked, and the left the answers, visually stage a kind of confrontation between the story the fiscal seeks to tell and the voice of the interrogated: here, the dialogic nature of the court narrative is vividly represented. Out of this, the fiscal has to create a single narrative combining the various voices of the witnesses, the reported direct speech of the various participants in each case, and the supposedly verbatim speech of the accused recorded during their interrogation and confession. The final sentences, produced by the Council of Justice members, usually copied the account directly from the fiscal's claims, with the verdict and punishment at the end. In thinking about how legal verisimilitude works in these records, I am thus most interested in the representation of direct speech and sentiment in the claims with conclusions and sentences, as they demonstrate the deliberate arrangement of narratives combined from various sources. The form of legal verisimilitude in these records draws both on the same central importance of speech as in the French inquisitorial system, but also on conventions of plausible storytelling that govern which reported quotations and other details make it into the final case narrative. In the following example, I demonstrate how various reports of verbally expressed sentiment are rewritten in compiling a claim and final sentence.

Jephta van Batavia, 1729

In 1729, Jephta van Batavia was accused of attacking an enslaved woman, Maria van Ceijlon, with whom he was seen as being in a relationship. The sentence in this case states that, in response to someone who tried to stop him, Jephta said, "Even if I am to be broken on the wheel, I shall murder her, I shall eat her heart, I seek my death [*Maske raadbraaken, ik sal haar vermoorden, ik sal haar het hert op vreeten, ik soek mijn dood*]" (Jephta van Batavia 1729).[61] The sentencing authorities, the Council of Justice, seem to have recognized the power of including this phrase, which increases the drama of his case against the accused, painting a picture of a jealous lover, driven beyond the point of reason, wanting to eat, or rather devour (*opvreeten* is a term used for animals, not people) his lover's heart. The set of documents about this trial in the Western Cape archives show that the council members, in their sentence, copied Jephta's supposed exclamation exactly from the claim made by the fiscal. Looking at the records of the interrogations and declarations in the case, though, we notice a curious set of circumstances pertaining to this supposed direct speech.

In the declaration by one of the witnesses, Johanna Lens, Jephta's words are as follows: "I shall murder her, I shall eat her lung, because I seek my death [*Ik sal haar vermoorden, ik sal haar long opvreeten, want ik soek mijn dood*]" (CJ 333, 313).[62] Here, two things change from the exclamation recorded in the claim and sentence. Jephta is seen as claiming to want to eat a *lung*, and a causal relationship is implied: he wants to eat her lung *because* he seeks his death. In the declaration by another witness, Barend Smit van Groningen, he claims that after he confronted Jephta, the latter replied, "Even if broken on the wheel, I seek my death: I shall murder her, I shall eat her lung" (CJ 333, 316). Both witnesses thus agree that it was the lung that Jephta wanted to eat, and Smit's testimony supports the suggestion that Jephta's desire for death precedes and perhaps causes his desire to eat Maria's lung. However, in the confession signed by Jephta van Batavia, compiled by the fiscal following the two witness statements, we read the first instance of the statement eventually recorded in the sentence: "Even if it means being broken on the wheel, I shall murder her, I shall eat her heart, I seek my death" (CJ 333, 317). The confession was read out to Jephta, who then has a chance to correct anything. He agreed with everything in the confession, except to ask that the following be added: that when he said, "I shall murder her, I shall eat her heart, I seek my death," he was "*beschonken*" (intoxicated) (CJ 333, 318). Jephta thus seems to have noticed the statement but chose to distance himself from it. In the final sentence, Jephta's edit, that he was intoxicated, is omitted, and the council members instead add that he uttered this phrase "in a rage" (*uit verwoetheijd*) (Jephta van Batavia 1729).[63]

This set of records demonstrates how slave sentiment is manipulated in service of narrative plausibility. The sentence "I shall eat her lung" is jarring: especially when combined with the clause "*because* I seek my death." This statement is difficult to understand figuratively. Rephrasing it to "I shall eat her heart, I seek my death" frames the utterance in the more familiar European tradition that connects the heart to affairs of passion and love. Jephta's own death is also reframed as a consequence of his murder that he is willing to accept, rather than the main reason for his actions. Earlier in the claim, the fiscal glosses a question allegedly posed by Jephta to Maria, "Why are you harming me?" (*waarom doet je mij quaad?*), which could have many possible interpretations, as "meaning with this that she had gone about or had carnal conversation with someone else than him," thereby establishing the narrative that this is a case of sexual jealousy (Jephta van Batavia 1729, 116). The fiscal here chose to read the relationship between Jephta and Maria, who as enslaved persons were not otherwise able to get their relationship legally recognized through marriage, as romantic, an affair of the heart. This reading allowed for what seemed to the fiscal to be the most plausible and convincing interpretation of the events.

The inclusion of Jephta's supposed direct speech here forms part of a system in which speech was both included, and sometimes manipulated, to form part of a verisimilar narrative of crime: here, one of love and jealousy. The reader is left, here as in the other records, with only vestiges of Jephta's actual speech act, since even the two instances of his claiming to want to eat Maria's lung are reported by witnesses. While we could link this threat to other threats of bodily mutilation and cannibalism found in the eighteenth-century legal archives, even an ethnographic understanding of the rituals and beliefs of this slave society would not produce a singular simple explanation of Jephta's supposed exclamation, and the emotions which may have motivated it.[64] I will return to Jephta's enigmatic claim in the conclusion to this chapter, reflecting on this urge to understand and reframe it as part of a familiar narrative.

Reijnier van Madagascar, 1749

In the cases I have examined thus far I focused on the claims and sentences produced largely by fiscals, combining other forms of testimony into a plausible narrative. I now turn to what we have seen referred to as the "queen of proofs": a confession. Reijnier van Madagascar was accused of attacking a slaveholder and liberating himself by running away. His confession was made in Dutch, which "the confessant speaks and understands reasonably well" (Reijnier van Madagascar 1749).[65] Reijnier had escaped, but he was recaptured and his confession recorded in January 1749, twenty years after the events detailed in it took place. As many, if not most, of the confessions and interrogations in the records of the Council of Justice were collected with the help of a translator, this extended untranslated confession offers an impression of greater immediacy and access to the enslaved confessor than other records. This is thus a case that allows me, tentatively, to speculate about the deployment of the conventions of legal verisimilitude by an enslaved person. In the same way that scholars have investigated the mediation of the conventions of the slave narrative and the genres it draws upon (the confessional, the abolitionist pamphlet, the travelogue, the religious conversion narrative, etc.) in the autobiographies of Equiano, Cugoano, Harriet Jacobs, and others, here my focus will be on the mediation performed by the form of the court record on the way Reijnier van Madagascar narrates an incident in his life. However, I steer clear of reading this as an autobiography. In an article addressing the question of how to work with the archives of enslavement, David Kazanjian cautions that "when we imagine enslaved lives as best recuperated or pictured by the 'autobiographical narrative,' we make a politically, culturally, and historically specific Anglo-American literary genre our norm and ideal."[66] Kazanjian argues for a speculative or philosophical reading of slave archives, saying that "we must read seemingly quotidian texts not only for the empirical information they offer about the lives their authors lived and observed, but also for the theoretical work they do—for the ways they speculate upon ontological, epistemological, and political questions."[67]

The confession as a genre—in legal, religious, and therapeutic contexts—has long been the subject of literary analysis, but the framework I find most useful for thinking through Reijnier's narrative is the work of historian Natalie Zemon Davis on sixteenth-century French letters of remission (letters written to the king to plead for pardon for a crime). Davis is struck particularly by the narrative form of these letters: "I marvel at the literary qualities of these texts, or, I might say, their 'fictional' qualities, by which I mean the extent to which their authors shape the events of a crime into a story."[68] These letters are also confessional, since the pleader has to first acknowledge guilt for the crime, explaining any extenuating circumstances, before asking for pardon. In her analysis, Davis pays attention to the following narrative strategies of the letter writers: "What they thought a good story was, how they accounted for motive, and how through narrative they made sense of the unexpected and built coherence into immediate experience."[69] It is in this vein, of asking how Reijnier structured his own narrative to tell a "good story" about his crime, that I will be reading his confession. Michel Foucault's insight that the confession is "of the order of drama or dramaturgy" (Foucault also examines confession in the context of the inquisitory legal system) is also helpful in terms of providing the vocabulary—that of the theater—to discuss the form Reijnier's confession takes.[70] The circumstances under which Reijnier performs this confession—captured, with the threat of execution hanging over him—as well as the amount of time that has passed since the events detailed underscore the fact that we cannot simply read this as a factual account of a specific event, but a feat of memory, imagination, and rhetoric, performed under duress and in fear.

Reijnier's narrative provides ample material for analyses of filial relationships under slavery, the role of women in controlling and disciplining the enslaved, and the bonds and rivalries formed between fellow slaves. The confession, however, also demonstrates that Reijnier is constructing his narrative according to similar conventions of legal verisimilitude we see in the other court cases, written by fiscals or council members. Reijnier's tactical deployment of the technique of reporting direct speech, though in line with the way speech is used in other court cases (as testifying to the plausibility of the event narrated), also perhaps allows him to speak of the cruelties of the system of slavery. While it is impossible to know the exact reasoning of the council members, we can speculate that Reijnier's confession was successful at both imitating and manipulating the conventions of the court, as he was sentenced to life imprisonment on Robben Island, rather than the death sentences that were usually imposed on enslaved persons who had attacked slaveholders. His case begins conventionally: "There appears before us, the undersigned delegates from the honourable Council of Justice at the Castle of Good Hope, Reijnier van Madagascar, bondsman [*lijfeigenen*] of the heirs of the late farmer Matthijs Krugel, 60 years old at a guess, who on the requisition of the magistrate [*landdrost*] of Stellenbosch and Draakensteijn, sieur Adriaan van Schoor, confesses how it is true" (Reijnier van Madagascar 1749).[71]

This introduction is standard across the cases I have looked at—enslaved people are introduced by stating their name and the slaveholder's name, along with their age. This legal ceremony also introduces the audience to this confession, the delegates of the Council of Justice, and invokes the authority of the magistrate of the region where Reijnier had lived. We now transition into the confession itself, recorded in the third person:

> That the confessant, now more than twenty years ago, because the wife of his above-mentioned master [*lijfheer*] beat the confessant's daughter, named Sabina, daily and without reason; and said mistress, who could not stand the girl, nonetheless and in spite of the confessant's many entreaties, would not agree to sell her under any circumstances, but instead, continually mistreated her; for, towards the evening on a certain Saturday, when the confessant came home from plowing and asked his fellow slave Manica, being the confessant's wife, for the used tealeaves of his mistress, this woman answered: "The *juffrouw* [mistress] drank no tea today, but wine" (Reijnier van Madagascar 1749, 264).

The direct quotation acts as an anchor in this story, moving Reijnier's tale from the iterative (Sabina was thrashed daily, and the female slaveholder refused to sell her, in spite of frequent entreaties) to the specific (the evening of a certain Saturday). When Reijnier starts quoting directly from what was said at the time, the narrative becomes more focused. Notice the exchange in which it is established that the woman had been drinking: rather than say that she was drunk, Reijnier describes a conversation with his wife in which he asks for tealeaves, and she tells him that "the *juffrouw* drank no tea today, but wine." This small detail, seemingly unconnected to the main narrative, is a much more effective way of communicating the woman's intoxication.

> The said woman [Manica] then narrated to him how his mistress had that day with a *sjambok* [whip], after first stripping said Sabrina naked and having her placed in a so-called *poolsche bok*,[72] thoroughly beaten her; she [Sabina] then ran from the house to behind a corral, from where the confessant himself brought her into the kitchen; and for this reason Sabina then wanted to run away, to which the confessant told her not to do so, but much rather go to her master and beg him for forgiveness (Reijnier van Madagascar 1749, 264).

The fact that Krugel's wife had first stripped Sabina naked and then had had her tied into a vulnerable, exposed position before beating her demonstrates a particularly sadistic streak, even bordering on sexual (this may also explain why she refused to sell Sabina, in spite of Reijnier's many pleas). Christine Walker, a historian of Jamaica, delves into the role of women in perpetuating the system of slavery in this British colony: "Free and freed women ... [proved] themselves to be every bit as calculating and brutal as the men with whom they shared the island."[73] It is not surprising to see that in the brutal slaveholding society at the Cape, violence was not purely a masculine weapon. Choosing to include these details, like the detail about the wine, helps Reijnier provide context for his own violent reaction, and is a more effective narrative strategy than the general description of the woman's behavior with which the confession started.

In the original Dutch, this has all been one long run-on sentence, and at this point, the second sentence in Reijnier's confession begins, "Whereas the confessant's fellow slaves, named Hans and Patas, seeing the continued maltreatment of his aforementioned daughter Sabina, often said to him: 'You are such an old man and have made it so that the farm is paid off, can plow and do all sorts of other work so well and can yet endure such maltreatment;

were this girl our daughter, we would have taught the *baas* [boss] something else'" (Reijnier van Madagascar 1749).[74]

We again have both iterative time (the continued maltreatment of Sabina, the slaves would often say to him) and one specific imagined quoted utterance. Reijnier imagines a play for the audience of his confession, in which his fellow enslaved are made to speak together, as a kind of chorus. The other men's words conflate three issues: Reijnier's strength (as demonstrated by his ability to plow), his age and position on the farm, and paternal responsibility. At first, the first two issues seem unrelated to the third, but Reijnier's choice to place them together in the imagined collective speech of the other slaves suggests that for him, they are inextricably linked. It is not just in his role as father that he reaches a breaking point, but also in his role as a slave: one that had established the farm and still performed many useful functions, including plowing (remember that he had drawn attention to the fact that he had just returned from plowing on the day this incident takes place). It may be that he considered the second, that of hardworking slave, to be a more legible role to the court, since paternal relationships between slaves were legally irrelevant: children took on the status (free or enslaved) of their mothers. Note the parallelism in the sentences ascribed to Hans and Patas—can plow (*kunt so well ploegen*) and can yet endure (*kunt dog . . . verdragen*). It is because of his excellent performance as enslaved worker that Reijnier's fellow enslaved seem to say that he should not be expected to endure Sabina's punishment. To us, it might seem as though Reijnier is muddling the narrative explaining his motivations here: did he react because he could no longer stand watching the abuse of his daughter, or out of pride, because his fellow slaves were mocking him? This case is telling because, to Reijnier, filial sentiment alone does not seem to be an adequate motivator. He adds the mocking voices of his fellow slaves to his confession, both as a form of character witness (this is how he incorporates the fact that he helped pay off the farm and was still a useful laborer, in spite of his age), but also to provide his paternal sentiments with external validation.

Here is the denouement of this case:

> And that, later on that very same Saturday evening, when both the confessant and the other slaves were all in the kitchen, the confessant's owner entered it, holding a broomstick in his hand, and beat the *meij* Sabina anew. As a consequence of this, the confessant, out of despair and heartache [*mismoedigheijd en hertseer*], took up a knife lying on the table in the kitchen and gave his aforementioned owner three

stabs with it, without being able to say where, seeing that the lamp was almost half burnt out. Upon this, the confessant immediately took flight over the plowed land of his master, where he hid for about a week, after which he betook himself to the Franschhoek mountains, and there, to the best of his recall, stayed for a time of sixteen years (Reijnier van Madagascar 1749, 264–65).

This is the most dramatic part of Reijnier's confession. Note how theatrically Reijnier sets the scene: All of the slaves on the farm are gathered in the kitchen, later the same night, when the slaveholder enters, holding a broomstick. The lights are low, the lamp is almost burned out. In "despair and heartache," Reijnier stabs his master three times. In looking at the French pardon tales, Davis unpacks the logic of minimizing culpability at work in these texts: the writers are not claiming to be innocent but making the case for their own pardon. Curiously, one feature shared between Davis's cases and Reijnier's confession is the insistence that the confessant "could not say where" they stabbed their victims. It seems as if not the act of violence itself, but the clarity or visibility thereof is at stake.

In this confession, we see both Manica and Hans and Patas invoked as witnesses. The narrative intriguingly shifts from the world of women (initially, the interactions between Manica, the wife, and Sabina are the focus of the narrative) to the world of men, as Hans and Patas are invoked as witnesses, and the final confrontation is between Reijnier and Matthijs Krugel. Domestic violence (notice Reijnier's use of the kitchen knife, and the intimate, half-lit scene of the kitchen) is displaced in the course of the narrative from the feminine realm to the masculine.

This confession by Reijnier van Madagascar thus demonstrates multiple ways in which the conventions of legal verisimilitude, in which the plausibility of a narrative is buttressed by as many details as possible, including reported direct speech, aids Reijnier in framing a confession that is convincing. Reijnier does not explicitly critique the system of slavery: rather, the expectation of legal verisimilitude established in the court records allows him to include imagined slave speech that undermines the institution of slavery by introducing an imagined outside observer of the actions of slaveholders. Neither Manica nor Hans and Patas express direct criticism of Matthijs Krugel and his wife in this little play, but their characters comment descriptively upon what they observe and through these descriptions highlight contradictions in the understanding of the enslaved as property and the enslaved as father.

Taking a step back, we can observe different kinds of discourses in Reijnier's confession. In the phrase *without being able to say where*, I have identified a certain formula at work, which suggests that this is something that Reijnier may have heard elsewhere, a phrase that had been established to have some exculpatory power. The first section of the confession ("There appears before us . . .") is likewise a formula, a legal one this time, that precedes every confession, and sets the frame for this tale as a legal one, beginning and ending with the stock phrases of the law ("Which I declare, [signed], C. L. Neethling, sworn clerk"). Reijnier's actual speech is rendered into the third person, such that we "hear" both his voice and the clerk's intermingled in the confession (did Reijnier actually describe himself as "taking flight" [*neemende de vlugt*], for example?). Of course, we also hear the speech ascribed to Manica, Hans, and Patas in this text, introducing them as separate characters contributing thoughts and information independent of the main narrator. We even catch a hint of the slaveholder's wife's negating voice, in the phrase *would not agree to sell her under any circumstances*. My process here is very similar to the discourse analysis that literary theorist Mikhail Bakhtin performs on extracts from various novels, in which he demonstrates the interpenetration of different forms of discourse, whether marked by quotation marks or not, in the novel. Reijnier's confession thus demonstrates the characteristic of language that Bakhtin calls heteroglossia (*raznorečie*) or the "social diversity of speech types," as Caryl Emerson and Michael Holquist also translate it.[75] Bakhtin further describes heteroglossia as "the social stratification of any single national language into social dialects, characteristic group behavior, professional jargons, generic languages, languages of generations and age groups, tendentious languages, languages of the authorities, of various circles and of passing fashions, languages that serve the specific sociopolitical purposes of the day, even of the hour."[76] While Bakhtin specifies that it is only in the novel (a genre that he, unlike most theorists of the novel, sees as originating in antiquity) that heteroglossia is "artistically organized," he adds that speech in law "calls for further study," a provocation I have taken up in this chapter.[77] One could perform the same kind of analysis (breaking up the record into its constituent social languages) on all of the court records I have included. Heteroglossia in these eighteenth-century records is a formal feature that allows for an enslaved speech effect to emerge, in which the enslaved are represented as speaking among other forms of official and unofficial speech. It presents an alternative to what Hartman calls the archive of slavery as a "death sentence, a tomb, a display of the violated body."[78] In this reading, the textual friction inadvertently enshrined in these legal records acts as a lasting monument, counteracting the exposure of the enslaved body to "the air and birds of heaven"—an act that confirmed ultimate judicial power over the body of the enslaved. These records then become a space where the law's authoritative voice can be tempered (though never erased) by the underlying murmur of exclamations, inexplicable phrases, and untranslatable words.

Slave speech, including expressions of love, passion, or self-pity, is recorded as evidence in these legal records: not as evidence of humanity, but simply evidence forming part of a believable narrative. The fact that these expressions of sentiment often arise from the cruelty of the system of slavery is not considered in these case narratives. The words of the enslaved are reproduced, rewritten, and sometimes reimagined in these records, and (as is the case for all forms of reported direct speech) they are thus highly vulnerable to manipulation. Yet, I suggest that the enslaved speech effect in the archives allows for a kind of opacity in these records. In making this argument, I am sympathetic to the claims of Hartman, Fuentes, Walter Johnson, and other scholars of slavery that any attempt to pinpoint the agency of the enslaved is rife with contradictions, as notions of agency often invoke liberal ideas of subjecthood that are incompatible with the lived experience of the enslaved.[79] As such, I avoid invoking agency in analyzing these documents—rather, drawing on the strengths of literary analysis, the textual friction I describe does not depend on the intention of the enslaved witness, or that of the recording fiscal. The proliferation of different voices in the court records allows for ambiguity, untranslatability, and glimpses of alterity to flourish, even in legal records that aim to establish a single, clear narrative leading to a single, clear verdict. These court records, while heavily invested in the criminalization and punishment of the enslaved body, allow for a more multifaceted, polyvocal figure of the slave to emerge through their frequent incorporation of imagined or reconstructed slave speech.

This concept of textual friction draws upon the work of several contemporary theorists of Black studies, using their insights into the work of addressing the archive of enslavement to frame an understanding of a kind of enslaved subjectivity that does not invoke agency. While different approaches to the archive of enslavement in the Black Atlantic have played out historically (from early studies focusing on the total powers of the slaveholders that reduced the enslaved to "obsequious, childlike, and helpless persons who embodied a pure extension of their masters' wishes" to social history approaches starting in the 1970s that focused on excavating forms of enslaved resistance), Hartman's anguish in "Venus in Two Acts" has been instrumental in inspiring different approaches to the archive.[80] In that 2008 essay, Hartman describes the archive as a site in which the "libidinal investment in violence is everywhere apparent," asking about the titular Venus whether it is "possible to reiterate her name and to tell a story about degraded matter and dishonored life that doesn't delight and titillate, but instead ventures toward another mode of writing."[81] This is fundamentally a question about the ethics of engaging the archives of enslavement—whether it is possible to go beyond the deathly logic of the archive-as-tomb: "How does one tell impossible stories?"[82] Every scholar of slavery has to engage with this question in their own work.

Hartman proposes what she calls "critical fabulation": "By playing with and rearranging the basic elements of the story, by re-presenting the sequence of events in divergent stories and from contested points of view, I have attempted to jeopardize the status of the event, to displace the received or authorized account, and to imagine what might have happened or might have been said or might have been done."[83] She adds: "Narrative restraint, the refusal to fill the gaps and provide closure, is a requirement of this method, as is the imperative to respect black noise—the shrieks, the moans, the nonsense, and the opacity, which are always in excess of legibility and of the law."[84] Historian Stephanie Smallwood, in reflecting upon her own reaction to Hartman's call, describes her own process of aiming to tell a history that "is accountable to the enslaved" as "theorizing what we might call the counterfact, by which I mean the fact that the archive is seeking to ignore, marginalize, and disavow—the detail it does not want to animate and make narratable."[85] The kinds of archives I work with here are different from those available to Hartman and Smallwood: the enslaved appear more robustly than they do in the lists of deaths, diseases, and violent crimes, or the diaries and letters of the slaveholders, that form the basis of their archival work. Yet, the question of engaging ethically with the violence of the archives cannot be eluded, and the temptation to see, in the recorded supposed direct speech of the enslaved, their actual voices is understandable, but also dangerous.

In the final chapter of *None Like Us*, Stephen Best takes up Hartman's challenge in response to the recording of rumors in court cases on slave insurrections. These are secondhand records of what the enslaved had allegedly said regarding emancipation: the anxiety in the slaveholding colonies being that abolitionist agitation in England had reached the colonies in distorted forms, leading to the belief that the enslaved would be freed imminently by an imagined benevolent monarch.[86] While the circumstances under which these forms of illicit enslaved speech, "loose talk," are recorded in the archives differ from the records I examine, Best offers an approach to these speech forms that resonates with my idea of the textual friction that surrounds the supposed recorded direct speech of the enslaved in the Dutch records. As he asks: "How does one leave aside the impression—the possibility, if even remote—that none of this was said? How can one write a history in the face of such doubt?"[87] He suggests that "we must strain to hear what is alien in the voice of the enslaved. This involves a necessary refusal to translate that foreignness back into our native tongue."[88] In order to approach this alienness, he proposes the idea of glossolalia: "A mumble that escapes the control of the speakers."[89] He concludes that "the slaves' intention do not so much matter; what matters is how rumor registers as metalepsis," with metalepsis here functioning as a break in the diegetic narrative, referring to a different narrative level, or an outside to the narrative.[90]

Working on different legal records, Best here intuits the same function I do for imagined recorded speech in the slave archive of the Dutch Cape of Good Hope: as exceeding the original purpose of forming part of a legal system of oppression and violence against the body of the enslaved. When we read, in Januarij van Boegies's case, that he, "all huffing and growling [*al pruttende en knorrende*] . . . said 'You have a soul, and I have a soul'" to the enslaved woman with whom he is described as being in a relationship, the accuracy of the recorded words perhaps does not matter as much as acknowledging what Hartman calls the "black noise," the rage or pain or other emotion that is suggested by this statement, which we cannot access (Januarij van Boegies 1755).[91]

To return to a case discussed earlier, the ghost traces of Jephta van Batavia's desire to devour Maria's lung can then also be read as a form of textual friction—a glimpse outside of the power of the legal system to contain and represent even the sentiments of the enslaved. It hints at a system of meaning outside of the European framework for understanding love: but it is a foreignness we, unlike the fiscal, should not try to tame or translate. Achille Mbembe warns about the risks of the official archive, and the historian's work with the archives: "The historian is not content with bringing death back to life. S/he restores it to life precisely in order better to silence it by transforming it from autonomous words into a prop on which s/he can lean in order to speak and write beyond an originary text."[92] This danger is unavoidable. But I hope there is also a possibility to attend to the autonomous words of the dead, even when they have been recontextualized here. In Jephta van Batavia's case, we need to linger in the moment when the limit of our ability to read, understand, and interpret the textual rendering of Jephta's words is made clear to us: a metalepsis, in Best's reading. The court records emerge out of the proliferation of different voices—Jephta's, the witnesses', the fiscal's, the council members'—and cannot be ascribed to a single controlling author or will. The inclusion of direct speech in these court documents, however, allows for this opacity—in the form of ambiguity, overdetermination, a refusal to signify—to arise.

To conclude, I juxtapose the examples of legal documents from the eighteenth-century Council of Justice I have examined in this chapter with a brief example from the nineteenth-century British Cape Colony's Council of Justice records, in which imagined direct speech by the enslaved is increasingly rare, to highlight the impact of reported direct speech. Here is an extract from the British Council of Justice records on a case of infanticide from 1823:

> That the Prisoner, supposed to be between Thirty and Thirty Five years of age, having left her Master's place situated in the District of George, about three o'clock on the 24th December last year, repaired to the place of Hendrik Van Huysteen, Field Cornet of the land behind said Bay, she there, in presence of a certain Carel Schaffer, acquainted the Field Cornet, at the same time delivering him a Clasp Knife and shedding some Tears, that she, through Heartsore and Grief, had cut the Throat of her Child named Baro with that knife because she, as well as the Child, were ill treated both by her Master and Mistress.[93]

It is significant that the British maintain the Council of Justice as a place where the enslaved are put on trial, alongside those who hold free status—this means that, even in the nineteenth century, we have much more detail about cases in which the enslaved appear than in most other British colonies (this was also the case for Ceylon and Mauritius, for example, where the British continued Dutch and French precedents of allowing the enslaved to testify in regular courts). However, the form and content of these cases change. The different kinds of discourse we see in Reijnier's confession, but also in the sentences and claims I quoted earlier, have been mostly flattened out into an official legal voice. Sentimental descriptions have not been erased from this account ("shedding some Tears"), but names, dates, ages, and times are scrupulously recorded and take the place of the direct quotations, details about clothing, and vivid descriptions of action that form the basis of earlier legal verisimilitude.

The only exception to the legal language in this extract is the word *heartsore*, a neologism in English that is a direct translation of the Dutch *hartzeer*. Yvette Christiansë, whose 2006 novel *Unconfessed* is a creative retelling of the life of the prisoner Sila van de Caab, describes this word as erupting from the testimony: "Even so, she [Sila] remains largely unknowable, the bearer of unbearable knowledge, the keeper of secrets, including, most powerfully, the meaning of a word that erupts in testimony, the word '*hartzeer*.'"[94] In this one word, appearing even more dramatically because of the bland legalese surrounding it, we can perhaps identify the voice of Sila. However, it is only in the contemporary novelization of this record that Christiansë is able to set Sila's voice among the heteroglossia of other voices.

Compare Cupido van Mallebaar's case narrative, with which I started this chapter, with that of Sila van de Caab. Remember Cupido showing the slaveholder five bullets and saying, "These bullets I made for myself"? While Sila's case is shocking, the narrative of Cupido's crime, in which we imagine ourselves capable of hearing his voice, along with the voices of the slaveholder and his wife, and their cruel laughter, is animated by the presence of these voices in a way that Sila's is not.[95] As Tannen writes, "The creation of voices occasions the imagination of alternative, distant, and others' worlds by linking them to the sounds and scenes of one's own familiar world."[96] For both the creators of these eighteenth-century records, and their readers today, the impact of direct speech lies exactly in its ability to bring together the world of the enslaved and their/our world. If back then this served to better convey a believable, convincing narrative about a crime, it now serves, perhaps, to allow us to imagine a break, something alien, a form of impossible speech, of "huffing and growling."

Of the enslaved individuals we have met in this chapter, Cupido van Mallebaar and Januarij van Boegies were sentenced to death, while Reijnier van Madagascar, Alexander van Couchin, and Jephta van Batavia were sentenced to harsh physical punishment and hard labor. We do not know the fates of others, such as Reijnier's daughter Sabina, or Maria van Ceijlon, who was stabbed by Jephta van Batavia. These individuals are quickly subsumed in the violence of the archives. In response to Gayatri C. Spivak's famous question about the speech of the subaltern, these records certainly do not contradict her position that the historic subaltern cannot speak. Like the Rani of Sirmur, Cupido van Mallebaar, Jephta van Batavia, and Reijnier van Madagascar can only leave imprints, tracks that are irrevocably distorted by passing through the Dutch imperial legal system and its archiving practices. However, I would add that archives do not distort in identical ways and that paying attention to the ways in which subalterns are imagined as speaking is important. These court records, though unique to the Dutch imperial world, can perhaps serve as a model for seeking out and identifying other kinds of textual friction in the forms taken by slave archives in other parts of the world, including the more familiar Anglo-American contexts: a challenge I take up in the next chapter, which focuses on the Cape Colony once it becomes British.

2. SILENCING THE ENSLAVED

The Aesthetics of Abolitionism in the British Cape Colony, 1795–1834

My Gun is Good and I am Likewise Good—GALANT (1825)

The trial began on March 14, 1825, at 10 A.M. Galant, formerly enslaved by the late W. N. van der Merwe, and eleven other accused (five enslaved men, one enslaved woman, five male Khoisan servants, and one male European settler) were accused of sedition and murder.[1] This, the final act of one of two large-scale revolts by the enslaved in this history of the Cape Colony, provides compelling reading. The main accused, twenty-six-year-old Galant, self-described in the trial as the "Captain" of the rebellion, is eloquent and thoughtful. During the trial, he frequently challenged other witnesses, including slaveholders. Galant's testimony reflects on various rumors circulating among slaves and slaveholders alike about the possibility of freedom for the enslaved at the Cape: he claims that he had reason to believe that the enslaved should have been freed by 1825.[2]

The trial records, including the testimony of the accused, take up more than 150 pages in the collected *Records of the Cape Colony*. None of Galant's eloquence makes it into the summary or claim written by the fiscal (prosecutor), however. In contrast to the eighteenth-century trial records I examine in the previous chapter, in which the fiscals would frequently choose to include extended quotations, few instances of direct speech are cited in the fiscal's claim. The first word we "hear" (or see cited) in the fiscal's claim is an instruction, from the other rebels, to Galant to "shoot."[3] Following that, we see Galant calling out to his fellow-accused Abel, "with a curse *Abel fire,*" and later, to another rebel, "*shoot him with the pistol that you have right on the head, for he is not yet dead.*"[4] The longest speech we read in the fiscal's statement is Galant saying, "*Whitehead I have already got, but now I must have Isaak van der Merwe and Jan Abraham du Plessis, my gun is good and I am likewise good.*"[5] In the fiscal's closing claim, none of Galant's statements explaining his actions, including his accusation that the slaveholder had earlier beaten his child to death, are cited, and the only word the fiscal wants to highlight from Galant's testimony is *war*: "One of the prisoners themselves, I believe Galant, called his act here in Court making war."[6] The purpose of the fiscal's inclusion of these specific instances of direct speech is clear: they demonstrate the violent nature of the insurrection and, specifically, Galant's role in inciting this violence. The enslaved are portrayed as only speaking the language of violence, rebellion, and sedition, not of family or reason. Slave testimonies, and speech attributed to the enslaved by other witnesses, are almost exclusively paraphrased, not cited directly.

This chapter pursues the question of how the enslaved are represented in colonial writings in the nineteenth-century Cape of Good Hope, increasingly referred to as the Cape Colony. As the colony makes a slow transition from Dutch to British rule, I ask what happens to slave voices and slave speech during this period, when the British slave trade is officially banned (1807) and the enslaved in the British Empire are emancipated (1834, though Cape slaves would serve a further four-year "apprenticeship" ending in 1838). Even as new British laws to ameliorate slavery take effect during this period, representations of slave voices largely disappear from both legal and administrative records, and instead, a sentimental image of the slave infiltrates both pro- and antislavery discourse. While the aims of these two movements are opposed, the figure of the slave as silent and helpless is surprisingly similar. The expressions of sentiment (love, pity, nostalgia, anger) that animated direct speech in eighteenth-century court records are replaced by sentimental descriptions of the enslaved as childlike, suffering, and either silent or crying inarticulately.

Writings by abolitionists, a slaveholder, and the civil servants working at the Office of the Registrar and Guardian of Slaves show that the enslaved are silenced in similar ways by pro- and antislavery activists and bureaucrats alike: through the erasure of their imagined direct speech in all these records. Though the disappearance of quoted direct speech by slaves may seem like a minor formal change, I contend that it is part of a larger process by which slave sentiments are increasingly ventriloquized by pro- and antislavery activists alike. The rendering of the enslaved as silent or inarticulate forms part of the racialization of the enslaved as "morally indebted, as fit for the toil of slaves, as permanently punishable, and as radically unassimilable into white settler society," as Kris Manjapra summarizes the effects of global colonialism during the age of empire.[7] The advocacy of abolitionists, while drawing on the speech of certain formerly enslaved persons like Olaudah Equiano, Quobna Cugoano, and Mary Prince, often silences or misrepresents the voices of the enslaved, performing a sympathetic substitution of the white body and the white voice.[8] One effect of this sentimental advocacy, as I will discuss in the next chapter, is that it eventually leads to widespread rejection of sentimental speech as an effective form of expressing grievances. In the absence of autobiographies by the enslaved from the Cape Colony, we are left with only these images or tableaus of silent slaves—most vividly represented in the reportage and poetry by Scottish abolitionist and Romantic poet Thomas Pringle. In the final part of this chapter, I investigate the relationship between this Romantic aesthetic of slavery and the more prosaic ledgers and account books in which the everyday administrative violence of slavery is recorded.

Great Britain seized the Cape of Good Hope from the Dutch in 1795 (as the French revolutionary army had invaded the Netherlands, this gave the British the opportunity to claim VOC territories), and it was initially unclear how long their occupation of the Cape would last. The Dutch Batavian Republic was reinstated as governing the Cape from 1803 to 1806, and, while the British retook control in 1806 (to prevent the French from seizing the colony), it was not until the 1814 Anglo-Dutch Treaty that the Cape Colony was officially ceded by the Dutch and acknowledged as a British colony. When the British first take over the Cape, the abolitionist movement was already well established in Great Britain and its colonies. Public agitation against the slave trade in Britain had surfaced in 1783, with the presentation of a petition by the Religious Society of Friends (the Quakers) to British Parliament, who also spearheaded the formation of the Society for Effecting the Abolition of the Slave Trade in 1787.[9] The 1780s and 1790s were key periods in the British abolitionist movement and debates around the future of slavery. In this light, the new British overlords of the Cape compiled a list of questions in preparing to take over the rule and governance of this slave-based society in 1797: "Is not this climate sufficiently temperate for the labor to be performed by white hands, if slaves were prohibited would not the white people become more industrious and useful—Does not the facility of procuring slaves &

the practice of employing them render the white inhabitants of the Country proud, slothful & brutal?"[10] The answer to these questions was declared to be an emphatic "no": as fiscal (prosecutor) W. S. van Ryneveld writes in his response, the colony considered slavery "a necessary evil," adding, "Yet, the business is done. Slavery exists and is now even indispensable."[11]

According to the 1808 census, 74,424 people lived in the Cape Colony: 29,768 slaves, 27,956 free inhabitants (including the formerly enslaved), and 16,700 Khoisan.[12] As John Edwin Mason points out, "Slavery dominated the Cape demographically, and in social, cultural, and economic terms as well."[13] As described in the previous chapter, the enslaved came from various Indian Ocean communities in South Asia, Southeast Asia, East Africa, and Madagascar. By this point many slaves were also "van de Kaap" (of the Cape), that is, born to slaves residing in the Cape Colony.[14]

While the deployment of sentiment in abolitionist writings in the Atlantic world has been extensively studied (the most famous example being Harriet Beecher Stowe's *Uncle Tom's Cabin*), and the dangers of this kind of writing have been well documented, it is worth taking a look at these sources from the Cape Colony.[15] When the British take over the Cape of Good Hope, they choose not to change the existing Roman-Dutch legal system extensively, though they do outlaw torture and some of the more brutal forms of capital punishment in practice under the Dutch VOC. This means that they inherit a legal system in which the enslaved are considered capable of testifying in court, and even testifying against Europeans. This is highly unusual in British colonies. Miles Ogborn writes the "oath-taking and evidence-giving were powerful sites of contested meaning and practice in the early modern Atlantic world," where restricting control of these speech acts was a cornerstone of colonial governance.[16] The stipulation, originally from Barbados, that governed the testimony of the enslaved in the Caribbean colonies, read that "no Person whatsoever shall be admitted as a Freeholder, or an evidence in any Case whatsoever, whose original Extraction shall be proved to have been from a Negro, except only in the Trial of Negroes, and other Slaves" (1720, slightly rewording an Act of Assembly passed originally in 1709).[17] It was expected that this clause be read out twice a year in all the island's parish churches. Even when this stipulation was changed in 1739 so that "Free Negroes, Indians, or Mulattoes" could testify against any other "free Negroe, Indian, or Mulatto" as well as enslaved persons, their testimony could never be admitted against "white Persons."[18] In the United States of America, the inadmissibility of testimony by the enslaved was enshrined in the statutes of slaveholding states.[19]

The Council of Justice at the Cape was thus very different than the slave courts in the British Atlantic, though other newly British colonies in the Indian Ocean had similar systems: in both Ceylon (captured from the Dutch) and the Mascarene Islands (taken from the French) earlier practices of allowing the enslaved to testify in the courts, and testify in cases involving slaveholders, were continued.[20] In other ways, however, the Cape Colony was increasingly brought in line with Atlantic British colonies. In 1826, the "Ordinance for Improving the Condition of the Slaves at the Cape of Good Hope" was approved, calling for the formation of an Office of the Registrar and Guardian of Slaves. Before the establishment of this office, the enslaved could lay complaints of ill-treatment against slaveholders with their local fiscals or magistrates, and, after investigation, these cases could be heard in front of the Council of Justice. After 1826 the Guardian (or Protector, as he was also called) of Slaves served as the first point of contact for slaves to make complaints: after investigation, his office could recommend that convincing cases be heard by the courts. In effect, this helped remove representations of enslaved voices from the court records. Poised between the two oceans, the Atlantic and the Indian, the Cape Colony, and the legacy of slavery at the Cape, would increasingly become enmeshed in a cultural imaginary that draws on the Black Atlantic for its frame of reference.[21] In the following section, I examine how abolitionist thought, originating in England and aimed at slaveholding in other British Black Atlantic colonies, began to reframe the Cape Colony in this more familiar model. This reframing had the unfortunate effect of also transplanting the image of the slave as silent and suffering, or as speaking only in certain circumstances when the enslaved voice is buttressed by that of the abolitionist.

The Abolitionist: Thomas Pringle

The Cape abolitionist movement is a belated development—almost nonexistent under the Dutch, antislavery texts from the Cape are rare.[22] When Thomas Pringle (1789–1834) published a report (first in the *New Monthly Magazine* and then in the Anti-Slavery Society's *Monthly Reporter*) in 1826 about slavery at the Cape, he argued that, while slavery at the Cape had popularly been portrayed as mild, "accounts which led to such a conclusion were founded either in gross ignorance or in willful misrepresentation."[23] The Cape thus offers a previously unexplored setting for the readers of these publications, a new site of outrage that Pringle was uniquely qualified to describe, having just returned from a six-year stint living in the colony.

Born in Scotland, Pringle had briefly worked as an editor of *Blackwood's Magazine* and the *Edinburgh Review* before deciding to move to the Cape Colony as part of a government incentive to settle the sparsely populated eastern borders of the colony. He recruited a party of twenty-five people, many of them family members, and became part of the more than five thousand Britons known as the 1820 Settlers, emigrating with free passage and grants of land along the eastern frontier. After two years of living on the Baviaansrivier, Pringle moved to Cape Town, where he cofounded the *South African Journal* and *South African Commercial Advertiser*. He attracted the ire of the governor, Lord Charles Somerset, through his advocacy for the rest of the 1820 Settlers, who were struggling to prosper on the remote eastern frontier, and returned to England in 1826 accompanied by his wife, her sister, and their servant, an orphaned African boy, Hinza Marossi.

While Pringle's abolitionist views were certainly not novel to the readers of the *Reporter*, Pringle did introduce these readers to the Cape Colony as an area of concern and, in so doing, launched his career as an abolitionist. After publishing this report in the *New Monthly Magazine*, he was appointed as the secretary of the Anti-Slavery Society and is remembered especially for his publication (with a heavy editorial hand) of the Caribbean enslaved woman Mary Prince's autobiography *The History of Mary Prince*.[24]

Dated January 5, 1826, Pringle's report on "Slavery at the Cape of Good Hope" sets out to describe the horrors of Cape slavery. Pringle uses detailed description of individual incidents to make his argument. In none of these descriptions (and his report contains nine of them, some of them written by other authors) is a slave directly quoted. At best, their words are paraphrased; at worst, they cry inarticulately. His first example goes as follows:

> In August, 1825, I was walking with a friend in the streets of Graaff-Reinett (a country town about five hundred miles from the capital), when we were accosted, in English, by a man of the Malay complexion. My companion, whom he addressed by name, asked how he came to know him. The man replied, that he had occasionally seen him at the house of his former master in Cape Town. On further inquiry, he told us the following story:- He was a slave, and had a wife and several children also in slavery. Being an expert waggon-driver, his master was offered a high price for him.[25]

The rest of the anecdote describes how the man was unwittingly sold and sent far away from his family and concludes, "The poor man appeared

Silencing the Enslaved · 53

extremely dejected, and his melancholy tale was afterwards fully confirmed to me by other authority."[26] This anecdote is a good introduction to the genre of the "melancholy tale" that fills this report, though the slave in this case is portrayed as unusually articulate. Pringle establishes the veracity of his tale by citing date and location and by assuring the reader that the enslaved man's tale had been confirmed "by authority." Slave accounts are seen as needing external verification: Pringle's edited edition of *The History of Mary Prince* is a prime example, where Mary Prince's account is buttressed by a slew of authentication, including a letter by Pringle's wife describing the "existence of marks of severe punishment on Mary Prince's body."[27]

The details included in the anecdote above are intended to testify both to the veracity of the incident described, but also to how deserving of sympathy the slave in question is: "On arriving in Graaff-Reinett, however, he . . . found that he was for ever separated from all he cherished on earth. Even some little property in money and clothes, which he had hoarded and left behind him, he has never been able to recover."[28] The slave's status as a married man, a father, someone who can speak English, and even someone who has demonstrated sufficient industry to accumulate a small amount of capital, is crucial to his claim on the reader's sympathy. The enslaved man here (notably unnamed, as are all the enslaved in Pringle's report) is described as "separated from all he cherished on earth" and as appearing "dejected"—sentiment functioning to portray the man as suffering, and deserving of sympathy. It is also no coincidence that this man's "wife and several children" are mentioned so prominently: as we will see, Pringle leans heavily on the image of the separated slave family to make his case against slavery.

Pringle's report is filled with similar examples, some taken from writings by other authors. The next account is from "the letter of a friend (Mr J.F. Thomas, of the English India Company's Civil Service)" (note the authority invoked already):

> While I was residing in the vicinity of Algoa Bay, there came to the house, late at night, an old slave woman, who had fled from the ill-usage of her mistress. She bore on her body marks of previous ill-treatment, having had three of her ribs broken at an earlier period of life. . . . Her dress was a filthy untanned sheep-skin petticoat, with a few old rags about her head, and a dirty sheep-skin thrown over her shoulders. She had absconded from her master's house the preceding night; and after concealing herself in the day-time, had made her way, the night following, to the house where we resided (106).

Thomas manages to convince the family to sell him the old woman, and (in the words of Pringle again), "The poor creature, thus emancipated, by the generosity of a stranger, now enjoys liberty and repose at the Missionary Institution of Bethelsdorp" (106). Authenticating details proliferate here: Algoa Bay, the Missionary Institution of Bethelsdorp, even the exact price Thomas paid. More particularly though, pay attention to the silencing of the enslaved woman (nameless) in the account. We presume she must have told Thomas the details about absconding from the slaveholder's house, hiding during the day, and so forth, but there are no traces of her voice left (in the previous anecdote, the slave is at least described as speaking several times, even though his story is paraphrased). Instead, her mute body—broken ribs, marks—and clothing—filthy, untanned, dirty—have to speak for her. These items also need to be ventriloquized by first Thomas, in his letter, and then Pringle, to the larger world. As Pringle remarks, "Examples, such as these, . . . might be adduced without end" in his report, which follows an additive logic, where anecdote follows anecdote in order to overwhelm the reader with evidence of "the wretchedness of slavery at the Cape" (106). Here follows two more, taken this time from a published account by Anders Sparrman (a Swedish naturalist, traveler, and early antislavery author) and quoted by Pringle:

> A female slave, who had been just bought at a high price, and rather prematurely treated with severity by her mistress, who lived in the Roode-zand district, hanged herself the same night out of revenge and despair, just at the entrance of her new mistress's bedchamber. A young man and woman who were . . . passionately fond of each other [asked the slaveholder to be allowed to get married, and he forbade it]. The lover was seized with a singular fit of despair; and having first plunged a dagger into the heart of the object of his dearest wishes, immediately afterwards put an end to his own life (108).

These anecdotes, about more anonymous slaves, are reminiscent of the court cases I examine in the previous chapter, which include far more details about the enslaved individuals under investigation. Sparrman's descriptions are comparatively generic and devoid of individualizing details.[29] Sparrman seeks to elicit the sympathy of the reader through the addition of explanatory phrases that hinge on ascribing specific emotions to the enslaved—the highly priced female slave, "out of revenge and despair," hangs herself; the lovers, "passionately fond of each other," also succumb to a "singular fit of despair." The emotions of the slaves are described as evidence of their humanity, in order to prove that the actions of slaveholders are inhumane. As Saidiya Hartman asks, though, about depictions of terror and suffering in American antislavery narratives, "Does the pain of the other merely provide us with the opportunity for self-reflection?"[30] In the examples included in Pringle's report, the (white, European, male) abolitionist acts both as ventriloquist for the enslaved, but also, crucially, as interpreter of their emotions. They speak sentiment on behalf of the slave: and this sentiment takes a particular form, solidifying around the image of the enslaved family. Note that the young lovers are portrayed as seeking to get married, and the refusal of this act of creating a family is what drives them to desperation.

Pringle ascribes the following anecdote, also included as a footnote in *The History of Mary Prince*, to "a letter of a friend of the writer, [written] while travelling in the interior of the colony."[31] This anonymity is already somewhat odd since he had been at great pains to name and describe his other sources and correspondents. The anonymous friend has remained unidentified, perhaps suggesting that Pringle may have invented this letter, given how perfectly the anonymous writer's words match Pringle's stated intentions in the report.[32] Regardless of its authorship, this letter presents a heart-rending description of an enslaved family at an auction:

> Among the stock of the farm sold, was a female slave and her three children. The two eldest children were girls, the one about thirteen years of age, and the other about eleven; the youngest was a boy. The whole family were exhibited together, but they were sold separately, and to different purchasers. The farmers examined them as if they had been so many head of cattle. While the sale was going on, the mother and her children were exhibited on a table, that they might be seen by the company, which was very large.[33]

The market or auction block is a frequent subject of abolitionist writings, as the site where the spectacle of the buying and selling of human flesh renders visible the inhumane logic of the institution of slavery, especially after the end of the transoceanic slave trade.[34] The continued state of bondage of those already enslaved can be least readily reconciled with the beliefs underpinning the banning of the slave trade at those instances where the enslaved trade hands on an open market.

Pringle adds this footnote to *The History of Mary Prince* in order to underscore the horrors of a slave auction depicted by Prince, perhaps feeling that her rather more subdued description ("it was a sad parting") did not do enough to excite the sympathy of her readers.[35] Alongside actively editing

Prince's account, these paratextual interferences by Pringle demonstrate his continued attempts to control the narrative, to validate it through his authority.[36] In this case, he seems to judge that Prince's verbal stoicism needed buttressing, perhaps reflecting his understanding of the conventions of abolitionist discourse in which the auction block becomes the perfect site for staging sentiment. The enslaved family here is exhibited "on a table, that they might be seen by the company"—but also by Pringle's readers, both of his report and of Prince's narrative, as witnesses to the continued barbarity of slavery.

"There could not have been a finer subject for an able painter than this unhappy group," the writer continues, providing a kind of ekphrasis of this imagined painting: "The tears, the anxiety, the anguish of the mother, while she met the gaze of the multitude, eyed the different countenances of the bidders, or cast a heart-rending look upon the children; and the simplicity and touching sorrow of the young ones, while they clung to their distracted parent, wiping their eyes, and half concealing their faces—contrasted with the marked insensibility and jocular countenances of the spectators and purchasers."[37]

One cannot miss the visuality of this description, heightened by the frequent references to eyes, looks, and gazing. The reader is called upon to visualize this scene, to meet the gaze of this anguished mother or watch as her children covered their faces. By calling the scene a fine subject for an able painter, Pringle's correspondent gestures to the potential aesthetic appeal of such a painting. One can thus ask about the aesthetics of abolitionism: what forms (of painting, sculpture, writing, etc.) were seen as beautiful, sublime, or moving?[38] We can extrapolate from Pringle's report that certain configurations, situations, characters, and scenes were viewed as more worthy subjects of the abolitionist's pen (and imaginary paintbrush): the slave family, and young slave lovers, being foremost among these.

Following this tableau, we are called upon to witness one more scene—not a static one this time, but one that involves an exchange: "While the woman was in this distressed situation she was asked, 'Can you feed sheep?' Her reply was so indistinct that it escaped me; but it was probably in the negative, for her purchaser rejoined, in a loud and harsh voice, 'Then I will teach you with the sjamboc' (a whip made of the rhinoceros' hide). The mother and her three children were sold to three separate purchasers; and they were literally torn from each other."[39]

The exact words of this purchaser are carefully recorded, as well as his (or her) final reply. The use of direct speech here creates a little play in order to make the scene more vivid, and believable, to the reader. Here, we only hear the slaveholder's voice: the enslaved woman's voice is "so indistinct that it escaped me." Even in this scene, the enslaved cannot be imagined as speaking. Pringle adds the clarifying note on the "sjamboc" as a touch of stereotypically African local color (in reality, it was exceedingly unlikely that a whip would be made of a rhinoceros's hide), but in all other aspects, this scene could have been set in any other British slaveholding colony (as Pringle's appending it to Mary Prince's account of her experience in Bermuda also demonstrates). Pringle's report increasingly familiarizes the Cape Colony to his antislavery audience, entering it into the cultural imaginary of the Black Atlantic.

In Pringle's entire report, we never have a single instance of direct speech by a slave; only slaveholders speak: "Never be kind, or speak kindly to a slave," we hear one English lady say to Pringle's relative. "I have found," she added, "by experience in my own household, that nothing but hauteur and harshness will do with slaves."[40] Sentiment is expressed through the descriptions of the enslaved, not in their own words.

In South Africa, Pringle is known more for his poetry (specifically his landscape poetry) than his later career as an abolitionist. J. M. Coetzee, in *White Writing: On the Culture of Letters in South Africa*, calls Pringle "the only Romantic writer of any attainment to have visited the Colony."[41] But, along with his abolitionist pamphlet, Pringle also wrote poetry about the enslaved and slavery. British Romanticism, which is undoubtedly the predominant influence on Pringle's poetry, has an ambivalent relationship to the abolition movement, with which, as Debbie Lee points out, it shares almost exact dates.[42] Lee points out the "common vocabulary of terms like 'slave' and 'master,' 'tyranny' and 'oppression,'" though Romanticists generally use these terms in "abstract and even universal ways, in the sense that everyone is a slave to something and seeking freedom from it."[43] The abstraction of bondage as a universal state of humanity thus allowed many Romantics to avoid grappling with the reality of slavery, which underpinned the society that supported them. William Blake's *Visions of the Daughters of Albion*, for example, can be read as both an allegory for the universal dangers of bondage and as a specifically abolitionist work that critiques both rapacious slaveholders but also hapless abolitionists who hesitate to take concrete action.[44] Blake, as well as other well-known Romantics such as Mary Wollstonecraft, Samuel Taylor Coleridge, and William Wordsworth, were active abolitionists, and Blake's illustrations for John Gabriel Stedman's *Narrative of a Five Years' Expedition against the Revolted Negroes of Surinam* (which he engraved at the same time as he was writing *Visions of the Daughters of Albion*) are important visual texts in the aesthetic history of slavery.[45] Pringle's poetry about slavery thus enters this larger tradition of Romantic poetry engaging with bondage, but Pringle uses his experience of living in a slaveholding society to frame his larger abstractions about the value of freedom within concrete descriptions of supposed encounters, and conversations, with the enslaved. His poetry alternates between looks and sounds (the visual and aural), and speech, language, and names (the verbal), drawing a line that does not fall neatly between slavery and freedom but establishes certain conventional rules for how, and when, imagined slaves can access the world of language and speech.

The importance of sight and appearance is established from the first stanza of Pringle's "The Bechuana Boy,"[46] where the speaker is introduced: "I sat at noontide in my tent / And looked across the Desert dun." The titular boy, on the other hand, is the looked-upon, described as "a swarthy Stripling . . . with foot unshod and naked limb." In the second stanza, however, the speaker's look is returned: "Then, meekly gazing in my face, / Said in the language of his race, / With smiling look yet pensive tone, / 'Stranger—I'm in the world alone.'" It seems that, in Pringle's poetry, there is not the same clear distinction between the speaking abolitionist and the silent slave as I have delineated in his prose writing. In the wider British abolitionist world, speaking slaves abound: both literally, in the sense of slave autobiographies, and figuratively, in imagined speech by slaves in abolitionist works where slaves are assigned direct speech. What Pringle's poetry highlights, however, is that the circumstances under which the enslaved are imagined as speaking are very often limited by certain conventions.

Here we thus have an instance of a slave who can speak, and is depicted as speaking—but, in "the language of his race," which the speaker would have to understand, and translate for the reader. Starting in the third stanza, the boy is invited to tell his story, his "hapless history." The poem depicts the familiar scene of the slave market: "When, with proud looks and gestures rude, / The White Men gathered round: / And there, like cattle from the fold, / by Christians we were bought and sold, / Midst laughter loud and looks of scorn— / And roughly from each other torn. / My Mother's scream, so long and shrill, / My little Sister's wailing cry." Pringle elicits sympathy for the captive boy through familiar appeals to sentiment: the enslaved family torn apart, screaming, wailing, and crying. It is worth noting that within the boy's tale, the world of the visual and aural, rather than the verbal, dominates: loud laughter and "looks of scorn," a "long and shrill" scream, a "wailing cry." This pattern is repeated throughout: the slavers are first discovered through their "wolfish howl of joy" and "their yell," and the captives hear "the wolf to his gorged comrade calling" and "a river sounding."

Once he has been bought, the boy befriends a baby Springbok, "although its dark and dazzling eye / Beamed not with human sympathy." The final insult is when "suddenly, with haughty look / And taunting words," the slaveholder tries to take away the buck. The boy escapes, and finds his way to the speaker: "Because they say, O English Chief, / Thou scornest not the Captive's grief: / Then let me serve thee, as thine own— / For I am in the world alone!" He concludes his tale with the same words with which he started it. In the final stanza, the speaker is reflecting back on this encounter from a later vantage point: "Such was Marossi's touching tale. / Our breasts they were not made of stone: / His words, his winning looks prevail— / We took him for 'our own.'" Here, finally, the "Bechuana Boy" is named as Marossi.

The poem is grounded in true circumstances: Pringle and his wife did return to England accompanied by an orphaned boy called Hinza Marossi, of whom he writes in his letters that he "was received by me as a little servant to Mrs. P, to whom he speedily became most affectionately attached; but as his intellect and disposition unfolded themselves, he exhibited so much amiable and excellent feeling, and good sense and delicacy, that he became to us rather a child than a menial attendant."[47] This has led researchers to refer to Marossi (who died from tuberculosis soon after arriving in England) as Pringle's "adopted son," though their true relationship is unknown as we have only Pringle's letters and poems as evidence.[48] There is, however, something distinctly sinister about the phrase *We took him for "our own"* when used in the context of slavery, suggesting as it does the ownership of another human being.

In *Imperial Eyes*, Mary Louise Pratt discusses the way in which abolitionist travel writing used the tropes of conjugal love "as an alternative to enslavement and colonial domination."[49] In her argument, "Transracial love plots [acted as] imaginings in which European supremacy is guaranteed by affective and social bonding." The protagonists in the travel book she discusses, the mixed-race woman Joanna and the white author Stedman, "are imaginary substitutes for Friday and Crusoe. In the transformation a fundamental dimension of colonialism disappears, namely, the exploitation of labor. The Joannas, like the Fridays, are property, yet they are not possessed for their labor power. The allegory of romantic love mystifies exploitation out of the picture." In Pringle's poem, there is no question of transracial love, but rather, a filial relationship is imagined between the Bechuana Boy and the "us" of "our own," which almost, but not entirely, obscures the relationship hinted at by the fictional Marossi's appeal to "let me serve thee, as thine own." The servant / adopted child trope also hearkens back to the Crusoe / Friday relationship evoked by Pratt: like Friday, Marossi is imagined as willingly serving the "English Chief" who saves him from "cannibals" (the wolfish slave traders), thereby substituting a positively valanced, reciprocal, filial servitude for the harsh conditions of enslavement. The suggestion that the Bechuana Boy offers to "serve" the speaker is reminiscent of Blake's "The Little Black Boy," which also ends with the titular figure saying he would "shade him [the English boy] from the heat" and "stroke his silver hair"—the love and shared joy between the two boys, and their supposed equality before God, undercut (arguably) by the servile gestures made by the Black boy.[50]

South African author Zoë Wicomb's 2020 novel *Still Life* is a postmodern engagement with Pringle's life, in which the ghosts of important figures in his life, like Mary Prince and Hinza Marossi, haunt his would-be biographer. The character of Marossi, upon reading this poem, says, "I see that the reiteration, the reply, 'We took him for "our own,"' complies with my stated wish to serve. In other words—and now it pierces my heart—they took me to serve them, according to my own wishes, or so the poem claims."[51]

It is instructive to compare "Bechuana Boy" with another one of Pringle's, "The Slave Dealer." Looks, speech, and names work somewhat differently in this poem, which starts, "From ocean's wave a Wanderer came, / With visage tanned and dun: / His Mother, when he told his name, / Scarce knew her long-lost son; / So altered was his face and frame / By the ill course he had run."[52] The poem is structured in a similar way to "The Bechuana Boy," with a very regular, simple, and striking rhyme and rhythm, and depicting one person (here, the slave dealer) describing past events to another (here, his mother). Like the speaker in "The Bechuana Boy," the mother in the beginning of this poem looks at the slave dealer, who, like the boy, is depicted as arriving—this time, from the ocean. The descriptor "dun" is even repeated, here referring to the "visage" of the slave dealer, not the desert. The first important difference to note is that the slave dealer introduces himself by name ("when he told his name"), though the reader never learns it—in "The Bechuana Boy," Marossi's name is only revealed at the end of the poem.

Whereas Marossi describes the sights and sounds he encounters while in the hands of the slave dealers, the slave dealer is haunted by "visions wild" that are, strikingly, populated with tactile description, outnumbering the sights and sounds: "'There's blood upon my hands!' he said, . . . It dropped from the gory lash, / As I whirled it o'er and o'er my head, / And with each stroke left a gash. / With every stroke I left a gash, / While Negro blood sprang high." The description here is less concerned with what the dealer saw and heard than in conveying what he felt: blood on his hands, the whip whirling overhead, the stroke, and the gash. This line, unusually, repeats—indicating the repetitive motion of striking and gashing skin, but also the irruption of this vision into the dealer's current thoughts: "for visions wild / Still scared good thoughts away." The vivid tactile description of torture is quite rare in Pringle's work: he is usually more concerned with depicting the emotional anguish of slaves separated from their families than the physical suffering of slaves.

This stanza reaches its crescendo with "That Woman's wild death-cry!" which starts the next stanza: "Her cry is ever in my ear, / And it will not let me pray; / Her look I see—her voice I hear— / As when in death she lay, / And said, 'With me thou must appear / On God's great judgment day!'" Here we have a return to Pringle's pairing of voice and look, familiar to us from "The Bechuana Boy," but whereas in that poem, words and looks separate the cruel slaveholder from the trustworthy Marossi, here the voice and look of the slave woman is part of a "vision" and is perhaps induced by the "hot fever" in the slave dealer's blood. The phrase that introduces the supposed words of the woman is instructive: "*As when in death she lay, and said . . .*" Having been told that her life ended in a "wild death-cry," it is implied here that the slave dealer imagined words emerging from her dead lips, a suggestion that is only strengthened by the biblical ring of the words she supposedly utters. Pringle here distances us from a speaking slave not only by having this story told by a slave dealer, but actively suggesting that her words were only ever uttered in his fevered imagination—that in actuality, she never uttered more than a "wild death-cry." The speaking slave is merely a device for the dealer's conscience to speak to and through him.

Pringle's two poems, about the slave and the slave dealer, together with his prose writings on slavery, demonstrate the limits of abolitionist empathy. The figure of the slave is much more likely to cry, scream, weep, and wail than speak, and freedom seems to be the necessary precondition for a slave to be able to speak, and be named. Slaves see and hear, but slave dealers feel and have the necessary mental and moral capacity to feel guilt over their actions, and envision divine punishment for them. Slaves have an intrinsic, unthinking honesty and purity about them, whereas slave dealers and slaveholders are cruel, but can reflect upon their cruelty. Both Marossi and the slave dealer tell their stories, but Marossi's is purely descriptive (and needs to be translated), whereas the slave dealer is concerned with the implications of all that he recounts. Marossi is the object of sentimental description, but not of identification, whereas "The Slave Dealer" presents a much more complex moral problem: while it is clear that the slave dealer did terrible things in the past, things that are depicted in clear and vivid language such that the horror of his actions comes through indelibly, the reader is also made to feel sympathy for his mother, "the woeful widow," seeking to save her son, and, in a complicated way, for the slave dealer himself, who now clearly regrets his actions and is haunted by them, even as he himself denies the possibility of salvation: "And now with God I have to deal, / And dare not meet his eye!" The slave dealer is a much more complex, and therefore human, figure than the figure of the slave, a silent, pure vehicle for suffering in these poems and writings.[53]

The Slaveholder: Samuel E. Hudson

"Reason told me . . . that the Horrors of Slavery was all a mischief so that my Aversion naturally wore off and those Tales of Woe and Cruelty appeared only as Chimeras to amuse Children."[54] So writes English immigrant S. E. Hudson (1764–1808), appointed as the First Clerk of the Customs in the Cape in 1798, reflecting on how, when he arrived at the Cape, he quickly became used to the idea of owning human beings, even though before he had been completely convinced by the writings of abolitionists. In turning to Hudson's writings, we are stepping back in time somewhat. Hudson's essay on the topic of "Slaves," written around 1806 but never published in his lifetime, is an attempt to justify what Robert Shell refers to as his "sea-change" from fervent antislavery believer to slaveholder.[55] Hudson references several prominent abolitionists, both those more famous ones in England and the few voices that were speaking out against slavery at the Cape by the time he writes this essay. His own prose demonstrates that he has mastered the same techniques as these authors, but marshals these sentimental descriptions of slaves in order to justify his slaveholding. He never attempts to argue that the enslaved are "strangers to every sentiment of compassion,"[56] as the *Encyclopædia Britannica* does: rather, he says, "Let those preach for ages upon the want of feeling in this race of Men. I have had proof [that] . . . convinces me that they are alive to all the sensibility which the White inhabitants of colder climates are so unwilling to allow them."[57] Hudson's defense of the legitimacy of slaveholding rests on a strong rejection of cruel behavior by slaveholders (his manuscript also resembles abolitionist writings in the large number of anecdotes about the cruelties of slaveholders he lists) and claims about his own benevolence and the happiness of his own slaves. This slaveholder's use of sentiment, I argue, echoes the language used by Pringle and other abolitionists, particularly in the silencing of enslaved voices, replaced by sentimental descriptions to talk about slaves.[58]

Notably, his description of his own relationship to the enslaved turns upon the sentimental image of the family: "I treat them as my Children and they return it with gratitude and affection. I have had repeated proofs of this when I have been confined to a sick bed (and) unable to assist myself my Slaves have been indefatigable in their Attendance and when I have suffered a momentary pang from the acuteness of my disorder, the big drops have chased each other down their sooty cheeks and their very looks expressed the thousand terrors that assailed them for fear of losing the Father in their Master."[59]

Hudson here paints an affecting verbal picture of a group of enslaved persons clustered around his sickbed, tears flowing down their cheeks, terrified that he would die. Rather than just stating that the enslaved are fond of him, he sets out to prove this through providing evidence of the ways in which the enslaved (all anonymous, of course) displayed these emotions. The image of family members surrounding a sickbed supports Hudson's assertion that he treats the enslaved "as my Children." Hudson here is appealing to the image of the family unit, and the sentiment attached to it, to justify his assumed ownership of these bodies. This mirrors the way the integrity of the enslaved family and the horror of family separation is one of the major motifs of abolitionist writings, as we saw in Pringle's account above. Hudson's imagery also sounds a warning bell regarding Pringle's use of filial sentiments to discuss his relationship with Hinza Marossi, the boy he takes back to England with him. Here, the childlike figures of slaves are threatened with separation from their father / slaveholder, the very thought driving them to tears. Hudson refigures himself as the savior of slave lives through his beneficent ownership: later in the document, before concluding with an anecdote about a cruel slaveholder who "has murdered several slaves," he says that "if I should [by writing this manuscript] . . . save from the merciless Lash or more cruel Sambuck one wretched Negro, I shall be amply repaid" (70). Returning briefly to the freedom-seeker Galant's trial (with which I started this chapter), we see the fiscal employing the same rhetoric of the family in his conclusion, expanding upon the feelings of the late slaveholder for Galant: "He could not conceive it possible that such a dreadfully wicked thought could enter into the heart of a slave whom he so favored, whom he considered as it were a member of his family, for whom he felt an attachment in his own heart because he was brought up and had grown up with him, and to whose irregularities he had even shewn [sic] indulgence by allowing him to have two instead of one Concubine."[60]

Hudson's manuscript is filled with further anecdotes aimed at demonstrating that he is a sympathetic slaveholder who abhors cruelty against slaves—anecdotes in which slaveholders speak, but slaves are silent, ill-treated figures. Like Pringle, he describes a slave auction: "They are brought to the Table and are made to show a variety of Anticks to the unfeeling Audience showing their teeth thrusting out their Tongues stretching out their Arms to their full extent and Jumping high as they can."[61] The enslaved are dismembered into their constituent body parts here—a writhing mass of bodies, thrusting, stretching, and jumping. Tongues and teeth appear but are not used for speaking. The silence of slaves is, in fact, explicitly described by Hudson, in a section on so-called Malay slaves. An enslaved man is sentenced to torture and death for murdering an old man he suspected of betraying him, and Hudson writes, "Amidst all the excruciating pangs of breaking his Arms Legs Thighs he never uttered a single groan or sigh but at each stroke an involuntary motion of the body was perceived. His Eyes rolled as if in the extreme of agony but no torture could draw from him a murmur of complaint, his Companions exulting at his dying like a true Malay" (51). Here, the enslaved body is almost literally dismembered—"Arms Legs Thighs"—Hudson in both cases seeming to lose control of his sentences by leaving out the commas separating the different actions or body parts. The enslaved, in this text, are an indistinguishable mass of body parts, silently suffering.

In another section, Hudson asks a hypothetical Dutchman what he thinks about educating slaves and transcribes his imagined reply: "Education! Do you suppose me Mad? learn a Slave to read and write? what? Put it in his power to do me every injury make known all my secrets. . . . No. No. The Sambuck is better than a Book for a Slave" (52). Much as though this imagined dialogue denigrates the Dutchman, he is imagined as speaking, holding forth: unlike the slaves. Other examples abound: "The poor Boy begged of his Mistress to forbear that the Maid was dying so much the better said the hardened wretch I now have my wish," (54) runs the conclusion of a tale about a harsh jealous female slaveholder who murdered a slave, the "Harpy," as Hudson calls her, imagined as speaking. Hudson enjoys repeating tales about cruel women: "Again a Mrs. Smith Wife to a Medical Man in Cape Town for some trifling fault had a poor wretch tyd up and by one of her own Slaves flogged 'till she died under the Lash tho' the wretch writhing in Agony declared She could bear no more give her more cried her Inhuman Mistress 'till the Slave hung her head upon her shoulder and . . . expired'" (55). Here, too, the enslaved woman's words are paraphrased ("declared She could bear no more") and the slaveholder's words quoted ("give her more").

In Hudson's document, a formerly enslaved man, Frank (also the only enslaved person named in this manuscript and identified by the editor Shell as the historical figure Frans van Bengal) is described as speaking to his own slaves: "If you serve me faithfully for so many years you are then free . . . if you act otherwise I shall sell you" (58). Rebellious "Hottentots" (indigenous Khoisan people) are also portrayed as delivering a long speech about their unfair treatment at the hands of the Dutch. The only slave figure who speaks is one who may not have been enslaved at all: purchased under dubious circumstances from an "unprincipled Dane" (66), the man had proclaimed his freedom for years, until one day, refused permission to spend a day away from the house, he snapped—"I am no Slave and yet you treat me as one" (66)—before stabbing the slaveholder. While denouncing this act of violence, Hudson's act of ascribing speech to the man suggests that he was inclined to believe him about his status as a free man.

These abundant examples of silent slaves raise the question: why do both proslavery advocates like Hudson and abolitionists like Pringle converge in their hesitancy to imagine enslaved speech? Clearly, the conventions of writing at the time still allowed for the use of direct discourse.[62] However, for Pringle and Hudson at least, speech is something that cruel slaveholders, former slaves, and nonslaves are depicted as doing, while the enslaved are imagined in touching, silent tableaus of suffering. Sentiment is displaced from represented speech to vivid visual description. For Hudson, the representation of the enslaved as childlike, dependent, and ultimately silent forms part of his justification for slavery: a form of racialization of the enslaved that depended not upon rendering them as brutal or without feeling (as some proslavery discourse did, of course, do) but as needing the paternalistic care of the slaveholder. The dangers of the kind of advocacy performed by Pringle, which creates similar tableaus of slaves needing saving, thus emerge. The silence of the enslaved in their writings allows Pringle and Hudson room to speak. The benevolent, paternalistic slaveholder and the benevolent, paternalistic abolitionist converge at this node.

We know that abolitionism often depended upon, and in fact sometimes deepened, an uneven power relationship between abolitionist and enslaved, or formerly enslaved (we can see this clearly in the paratextual apparatus surrounding accounts written by former slaves, and especially women, such as the heavily edited edition of *The History of Mary Prince*). The problem is intensified in the Cape Colony, however, where no self-narratives by the enslaved have been found, and so we are dependent upon these imperfect accounts by people speaking for the enslaved.

Specifically, I have sought to draw attention to the role played in these texts by the absence of imagined direct speech by the enslaved. This marks a real difference from the records of the eighteenth-century Dutch Council of Justice examined in the previous chapter, where slaves are imagined as speaking, and, frequently, as expressing sentiment. What happens to these representations of speaking slaves in the period after the Dutch relinquish control of the Cape of Good Hope? In the following section, I demonstrate that while direct speech by the enslaved is still recorded in the court records of the time, the creation of new institutions aimed at the amelioration of slavery results in the imaginative silencing of the enslaved. As expressions of sentiment are increasingly deployed in debates for and against slavery, they disappear from court records and other administrative documents, which rely on what we now think of as the bland language of bureaucracy—of dates, prices, and enumeration—in order to record accounts of slavery.

The Court and the Civil Servants: The Office of the Registrar and Guardian of Slaves

Author Yvette Christiansë is acutely aware of the silences of the archive. Tracing the records related to one court case, of Sila/Drusilla/Drucila, an enslaved woman sentenced to death for the murder of her son, Baro, she argues in "'Heartsore': The Melancholy Archive of Cape Colony Slavery" that "one must learn how to listen to echoes of subjects for whom one might not have an adequate language; one must also learn how to discern what they might have been trying to say within the statements attributed to them (but that could very well represent the redactions of colonial officials—notaries, court reporters). In addition, one must prepare to hear and interpret any echo of the unsaid as something that could be nothing more than a trace."[63] Christiansë draws on one word from the Council of Justice records from 1823, *hertzeer*/heartsore, in the following sentence: "She thereupon rubbed the child with fat which she had scraped from her bread for the purpose,—[and] while she was so employed the child fell asleep, [and she] through heartsore and grief, cut the child's throat with a knife which she had with her."[64] Court conventions had by this point largely eliminated the inclusion of direct speech by enslaved in the court records, such that this description, based on the declaration of the law official who had arrested Sila, is framed in the third person. In his own statement, the official states that "she, through heartsore [*hartzeer*] & grief, had cut the throat of her child named Baro with [the clasp] knife."[65] As Christiansë points out, the word *heartsore*, or *hartzeer* in the original, "appears to come directly from Sila; it is strange and, especially its transliteration, doubly foreign. The word seeps out across the official documents. It will not be contained. It echoes within the archive—excessive, dangerous, and struggling." Based on this uncontainable, dangerous word, Christiansë writes a compelling novel, *Unconfessed* (2006), about Sila's attempt to be heard within the structures of the court. Even as Sila was silenced, and eventually disappears, her traces evoke this fictional afterlife.[66]

In the year following the trial of Galant and others, on June 19, 1926, the "Ordinance for Improving the Condition of the Slaves at the Cape of Good Hope" was approved, calling for the formation of an Office of the Registrar and Guardian of Slaves. As mentioned earlier, this marked increased legal standardization of the British slaveholding colonies during the period between the end of the slave trade and the emancipation of the enslaved. Before 1826, the enslaved could go directly to their local magistrate or fiscal with complaints against other slaves, slaveholders, or other inhabitants of the colony. After investigation, these cases could be heard in front of the Council of Justice. After 1826 the Guardian of Slaves served as the first point of contact for the enslaved to make complaints, which were recorded in a complaints daybook; after investigation, his office could recommend that convincing cases be heard by the courts. He also had to be present at all trials involving the enslaved. Based on the complaints listed in his first report, most complainants wanted to contest their enslavement, arguing, using the various rules on manumission, that they were unjustly enslaved, whether because they had arrived in the colony after the abolition of the slave trade, or the slaveholders had willed that they should be freed, or they had paid off an agreed-upon amount.

In the first report penned by G. J. Roberts, the newly appointed Registrar and Guardian of Slaves in January 1827, he complains:

> A very considerable portion of my time has been occupied in hearing the complaints of Slaves; and as the greater part of them (particularly those from the country) are unable to speak or comprehend English, and many of them are ignorant of the Dutch language also, the taking their own statements, and depositions of their witnesses, necessarily occasions great trouble in interpreting and explaining, and much of the time and

attention of the whole of the persons composing the establishment of my office is drawn off or absorbed thereby, and the course of the business of the Registrar's duties greatly interrupted and impeded.[67]

The introduction to Roberts's report transports us to the moment in which these complaints were made: the translating, interpreting, and explaining that this involved. What, for him, is a logistical challenge becomes a formal challenge for those reading these complaints today: the individual voices of the enslaved he describes as testifying in various tongues are smoothed out, interpreted into conformity. The eighteenth-century fiscals whose court records I examined in the previous chapter faced the same problem in terms of linguistic diversity, but the inclusion of direct speech, even if imagined, in those records results in rich, heteroglossic textual inscriptions of slavery. The records from the Registrar and Guardian of Slaves's office are written in a more neutral third-person style, simply reporting the facts of each case without including quotations from any of the participants, and with traces of the linguistic diversity described in the passage above almost entirely erased.

This is not to say that Roberts's report does not make for fascinating, and disturbing, reading: we meet, for example, an enslaved man named Kakerlach (Cockroach), as well as a woman who wishes to lodge a complaint of ill-treatment against her mistress—who is also her sister. These brief passages evoke a world of cruelty. Nevertheless, they do so in the placid prose of the bureaucrat:

> 12. 21st August 1826. Candace, of the widow Thomas Beedlestone, represented that her mistress (who is her sister) had ill-treated her, and threatened to sell her, although she was not purchased by the late Thomas Beedlestone with the intention of being sold, but, as he informed her, for the purpose of being made free as soon as she had refunded the purchase money, being 1,800 rixdollars. According to a written statement produced by her she had repaid, on the 31st July 695 rixdollars; and she further stated that she was still hired out at 20 rixdollars per month, which becoming due on the 31st August would increase the sum to 715 rixdollars; that William Spratt, with whom she cohabited, was willing to pay 500 rixdollars for her freedom, and that he would then have her christened, and marry her.[68]

In this particular case, the Guardian found that while witnesses supported Candace's statement regarding the intentions of Thomas Beedlestone, she had not paid off the majority of the amount owed, and so had to remain with her abusive slaveholder/sister. The tragic entanglements of slavery do shine through the flattened official prose, but the third-person rendering of Candace's complaint never allows her the possibility of speaking for herself (even imaginatively). This is, however, a very different image of the family than the one evoked by Pringle and other abolitionists: both arguably more disturbing than the scene of an enslaved family separated at auction, but also more morally complex. The romance in this situation is also not simply a matter of passion or love, but of money: her lover is willing to pay for her freedom (though not enough to satisfy her sister) before marrying her. This set of circumstances does not make for a straightforward tale about slavery as favored by Pringle.

Another example of how the complexity of familial and romantic relationships is recorded in a depersonalized manner in the records of the Office of the Registrar and Guardian of Slaves reads as follows: "42. 19th December 1826. Rachel, of the Widow Ryk le Sueur, represented that she had for six years been allowed to hire herself out to the man with whom she cohabited, at 18 rixdollars per month, but as he was no longer able to pay that sum, her mistress refused to receive less from him, and let out complainant to another person for 12 rixdollars per month, which sum the man had before offered to pay on her behalf. Report: Investigation will be made into this case."[69] Here, too, we can only guess at the circumstances that lead to this complaint: any hint of sentiment and individual expression is completely removed from this description. "Investigation will be made into this case," promises the passive voice of the Guardian of Slaves. In the case of another enslaved woman named Rachel, we read at least a trace of sympathy in the report:

> 37. 15th November 1826. Rachel, of the estate of the Widow J. P. Naude, represented that she was blind, and on that account her mistress had bequeathed her half her property, but that the executor to the estate had refused to support her, although she was unable to earn her own livelihood. Report: This case being connected with No. 30 [a group of slaves who could not be manumitted until their late owner's debts had been settled], the Guardian has not yet had it in his power to obtain any relief for the apparently unfortunate complainant.[70]

"The apparently unfortunate complainant"—this is as much sentiment as these records are allowed to express. The language of sentiment, in this period, seems to have become exclusively the purview of abolitionists and proslavery advocates, such that it needs to be scrubbed from official records, which are written in as neutral a tone as possible. Expressions of sentiment had been weaponized by debates on abolitionism in a way it had not been in the eighteenth-century Dutch Cape of Good Hope (which lacked a robust antislavery movement), which resulted in this sharp distinction in the ways the enslaved are portrayed in legal or official versus broader public discourse.

Much as though the reports filed by the Guardian's office erase the individuality and linguistic ability of the complainants by flattening out the prose into bland officialese, however, the description by the Guardian of the process of collecting evidence reveals traces of the linguistic polyphony that must have filled the office. In Roberts's second report, he continues to complain about the lack of manpower in his office, requesting the assistance of someone with more legal knowledge to help him with manumission claims. His letter reveals him to be a poor ally to the enslaved, as he is inclined to question the veracity of their statements and distrust their motives. Of enslaved claiming to have been sold in the colony illegally, he writes, "Their cunning in concealing, under assumed ignorance, that which they do not wish to be known, and in evading questions which would expose their inconsistency, renders their depositions at all times doubtful."[71] As a Guardian of Slaves, we may suspect that Roberts was not particularly attentive to his duties of protecting and guarding the interests of the enslaved. But perhaps his office's more important and lasting impact was in the first part of its title: *Registrar*. As keepers of slave records, Roberts's office managed to preserve more than just the dry data of slavery: deaths, sales, and manumissions. In these records, some of the individuality of the experience of slavery has also been preserved. In the following section, I question whether archival records can be considered as aesthetic objects in their own right. If Pringle's poetry and prose espouses an aesthetic in which slaves are silent, passive observers and sufferers, pictured in wordless tableaus, what alternative does a ledger page, detailing the sale of enslaved persons, present?

Aesthetics of the Ledger

On the back of a page from a ledger listing the number of enslaved registered at the Cape of Good Hope from August 1833, one finds a curious drawing (figure 2.1). It depicts an elegantly dressed man, seen from the side, his hair combed back, in a relaxed *contrapposto* pose with his one visible hand in his pocket, his back foot dropping slightly below the plane where it would realistically be grounded. Emerging from his front, as if walking on his side, is the head of a lion, facing in the same direction as the man, and sharing some of his facial features: its mane is drawn with the same rapid upstrokes

FIGURE 2.1. Lion Man, "Return of the number of Slaves Registered at the Cape of Good Hope on the 31st August 1833 divided according to age into Seven Classes," reverse. In "Various Slave Returns, 1816–1834," Slave Office (SO) 7/36, Western Cape Archives and Records Service, Cape Town, South Africa.

as the man's hair; its eye is the same shape and size as his. The back of the lion is not drawn, so its head floats unmoored, seeming to emerge, almost libidinally, from the man's midsection.

Looking at the full page on which this is drawn, the other side of the page contains a series of regular box-like shapes in a line, with shading above them, that suggest an attempt to create a horizon for this drawing: perhaps a fence that hints at the background against which this lion-man is taking a walk (figure 2.2). But the frame is disrupted by a vertical line of text that cuts through the plane of the artwork, impossible to ignore: "The highest

FIGURE 2.2. Lion Man Landscape, "Return of the number of Slaves Registered at the Cape of Good Hope on the 31st August 1833 divided according to age into Seven Classes," reverse. In "Various Slave Returns, 1816–1834," Slave Office (SO) 7/36, Western Cape Archives and Records Service, Cape Town, South Africa.

sum given for a Cook was £383 & 5 sh str. (Bundle no 3743 [?]) & the lowest Sum 24£ sterling bdl no 1516." Some slight smudging in the middle section suggests why this piece of paper was considered spoiled and could be turned to drawing practice. A casual pen drawing by a bored clerk, this page was bound up and included in a folder on "Various Slave Returns, 1816–1834."[72]

The enslaved are not the subject of this sketch, but intrude upon it through a ledger column: a form frequently occupied by the enslaved in the archives. The ledger is the quintessential form of empire, even more so than the travelogue or the landscape poem. These latter forms are more evocative, so that we associate them more vividly with empire and colonialism: but day-to-day imperial governance took the form of ledgers, logbooks, daybooks, lists—columns of people (free and enslaved), transactions, and other organizational details. As Stephanie Smallwood argues of the Atlantic slave trade, "The ledger's double-entry pages and the neat grid of the invoice gave purposeful shape to

Silencing the Enslaved · 73

the story they told. Through their graphic simplicity and economy, invoices and ledgers effaced the personal histories that fueled the slaving economy."[73] On the reverse side of the page featuring the lion-man drawing, we find the following ledger page: "Return of the number of Slaves Registered at the Cape of Good Hope on the 31st August 1833 divided according to age into Seven Classes" (figure 2.3). With its juxtaposition between figurative arts and the ledger column, the lion-man, a negligible piece of archival ephemera, bundled up by accident, is a productive place from which to interrogate the aesthetics of slavery.

So how can we read this lion-man, a simple doodle by a clerk working in the office responsible for recording the prices received for enslaved persons? Is this nothing more than an example of the banality of evil? It may not be a coincidence that the ledger column that survives on this page refers to cooks specifically. The placement of the lion's head as emerging from the stomach of the dandy figure is thus less libidinal than gastronomical—a suggestion that underscores the fact that we should not be able to view this sketch as divorced from its context in the slave ledger, on a page detailing the prices fetched by enslaved cooks. The lion emerges, perhaps, as an unconscious reflection of the work this clerk does day after day, adding up the sales of human lives. The image of the Cape dandy and the column from the slave ledger are inextricable, both constituting Cape society and making up the cultural imaginary of that society. The clerk embodies the administrative violence necessary to maintain the system of slavery. The ledgers of the Slave Office are as implicated in the violence of slavery as the Council of Justice, but the manifestation of this violence has become nothing more than a list of figures: "Males: from 1 to 6 years; from 6 to 10 years; from 10 to 25 years; from 25 to 35 years; from 25 to 45 years; from 45 to 50 years; from 50 years Upwards," in this example.[74]

A significant challenge of working with slave narratives, as Simon Gikandi notes in his article "Rethinking the Archive of Enslavement," is the difficulty of accessing the experience of the enslaved person while "in bondage."[75] Autobiographies are necessarily a retrospective genre, written, or dictated, after the enslaved individual has become free. In both Hudson and Pringle, we see something similar: slaves can be imagined as speaking after they have been freed, but not while they are in bondage. Gikandi turns to what he calls "third texts," written neither by slaveholders nor the enslaved (such as a history written by a Moravian missionary seeking to convert the enslaved, who records the oral testimony of the enslaved persons he interviews) to supplement the official archive. The court documents I examine in

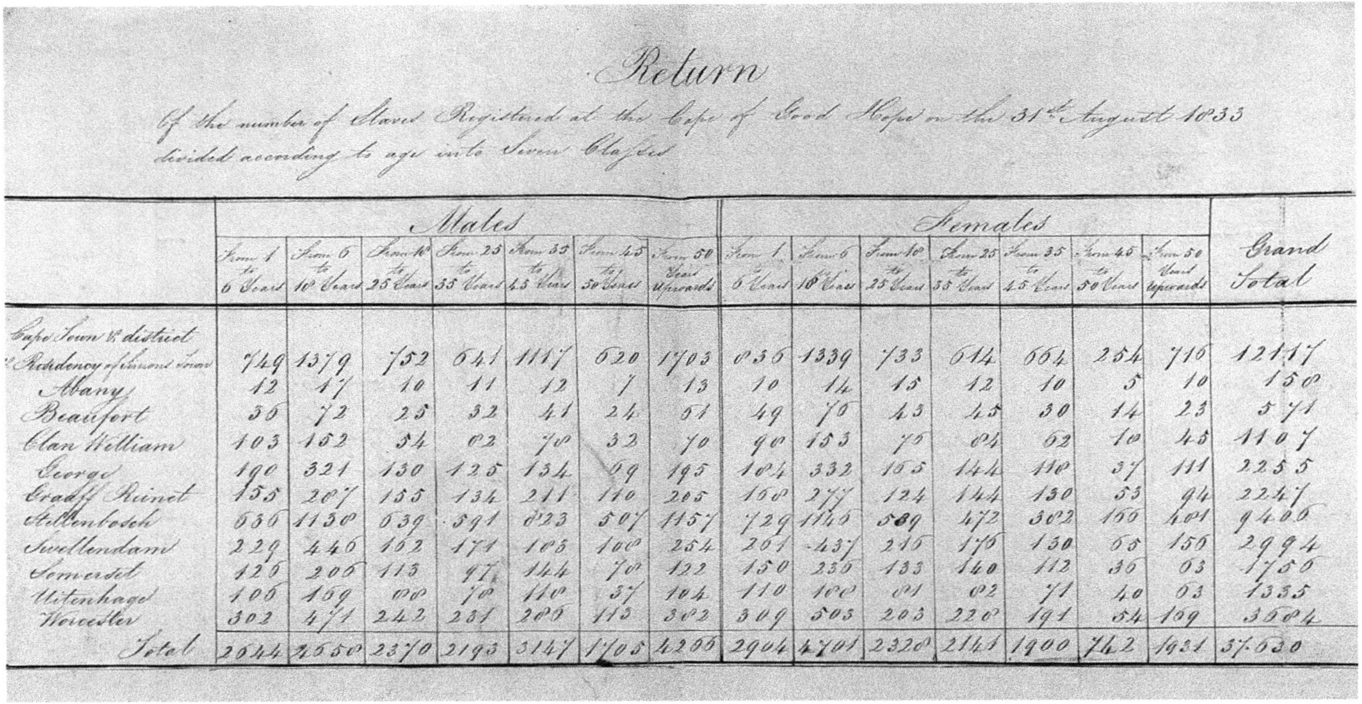

Return

Of the number of Slaves Registered at the Cape of Good Hope on the 31st August 1833 divided according to age into Seven Classes

	Males							Females							Grand Total
	From 1 to 6 Years	From 6 to 10 Years	From 10 to 25 Years	From 25 to 35 Years	From 35 to 45 Years	From 45 to 50 Years	From 50 Years Upwards	From 1 to 6 Years	From 6 to 10 Years	From 10 to 25 Years	From 25 to 35 Years	From 35 to 45 Years	From 45 to 50 Years	From 50 Years Upwards	
Cape Town & district & Residency of Simons Town	749	1379	752	641	1117	620	1703	836	1339	733	614	664	254	716	12117
Albany	12	17	10	11	12	7	13	10	14	15	12	10	5	10	158
Beaufort	36	72	25	32	41	24	51	49	76	43	45	30	14	23	571
Clan William	103	152	54	82	78	32	70	98	153	76	84	62	10	45	1107
George	190	321	130	125	134	69	195	184	332	165	144	118	37	111	2255
Graaff Reinet	155	207	155	134	211	110	205	168	277	124	144	130	53	94	2247
Stellenbosch	636	1138	639	591	823	507	1157	729	1146	589	472	382	166	481	9406
Swellendam	229	446	162	171	185	108	254	261	437	216	176	130	66	156	2994
Somerset	126	206	113	97	144	78	122	150	236	133	140	112	36	63	1756
Uitenhage	106	169	88	78	118	37	104	110	188	81	82	71	40	63	1335
Worcester	302	471	242	231	288	113	382	309	503	203	228	191	54	169	3684
Total	2644	4558	2370	2193	3147	1705	4266	2904	4701	2328	2141	1900	742	1931	37.630

FIGURE 2.3. "Return of the number of Slaves Registered at the Cape of Good Hope on the 31st August 1833 divided according to age into Seven Classes." In "Various Slave Returns, 1816–1834," Slave Office (SO) 7/36, Western Cape Archives and Records Service, Cape Town, South Africa.

the previous chapter, in which the enslaved are portrayed as speaking subjects, are another source where the stylistic conventions of the court allowed for the imagination of the voices of the enslaved. It is harder, though, to know how to approach other forms of documentation, like the slave return books, noting the prices fetched by the enslaved on auction, or the slave complaints daybook, which consists of summaries of complaints listed in ledger format (date, name, description of complaint). Black studies scholar Katherine McKittrick refers to similar documents from the Atlantic archive as the "absolutely economic, the mathematics of the unliving," positing that "breathless, archival numerical evidence puts pressure on our present system of knowledge by affirming the knowable (black objecthood) and disguising the untold (black human being)."[76]

One haunting example from the Cape archive of slavery would be the document used to tally the enslaved, divided into two halves ("males" and "females"), with a small dash made in each square, each dash representing one person (figure 2.4). Is it obscene to suggest that the horror of this image could produce something like an aesthetics of the ledger? To view its symmetrical halves, in which the slight variations to each slanted dash create the mesmerizing suggestion that at any moment a pattern might emerge, might coalesce and jump from the page, as a form of art? Is this any more obscene than finding beauty in J. M. W. Turner's famous painting *Slavers Throwing Overboard the Dead and Dying—Typhoon Coming On* (1840)? Or more obscene than Pringle's poetic meditations on the experience of slavery, or his affective imaginary tableau of a mother being separated from her children? What would it mean, in this case, to "ethically engage with mathematical and numerical certainties that compile, affirm, and honor bits and pieces of black death," in McKittrick's formulation?[77]

Gikandi has written in *Slavery and the Culture of Taste* about one aspect of the aesthetics of slavery: the art resulting from and inspired by the slave trade. He shows how the presence of slave figures in a painting often acted as a symbolic marker of wealth and, therefore, culture.[78] Abolitionists, on the other hand, were often invested in the mimetic function of painting: its ability to bring to life the horror of scenes of torture, cruelty, and debasement. Lynn Festa discusses Josiah Wedgwood's medallion depicting a kneeling slave and the question—"Am I not a man and a brother?"—describing it as follows: "Depicted in a pose of supplication, the slave begs rather than demands, kneels rather than revolts. Isolated and abject, he is in no position to unite in revolution and therefore poses no threat to the reader's contemplation of his suffering."[79] The slave figure here literally becomes a "sentimental

FIGURE 2.4. "Cape Town: Number of Males/Number of Females." In "Various Slave Returns, 1816–1834," Slave Office (SO) 7/36, pg. 183, Western Cape Archives and Records Service, Cape Town, South Africa.

object," a source of pleasure as "images of a victimized other affirms the wholeness of the self," in Festa's reading.[80] The tableau of the slave auction depicted by Pringle's correspondent, and imagined by him as the subject of a painting, is part of this larger tradition of abolitionist aesthetics, in which the suffering of the abject slave may serve a political purpose, but also serves as a source of pleasure.[81]

"When danger or pain press too nearly, they are incapable of giving any delight, and are simply terrible; but at certain distances, and with certain modifications, they may be, and they are delightful," writes Edmund Burke of the experience of the sublime, "the strongest emotion which the mind is capable of feeling."[82] Given the aesthetic distance between the enslaved experience and that of the reader, the Romantic poet Pringle's invocation of the horrors of slavery experienced by Marossi, or his description of the slave auction, perhaps partake of this sublime delight—the "pleasure, which cannot exist without a relation, and that too a relation to pain."[83] Turner's 1840 painting of the slave ship *Zong*,[84] a belated antislavery gesture given that slaves had been emancipated in 1834 in the British Empire, emphasizes this link between the depiction of slavery and the sublime as it depicts violently roiling waves and a turbulent ocean. In a 1989 review of an edition of Pringle's African poems, J. M. Coetzee writes of "The Bechuana Boy" that "its diction draws us away from the specificity of Africa towards a generalized landscape of the Romantic sublime dotted with the more celebrated African mammalian fauna," concluding that Marossi is "a figure already prepared in the European imagination for discovery in Africa (his fawn, exotic equivalent of the lamb, is a giveaway, a merely literary emblem of pastoral innocence)."[85] More than simply drawing on pastoral imagery though, Pringle draws on wider abolitionist tropes circulating in Britain. As Hartman explains, "The lure of the pastoral is in reconciling sentiment with the brute force of the racial-economic order. Thus, the brutality and antagonisms of slavery are obscured in favor of an enchanting reciprocity. The pastoral renders the state of domination as an ideal of care, duty, familial obligation, gratitude, and humanity."[86] Writing on colonial art from the Cape Colony, Gabeba Baderoon makes a similar argument about the depiction of slavery as leaning on European conventions, in this case, the picturesque: "In the dominant picturesque mode seen in landscape paintings in the nineteenth century, the violence of the slaveholding Cape Colony was rendered into a pleasing and domesticated view. In contrast to indigenous people, who resisted forced labour ... 'Malay' slaves were portrayed in such paintings as skilled, reliable and compliant, while also mysterious and exotic."[87] Pringle's abolitionist pastoral and the slaveholder Hudson's familial idyll partake of the same aesthetics, of familiarizing and domesticating the violence of enslavement.

In *Zong!*, lawyer and poet M. NourbeSe Philip turns to the legal decision from the 1781 *Zong* tragedy, *Gregson v. Gilbert*, in which at least 150 enslaved persons were thrown overboard so that the shipowners could claim their insurance value. She manipulates the actual text from the legal decision in various ways ("I . . . literally cut it into pieces, castrating verbs, suffocating adjectives, murdering nouns, throwing articles, prepositions, conjunctions overboard, jettisoning adverbs") to turn it into poems.[88] She also adds West African names to the bottom of the page, as unnumbered footnotes, in the first poem cycle, "Os," in response to the fact that the names of the enslaved were never recorded: "Idea at heart of the footnotes in general is acknowledgement—someone else was here before—in *Zong!* footnote equals the footprint./Footprints of the Africans on board the *Zong*."[89] She thus creates a counterarchive of this incident: "A recombinant antinarrative. The story that can't ever be told."[90] Jenny Sharpe, in *Immaterial Archives: An African Diaspora Poetics of Loss*, points out that some of the poems in *Zong!* "appear on the page as columns of words mimicking the neatly-written ledger recording Africans as commodities."[91] Sharpe suggests that Philip's work provides an alternative to engagements with the archives of enslavement that focus negatively on the silences and absences built into these records: "*Zong!* not only questions the ability of language to deliver the meaning of the 'ineffable,' scenes of massacre, terror, displacement, and dislocation; it also constitutes the search for a new and different kind of speech/language for speaking/writing the memory that silence holds."[92] One cannot help but read Philip's work as a critique of the romanticizing gesture of Turner's painting, and others like it. To posit an alternate aesthetic theory of the slave archive is to suggest that the sentimental tableaus of abolition obscure the harsh everyday administrative cruelty of the system of slavery, the reality of which is, perhaps, more accurately depicted by the dashes counting off the enslaved in an administrative ledger.

The sentimental mode of abolition art is thus associated with the aesthetically pleasing effect of the sublime: terror, but at a distance. The aesthetics of the ledger page steps away from the sentimental—a mode that, as we have seen, is too easily captured by those in power, available to the slaveholder as readily as to the abolitionist. It is worth comparing this page to another well-known work in the aesthetics of slavery and abolition: the famous diagram of the slave ship *Brookes*. Cheryl Finley, in *Committed to Memory: The Art of the Slave Ship Icon*, examines both the use and circulation of the diagram at its time of publication (in the late eighteenth century), and the afterlives of this icon in contemporary works of art. She refers to it as originally intended as an "'anti-art' image . . . a brutal, painful, and political image, a calculated outrage, even an obscenity."[93] The first version of this diagram was titled *Plan of an African Ship's Lower Deck with Negroes in the Proportion of Only One to a Ton* and was conceived and printed by the Plymouth Committee of the Society for Effecting the Abolition of the Slave Trade in England, in 1788, though the more well-known version is the 1789 *Description of a Slave Ship*, designed and circulated by the Society for Effecting the Abolition of the Slave Trade, based in London. Finley argues that the power of the drawing lies in its simplicity or even crudeness: "Even though the figures are meant to represent people, they are the human cargo and thus are shown stacked like barrels or some other inanimate, nonliving commodity. Here the power is achieved not by some completely new conception but by a classic revelation of economic and human reality. What is invisible and hidden is made visible. Not only does the plan expose what is hidden below decks, it also engages the numerous ship plans/packing lists that label what is placed in the ship's holds."[94] Like the *Description of a Slave Ship*, the power of the ledger page from Diverse Slave Returns (1816–1834) lies in its abstraction and simplicity. It cannot fail to mesmerize the viewer, who is invited, almost forced, to reverse the process of its creation, during which human beings were translated into dashes on the page. While the effects on the reader/viewer are quite different, this ledger page also leaves the contemporary viewer with a sense of textual friction that is reminiscent of the effects of the represented direct speech of the enslaved discussed in the previous chapter.

For each dash, on either the "male" or "female" side, the mind tries to conjure a body, a face, a life story: an impossible task, and yet it is also impossible to turn away from this page. The tension, and thus the horror, in this image lies in this connection between a dash on the page and a human being. The page as a whole is overwhelming: one can see it either as a single image, in which case one instinctively seeks patterns, or you can focus in on each dash individually, at which moment the page as a whole dissolves. Unlike the *Description of a Slave Ship*, one cannot ascribe any aesthetic intentionality to this image though—its original purpose was to serve as a counting aid, and any affect that it invokes in the viewer exists outside of its original intent. I am not sure whether we can call it an artwork, and, again unlike the *Description*, it is unlikely to have served any political purpose, even had it somehow escaped the boundaries of the slave ledgers at the time. For the contemporary viewer, the ledger page certainly generates an affective response, but still, I hesitate to call it a work of art. Rather than positing that it represents an aesthetic of the slave ledger, I suspect that it rather invites an aesthetic engagement with the archive: whether simply by sitting with the horror of encountering this ledger page, or, more robustly, encouraging contemporary artistic responses to it. Finley suggests that much of the power of the slave ship icon lies in its afterlives: a "ritualized politics of remembering" she calls "mnemonic aesthetics" that have ensured that the slave ship icon lives on today in many forms, from T-shirts and stamps to reenactments, as well as in many serious engagements by diasporic artists.[95] One cannot control the afterlife of an image, and in some of these cases, it may have been deployed in ways that are more cynical than others: but it remains a potent icon for referencing the dehumanizing slave trade today. One can perhaps imagine that the ledger page of slave returns could be reinvented in the same way, in a context where the legacies of slaveholding loom large.[96]

In suggesting that this ledger page may, in the future, become the basis for art, I am reneging on the responsibility of fully grappling with it myself.[97] But there is a limit to what can be done in the space of an academic monograph, a form that partakes in what McKittrick calls a "monumental system of knowledge that is fueled by colonial and plantocratic logics," questioning, as she does in *Dear Science*, "the analytic work of capturing, and the desire to capture, something or someone."[98] And perhaps the only service I can offer to those enumerated in the tallying of the enslaved is to publish the ledger page, so that others can work with it. Sharpe suggests that contemporary Caribbean writers and artists "disrupt, bend, and break the categories of archival knowledge," revealing "silences not to be absences, and the invisible as not the same as what cannot be seen."[99] In leaving this chapter on the possibilities of contemporary art to transform the archives, I thus propose a different viewpoint on the silencing of the enslaved I diagnose in the first part. Rather than the inarticulately suffering enslaved mother imagined by Pringle and his fellow abolitionists, or the grateful, childlike, and, again, silent slave described by the slaveholder Hudson, these other records and ledgers have the power to introduce unsettlingly silent figures, not speaking but present, bearing witness. While the silence of Pringle's and Hudson's enslaved figures is rendered all but unnoticeable through the babble of other voices, slaveholder and abolitionist alike, the silence of the ledger page is deafening.

3. "GRIEVANCES MORE SENTIMENTAL THAN MATERIAL"

Representing Indentured Labor in Natal, 1860–1915

Who can speak, and how? Demand for labor continued to shape the depiction of subaltern speech in the Indian Ocean world after the end of slavery. In the period following emancipation in the British Empire, British colonies increasingly relied upon a different system of transported bonded labor in the form of indenture. The term *indenture* literally referred to the serrated edges—teeth—of a contract or document, two copies of which were written on the same piece of paper and then cut with a jagged edge, so that the two pieces matched. This term was initially used for the contract between an apprentice and the master craftsman responsible for their training. Once the period of indenture was completed, the master would hand back his half of the contract such that the apprentice could "take up his indentures," signifying that the former apprentice's training was considered complete.[1] Starting in the seventeenth century, the meaning of this term shifts from a period of training to a specified period of labor, whereby workers signed indenture contracts to labor for a period of time in another part of the world in return for passage (usually including return passage) and wages. The system of indenture was particularly important to the economic growth of European imperial powers after emancipation, when many colonies where slavery had been the main source of labor began contracting indentured laborers to perform the same work. While in practice many indentured laborers experienced the same violence and exploitation that marked slavery, indentured laborers had certain legal protections in place that were absent for the enslaved. The system was primarily distinguished from slavery by the existence of the indenture contract. One could thus only contract laborers for a certain period of time, and workers were promised wages. Moreover, one could not be born into indenture: the children of indentured laborers were not indentured.

In the nineteenth-century Cape Colony examined in the previous chapter, both abolitionists and proslavery advocates spoke for the enslaved, resulting in the dominant image of the slave as silently suffering. The historical shift in labor practices from using enslaved labor to contracted labor brought along legal changes to the forms of officially recognized speech available to indentured laborers, and a concomitant shift in the imagination of the figure of the indentured laborer. I chart the depiction of the indentured laborer, and specifically the speech of the indentured laborer, across political and legal archives, in the same way I had examined the legal archives of the Cape Colony and the political writings of abolitionist and proslavery authors in the previous chapter. The first part of this chapter focuses on the figure of the indentured laborer as imagined in the political writings of Mohandas K. Gandhi, before turning to legal complaints filed by indentured laborers in Natal, South Africa. While the formal constraints of treatise or legal complaint as genre shape the representation of the indentured laborer in these texts, these texts also reflect historical shifts in what kinds of speech are legible to authorities. Gandhi thus had to deploy different strategies of representation in his pamphlet regarding the treatment of Indians in South Africa than abolitionist Thomas Pringle did in his pamphlet on slavery at the Cape. The key to understanding these strategies of representation lies, I argue, in a distinction Gandhi makes between *sentimental* and *material* grievances. This chapter demonstrates that appeals to the sentiments of contemporaneous readers, whether political authorities or the general public, were seen as less effective than concrete demonstrations of material harm. In the final part of the chapter, I shift to contemporary debates around the representation of indentured labor (as either a "new system of slavery" or as strategic labor migration), using sources from different empires to suggest that the afterlife of the sentimental depiction of the enslaved by Black Atlantic abolitionists continues to affect the representation of indentured diasporas. If, as I suggest in the previous chapter, Pringle's pamphlet on "Slavery at the Cape of Good Hope" marked the entry of the Cape Colony into the imaginative sphere of the Black Atlantic, Gandhi's writings and the other texts examined here reinscribe the Natal colony into a complex web of diasporic relationality in the Indian Ocean.

Laborers traveling under indenture contracts came predominantly from China and South Asia in the nineteenth century. Through this system, perhaps five hundred thousand Chinese indentured laborers traveled to Cuba, Mauritius, Peru, Australia, and the Hawaiian Islands in the 1840s, to the Philippines, Siam, and Sumatra later in the nineteenth century, and, early in the twentieth century, to the Transvaal (South Africa) and France. Chinese indentured migration continued until the 1920s. The South Asian indentured labor diaspora also emerged after emancipation, with the first indentured laborers traveling to Mauritius and its dependent islands in 1835, and the final indenture contracts ending in the 1920s. Around 1.5 million South Asian indentured laborers were transported to the Mascarene Islands, British and Dutch Guiana, Trinidad, Jamaica, and other British Caribbean islands, the French Caribbean, Fiji, British East Africa, and Natal. These laborers embarked mainly from Karikal (Karaikal) and Madras (Chennai) in South India and Calcutta (Kolkata) in the north. A more informal system of labor migration, called *kangany* ("foreman" in Tamil, for the person who served as both recruiter and supervisor) or *maistry* (from the Portuguese for "master"), in Malaya and Burma involved recruiters specifically sent to enlist individuals from their own families or regions. Many laborers from British India recruited through these more informal systems of *kangany* or *maistry* were also transported to Ceylon. During the period of Chinese and South Asian indenture, a smaller number of Japanese migrants also traveled to Hawai'i, the United States, Peru, and Brazil under indenture contracts.[2]

In South Africa, the British in the Cape Colony had inherited from the Dutch a system that in some ways foreshadowed indenture: called the *inboek* (booking-in, referencing the necessity of recording the names of these individuals in a book held by the Magistrate) system, it involved children of the Khoisan indigenous groups being registered (using various degrees of force or coercion) to work on a particular farm until they reached the age of twenty-five. This system was curtailed in 1828.[3] Other Indian Ocean systems of coerced labor that prefigured indenture include South Indian slavery, as well as the *engagé* system, which involved the recruitment of liberated East African and Malagasy slaves to work on various islands in the French Indian Ocean empire.[4] Clare Anderson, furthermore, argues that the network of penal transportation in the Indian Ocean world provided the model—"discursively, institutionally, and imaginatively"—and some of the infrastructure for the transportation of indentured laborers starting in 1835.[5] The East India Company had, prior to being replaced by the government of British India in 1858, deported numerous South Asian convicts to work in the Straits Settlements (Penang, Malacca, Singapore), Burma, Bencoolen, and Mauritius, and, following the 1857 Mutiny, the Andaman Islands. Anderson's article shows how both the practice and the language of indenture can be traced back to penal transportation: for example, even the term *kala pani* (black water), now associated with the experience of crossing the ocean as an indentured migrant, originally described the fear of this same experience as a convict.

The South African colony of Natal was colonized by Great Britain in 1843 (having been initially settled by early Boer expansionists in 1839 and called the Republic of Natalia). From 1843 until the end of the second South African War in 1902, the colonial territories of South Africa comprised two British colonies, Natal and the Cape Colony, and two Boer Republics, the Orange Free State (Oranje Vrijstaat) and the South African Republic (Zuid-Afrikaansche Republiek). In 1860, the colonial government of Natal entered into agreement with that of British India to transport indentured laborers from British India to Natal, initially on three-year contracts, in order to work predominantly on sugarcane plantations.[6] The agreement regarding indenture remained in place (with some modifications and occasional suspensions) until 1911, when the recruitment and transport of Indian indentured laborers to South Africa was officially ended, with the final contracts ending in 1915. During this period, 152,184 South Asian laborers traveled to Natal under indenture contracts.[7]

Material Grievances in Political and Legal Discourse in Natal

Gandhi, who lived in Natal from 1893 to 1914, is perhaps the most well-known advocate for indentured laborers in South Africa, though much of his work on their behalf took place during the latter part of his South African period, and he was initially reluctant to include them in his campaigns.[8] His writings reveal that this initial reluctance had much to do with the perceived insult of the term *coolie*, which he saw as applicable only to indentured laborers, being applied to all South Asians in South Africa. In one letter, written just four months after his arrival in South Africa, he writes:

Sir,—You will oblige me by kindly allowing me to say a few words about the Coolie controversy that is being carried on in your paper; not that I want to join the fray but with a view to remove some of the misunderstanding that prevails with regard to the coloured people. . . . The word Coolie is a term of contempt when applied to those who have not come under the Immigration Act, and it is a pity that every coloured man passes generally for a Coolie. It will have been seen that no Indian is a Coolie by birth. Any Indian is a Coolie who has come under the Immigration Act, and ceases to be one when he has finished his agreement. This is as it should be.[9]

This letter appears in the *Transvaal Advertiser* on September 5, 1893, and in it, Gandhi expresses approval of the term *coolie*, if used for "indentured Indians who have come under the Immigration Act," but argues that an Indian "ceases to be one when he has finished his agreement." In this argument, indenture isolates the indentured laborer from the Indian community, separates them and confines them to a different nomenclature, that of the coolie. "No Indian is a Coolie by birth"—one just inhabits the term for a while, at the conclusion of which, the proper name *Indian* can be reclaimed. Gandhi is primarily objecting to the term *coolie* being used for those South Asians who had not come to Natal under indenture contracts, or those whose contracts had expired. In the South African parlance of the day, these were referred to as Passenger Indians (who had paid for their own passage to Natal) or Free Indians (those previously under indenture contracts or born to indentured laborers).[10]

The word *coolie* is a particularly briny South term, originating and circulating in maritime contexts and various languages, and tracing the intersections between various forms of coerced labor. As Lisa Lowe argues, "The great instability and multivalence of the term coolie suggests it was a shifting, historically contingent designation for an intermediary form of Asian labor, used both to define and obscure the boundary between enslavement and freedom."[11] The origins of the word *coolie* are debated, but the most widely accepted hypothesis is that *coolie* originally came from the Tamil word கூலி (*kūli*), meaning "wages" or "hire," and was spread by Portuguese merchants throughout the Indian Ocean world.[12] *Coolie* first appears in South African records in the context of slavery: in the Dutch eighteenth-century court records I examine in chapter one, *koeli-geld* or "coolie-money" refers to the money slaves can earn for themselves (or, frequently, for the slaveholder) by hiring themselves out for a day.[13]

While Moon-Ho Jung argues, in reference to the use of the term *coolie* for East Asian migrants in an American context, that "coolies were never a people or a legal category," in Natal, the term *coolie* was initially used in legal statutes.[14] The law that originally allowed for the introduction of indentured labor in Natal was titled "Law No. 14: Law providing for the Introduction of Coolies into the Colony of Natal at Public Expense, and for the Regulation and Governance of such Immigrants," and Law No. 15 of 1864 is titled "To Raise a Loan for the Introduction of Coolies into the Colony of Natal."[15] A commission appointed by the Natal government to report on indentured laborers in South Africa in 1872 was titled The Coolie Commission: The 1872 Commission of Inquiry into the Condition of the Indian Immigrants in the Colony of Natal. When Gandhi argues for the "proper" use of the term *coolie* as referring to someone under an indenture contract, he thus reflects the existence of these legal statutes, in which *coolie* refers to a certain clearly defined type of Indian immigrant.

The Coolie Commission was conducting an inquiry into the treatment of South Asian indentured laborers in Natal after several complaints were lodged by returning indentured laborers in Madras and Calcutta, including of poor working conditions, physical punishments, inadequate food and lodging, and nonpayment of wages. Ann Laura Stoler points to the importance of such colonial commissions—in her words, they "produced new truths as they produced new social realities" and "wrote, revised, and over-wrote genealogies of race."[16] The commission interviewed thirty-six witnesses—thirty employers, three government officials, and only three indentured laborers. One of their recommendations is that the term *coolie* be dropped from official discourse: "There is no doubt that the term is galling, and a source of annoyance. We would suggest that the term 'Indian Immigrants' be substituted for that of Coolie in all official documents, and that the designation 'Coolie Agent' be changed to that of 'Protector of Indian Immigrants.'"[17] This concession is framed as responding to a grievance on the part of indentured laborers. The authors of the report state that "on many estates this term was mentioned to us, in our conversations with the Coolies, as one of their objections to the Colony."[18] It is clear, however, from Gandhi's writings on South Africa, that the removal of the term *coolie* from law did not remove it from public discourse about indentured laborers, and about British Indians more generally.

In an 1896 pamphlet, written while he was briefly back in India and titled *The Grievances of the British Indians in South Africa: An Appeal to the Indian Public* (usually referred to as the *Green Pamphlet* because of the color of its cover), Gandhi expands on his critique of the word *coolie*: "These offensive epithets have become so common that they (at any rate, one of them, 'Coolie') are used even in the sacred precincts of the courts, as if 'the Coolie' were the legal and proper name to give to any and every Indian. The public men, too, seem to use the word freely. I have often heard the painful expression 'coolie clerk' from the mouths of men who ought to know better."[19] As in his earlier letter, Gandhi is offended by the confusion of the term *Coolie* with the term *Indian*.

In the pamphlet, Gandhi seeks to differentiate between traders and indentured laborers on the one hand, but also between South Asian and African inhabitants of the South African colonies. He claims that anyone would be able to tell the difference between an indentured Indian and an Indian trader on sight, since "the indentured Indian never is dressed in a fashionable dress" (367). South Asian indentured laborers are, however, distinguished from Africans in terms of their work ethic. Protesting the registration of indentured laborers alongside Africans, Gandhi says that "there is a very good reason for requiring registration of a native in that he is yet being taught the dignity and necessity of labour. The Indian knows it and he is imported because he knows it" (367). Sukanya Banerjee, in *Becoming Imperial Citizens: Indians in the Late-Victorian Empire*, writes about Gandhi's strategies for differentiating the South Asian trader class (Passenger Indians) from indentured laborers, focusing on the aspects of character, cleanliness, and creditworthiness. Banerjee argues that indentured laborers were "both indispensable to—and unrepresentable within—the rhetoric of imperial citizenship" for Gandhi, in order to describe their curious position (both central but also disavowed) within his rhetoric: the labor performed by the indentured laborers justifies their being in Natal in the first place, but also renders them beneath the Passenger Indian class in terms of marks of civility (like clothing).[20]

Gandhi is thus both invested in maintaining the difference between coolies and Passenger Indians, while also (the primary objective of this pamphlet, as indicated in the title) bringing home to the reader the "Grievances of the British Indians in South Africa"—here, British Indians being a larger category under which both Passenger Indians and indentured laborers are subsumed. What are these grievances? Gandhi makes a crucial distinction early in the pamphlet between sentimental and material grievances, by claiming that the secretary of state for the colonies, Joseph Chamberlain, "is said to have stated that our grievances were more sentimental than material and real and that, if he could be shown any instances of real grievance, he should deal with them effectively."[21] The phrase *sentimental grievance* at the time frequently appears in opposition to "real," "material," "practical," "substantial," "genuine," or "positive" injuries, and bespeaks a grievance that is only perceived by the sufferer, not actually experienced.[22] As the term *material* suggests, one has to establish that real, by which is usually meant financial, harm befalls the victim because of this grievance. Gandhi explains that in order to give "proof of real grievances and to strengthen the position of the advocates of our cause in India, I shall beg leave to cite my own testimony and that of those who have undergone grievances personally."[23] The purpose of the pamphlet is thus to establish that British Indians in South Africa have suffered real, material grievances, and not merely sentimental ones.

It is thus surprising that Gandhi chose to begin the pamphlet by quoting a letter of his to the Natal legislative assembly listing all the verbal insults directed toward South Asians in South Africa in the press: "Here are a few samples. 'The real canker that is eating into the very vitals of the community', 'these parasites', 'wily, wretched semi-barbarous Asiatics', 'A thing black and lean and a long way from clean, which they call the accursed Hindoo', 'He is chock-full of vice and he lives upon rice. I heartily cuss the Hindoo', 'Squalid coolies with truthless tongues and artful ways'. The Press almost unanimously refuses to call the Indian by his proper name. He is 'Ramysamy'. He is 'Mr. Samy'. He is 'Mr. Coolie'. He is 'the black man'" (360).

Gandhi's argument, however, depends on proving that these verbal insults, rather than merely harming the feelings, or sentiments, of the British Indian population in South Africa, actually have material detrimental impacts. For every insult Gandhi and his associates suffer in these pages, the physical rather than the emotional toll is stressed: "The hotelkeeper would not allow him a room in his hotel and he had to sleep in the coach, shivering the whole night with cold. And the winter in that part of Africa is no joke," for example, or "in Field Street, Durban, last year during Christmas time, some youths threw burning crackers in the Indian stores doing some damage. Three months ago, in the same street, some youths shot lead bullets into an Indian store with a sling, hurting a customer who nearly lost his eye" (361). The intense cold, the damage done to the stores, the customer who nearly loses an eye: these are tangible instances of harm demonstrating that discrimination goes beyond words to deeds with material consequences.

In the *Green Pamphlet*, Gandhi thus has a vested interest in steering clear of depictions of British Indians in South Africa that appeal primarily to the sentiments of the reader. The perceived antipathy toward "sentimental grievances" he describes is a result of the many years of abolitionist campaigning, which resulted in a suspicion of sentiment in political discourse.[24] Gandhi spends relatively few pages on the plight of indentured laborers, but toward the end of the pamphlet, expresses one specific request related to indenture: he asks that "the Protector of Immigrants should be a man knowing the Tamil and the Hindustani languages and should, if possible, be an Indian," adding that the "present Protector is an estimable gentleman. His ignorance of the languages, however, cannot but be a serious drawback."[25] The Protector of Immigrants was the person tasked specifically with protecting the interests of indentured laborers, and hearing their complaints. Gandhi explains this request by discussing one particular incident concerning his interactions with an indentured laborer.

In this passage, pay attention to how Gandhi depicts the speech and silence of the indentured laborer, a man named Balasundaram:

> An Indian named Balasundaram was, in 1894, so ill-treated by his master that two of his teeth were nearly knocked out; they came out through his upper lip causing an issue of blood sufficient to soak his long turban in it.... The man went, then, to the Magistrate who was much moved at the sight. The turban was kept in court and he was at once sent to the hospital for treatment. The man after having been kept in the hospital for a few days was discharged. He had heard about me and came to my office. He had not recovered sufficiently to be able to speak. I asked him, therefore, to write out his complaint in Tamil which he knew. He wanted to prosecute the master so that his contract of indenture might be cancelled. I asked him if he would be satisfied if his indenture was transferred. On his nodding consent to what I said, I wrote to his master asking if he would consent to transfer the services of the man. He was at first unwilling but subsequently consented. I sent the man also to the Protector's office with a Tamil clerk of mine who gave the man's version to the Protector.... The man was then said to have compromised and to have given the Protector a written document to the effect that he had no complaint to make. He sent me a note to the effect.... To proceed, however, with the painful story, naturally the note sent a shock through my body. I had hardly recovered when the man came to my office crying and saying the Protector would not transfer him. I literally ran to the Protector's office and inquired what the matter was. He placed the written document before me and asked me how he could help the man. He said the man should not have signed the document. And this document was an affidavit attested by the Protector himself. I told the Protector that I should advise the man to go to the

> Magistrate and lodge a complaint.... The magistrate treated us quite differently. He had seen the man while the blood was yet dripping from his lips.... The master said he gave provocation. The Magistrate retorted: "You had no business to take the law in your own hands and beat the man as if he were a beast."... This is only a typical instance showing how hard it is for the indentured men to get justice (373–74).

At first glance, this incident seems to have little to do with whether the Protector of Immigrants speaks Tamil or not—the more sympathetic magistrate, after all, is presumably also ignorant of these languages, but still sympathizes with the indentured man: crucially, because he had witnessed the man "while the blood was yet dripping from his lips." However, this anecdote stages a delicate movement between the language of speech, writing, and the physical evidence of the body, in which the evidence of the body is shown to outweigh other forms of language.

As a result of his injuries, Balasundaram literally cannot speak. We never hear Balasundaram's voice in this description, and it is the voice of the liberal magistrate that is quoted instead, saying, "You had no business to take the law in your own hands and beat the man as if he were a beast." On the other hand, the body and clothing of the indentured laborer testify on his behalf: note the importance of the bloody "long turban," kept in court as evidence, and the detailed description of Balasundaram's injury: "Two of his teeth were nearly knocked out; they came out through his upper lip causing an issue of blood." It is the "sight" of this bloody face that remains with the magistrate, convincing him to take Balasundaram's side. In the *Green Pamphlet*, Gandhi largely uses the figure of the indentured laborer as a foil for the educated, well-dressed Indian trader, and this depiction of an oppressed, helpless, bloody-turbaned laborer does not necessarily contradict these earlier descriptions of indentured laborers.

However, Gandhi complicates the depiction of Balasundaram as silently suffering in several ways. Firstly, while Balasundaram does not speak, he is shown to be writing "out his complaint in Tamil which he knew." He is thus able to express his desires, and is also shown in conversation with Gandhi, nodding his consent to his suggestion of a transfer. Balasundaram is thus represented as capable of communicating, and making his desires clear. Notes, letters, and documents proliferate in this passage, demonstrating the importance of writing in dealing with colonial bureaucracies and thus implicitly lending importance to Balasundaram's act of writing. Bodily evidence, too, is not something that is only restricted to a form of expression for the indentured laborer: Gandhi inserts his own body into the narrative, claiming that the note from the protector "sent a shock through my body" and that he "literally ran" to the protector's office. Gandhi's use of his own body in this passage perhaps runs the same risk of rhetorical substitution as abolitionist discourse, in suggesting that the pain he felt in living through this "painful story" was in some way similar to the pain experienced by Balasundaram.[26] However, rather than eliding Balasundaram's body, and his suffering, Gandhi's rhetoric here actually amplifies the evidence of the suffering, bloody-faced Balasundaram by adding the testimony of his own body, and therefore underlining the validity of bodily evidence, in conjunction with writing.

While the renewed focus on the language of feeling is perhaps surprising here, given Gandhi's focus on material rather than sentimental grievances in the pamphlet, Gandhi's shock and (emotional) pain is subsumed under Balasundaram's real, bodily injuries. Gandhi's focus on material grievances, then, explains the centrality of Balasundaram's injured face to this description. Gandhi claims that he tells this story as "a typical instance showing how hard it is for the indentured men to get justice," but of course, there is also another message, to Chamberlain and his fellow skeptics, imbedded in this narrative. While the protector is an example of someone who, in order to make his own job easier, simply accepts the written document that he is given, the magistrate, because he has seen with his own eyes the physical evidence of the real, material injuries suffered by this British Indian in South Africa, questions the signed piece of paper and the testimony of the man's employer, notably exclaiming that the man's crime was to "beat the man as if he were a beast." This is very much in line with Gandhi's rhetoric throughout this pamphlet, which serves to establish that the insults he documents on the first page, including "parasites" and "thing," while seemingly injurious only to the sentiments of British Indians, actually lead to material harm. Recalling his catalogue of insults, Gandhi laments at one point in the pamphlet that "but, then, the Indian in South Africa is not credited with any feelings. He is a beast, 'a thing black and lean', 'the Asian dirt to be heartily cursed.'"[27] Sentimental and material grievances, Gandhi finally demonstrates through his subtle rhetoric in this pamphlet, are not as clearly delineated and separable as Joseph Chamberlain and his ilk suggest.

The figure of the indentured laborer in Gandhi's *Green Pamphlet* is thus particularly complex. In the Balasundaram passage, an indentured laborer's injured face becomes a metonym for the material grievances suffered by British Indians—but his face, and body, need to be vocalized through Gandhi, the representative of the educated class of Passenger Indians. Gandhi thus in one way stands in a similar relation to indentured laborers as earlier white abolitionists, like Pringle, had been to the slaves they represented. In his pamphlet, Gandhi draws direct links between the treatment of British Indians in South Africa and the earlier treatment of slaves in the British Empire: "For a good Christian gentleman it is as natural to see nothing unjust in the persecution of the Asiatic as it was in the olden days for the bonafide Christians to see nothing wrong or un-Christian in slavery" (385). Here, however, the comparison between Gandhi and the abolitionist figure breaks down because of the racial hierarchy of the British Empire, which does not allow Gandhi the same authority as the white abolitionist. Gandhi is also part of the British Indian population in South Africa that is being mistreated, and he objects specifically to the ways in which all British Indians were being persecuted as if they were all indentured laborers. Gandhi both wants to maintain the difference between indentured and nonindentured Indians on the basis of civilization, while also arguing that all of them face forms of discrimination in South Africa that need to be redressed.

The pamphlet form shapes some of Gandhi's rhetorical choices. It aims to inspire righteous outrage and engender reform by reporting to its readers on the experiences of British Indians in South Africa, drawing largely on a series of anecdotes in order to make arguments. Gandhi quotes extensively from other sources in order to support his own testimony with that of other, supposedly authoritative, voices. The pamphlet is explicitly addressed to its subcontinental audience ("An Appeal to the Indian Public"), but its secondary audience is clearly readers in England. Since the earlier letter to the legislative council of Natal, in which Gandhi had described the terms of abuse directed at Indians in South Africa, had proven to be unsuccessful (with Chamberlain decrying the grievances as sentimental rather than material), Gandhi has adjusted his rhetoric to demonstrate the concrete, material effects of the verbal discrimination he had described earlier. In the following section, I trace how indentured laborers themselves presented their grievances to the Office of the Protector of Immigrants.

"Two Marks Shown": The Language of the Contract in Complaints of the Indentured

Examples of legal complaints lodged by indentured laborers offer contemporary readers some limited access to how these men and women framed their own suffering within the constraints imposed by this genre. The Office of the Protector of Immigrants served, after 1872, as the first resource for indentured laborers seeking to lay complaints. These complaints, brief as they are, support the trend indicated by Gandhi's *Green Pamphlet*, in which material complaints are most legible and convincing. For example, Hureebhukut's deposition, dated February 10, 1877, reads:

> I am an indentured Coolie and work for Mr. Thomas Brown, Umgeni Sugar Estate. . . . Again at muster on Saturday morning I told the manager and sirdar that I was sick, suffering from loose bowels and was not able to work. So I went to my hut (;) about an hour after (,) the same white man came to my hut. I was at that time just entering my hut when he (the white man) caught me by the neck, and struck me three times on the back with a stick (two marks shown) after which I snatched away the stick and ran into the cane. I went to Verulam court on Monday morning and at 9 a.m. I met the Indian constable there who said the magistrate is not here today, come tomorrow, and on Tuesday when I went to the court house, the same Indian constable told me that the magistrate would not be in that day also, and said try and come again tomorrow. I went the next day and made my statement to the interpreter of the court, after he had taken down all that I had to say, he told me to go back to my master's estate. I said I would not go back till my case was settled, and if I did not get proper satisfaction I would go to the Protector of Immigrants at Durban (,) which I have done. I have been twice during the Christmas month to complain at the Verulam court, and the first time the interpreter would not take down my complaint but he did so the second time I went with a large mark on my left shoulder.[28]

Hureebhukut lays out the difficulties faced by indentured laborers in making their complaints legible to legal authorities. He is at the mercy of the whims of officials: the magistrate is not at work at the times he is expected to be, the constable is profoundly unhelpful, and the interpreter tells him to go back to his employer's estate. Written a few years before Gandhi's *Green Pamphlet*, Hureebhukut's deposition demonstrates that, in many cases, the literal ability of indentured laborers to speak was almost irrelevant when faced with constables, magistrates, and interpreters—the latter especially important, as the interpreter is the necessary link that should make indentured speech comprehensible to the law. The final sentence here is thus particularly damning, as we see the interpreter refusing to take a statement until the indentured laborer appears with material, bodily evidence: "A large mark on my left shoulder." In this context, Gandhi's description of his interaction with

Balasundaram is shown to be typical, in that the bodily evidence of the indentured laborer is esteemed far more highly than his speech.

Hureebhukut's deposition also frames his experience in the language of the contract. He identifies himself as an "indentured Coolie," notes his place of work, and is very clear in noting days and times of specific events. Other documents will underscore how important this framing in terms of laws and contracts becomes in rendering a complaint legible to authorities. Another case, recorded by the office of the Protector of Indian Immigrants, involved an indentured man named Bhagoo. He is one of five men who laid complaints against a particular employer in February 1884.

This narrative is particularly striking for the way in which sentiment is erased:

> I am indentured to Mr. J. Meikle. Five of the men who were assigned with me ran away as they were ill-treated, and about a fortnight ago one of my sons named Augna (25980) about 10 years of age left the estate and has not been heard of since. The circumstances of his leaving were, he had 50 sheep to look after and one evening one did not return with the rest, the boy also through fear stayed away. The missing sheep afterwards returned and the boy also. The next morning Mr. Meikle with Mrs. Meikle's approval tied the boy's hands together with a strap and hung him naked to a rafter in the dining-room and thrashed him with a hunting crop. The boy was kept hanging for an hour about two feet from the ground and when breakfast time came he was taken down and sent off with the sheep as usual. He went but as stated never returned.
>
> For one week before I left the estate search was made for the boy when off work but he could not be found. On two occasions after the boy left and could not be found, Mr. Meikle beat me and my wife suspecting that we took food to the boy at night. I am served with (Junari) Kaffir Ammabella [a type of staple] one month; and with mealy meal another; I also get salt and dhal but no fish, ghee or rice. I work seven weeks for a month's wages. This has been the case for the last 2 years. When I went first to the estate I worked only 4 and 5 weeks to a month. I have not received any wages for 4 months.
>
> Not a day passes without one or another of the Indians on Mr. Meikle's farm being thrashed. I have often lost clothes, pots [unclear] from my house while at work but can never find out who takes them. My house is daily searched by Mr. and Mrs. Meikle and the children. I work a

> portion of the day on Sunday. No extra pay is given for Sunday work. The other Coolies on the estate witnessed my son being beaten. I refuse to return to the estate.[29]

Bhagoo describes his son's punishment in great detail: the rafter, the time of day (breakfast), and the hunting crop all add to the materiality of the description. Rather than lingering on the emotions that their son's disappearance may have caused him and his wife, Bhagoo moves on to other forms of material evidence: he lists the precise kinds of staple foods they are provided (presumably to stress that he could not have been feeding his son, as he was accused of doing) and then other grievances against Meikle. He concludes by invoking other witnesses: "The other Coolies on the estate witnessed my son being beaten" before stating that he refuses to return to the estate.

Bhagoo's complaint is rather unfocused: is he objecting to the physical maltreatment his son suffers, the fact that his son still hasn't been found, the quality of food he receives, or his wages and lack of rest days? Seen in the context of other complaints and of Gandhi's later *Green Pamphlet*, however, Bhagoo's impulse to list as many grievances, in as much detail as possible, begins to make sense as a reasonable strategy for an indentured laborer confronting the law's refusal to hear his voice. Even if he does feel anxiety about his son, or anger at the way he was beaten, these emotions are not seen as relevant to his legal complaint.

We can better understand Bhagoo's impulse by turning to a different set of letters from the early years of indentured labor in Natal. Again, we catch only a fragmentary glimpse of the indentured laborer, Bundhoo, in these accounts, which consist of two letters written by his employer, a Mr. J. Gordon, and a minute from the Resident Magistrate of Durban to the Protector of Immigrants in that same city. The facts of the case seem to be that, following the death of his son on December 20, 1876, Bundhoo, his wife, and two children left Gordon's farm in March 1877 and were subsequently arrested for being away from their place of employment without a pass. Bundhoo appeared before the magistrate on March 19, having walked (with his family) from Pietermaritzburg to Durban.

When Gordon learns that Bundhoo and his wife had been arrested, he responds by writing the following:

> Sirs
> I have received your letter informing one that Bundhoo wife & 2 children is arrested. They deserted my service on the night of the 12 of this month. This is the second time they have deserted. They make the death of their

boy an excuse for going away. The first time they went they stayed eight days & come back of their own accord. They are a very troublesome lot & I don't think they will ever do one much good.[30]

Gordon's wording here is key: "They make the death of their boy an excuse for going away." Sentiment over a dead child is relegated, in this employer's words, into no more than an excuse. He insinuates that this is simply part of a larger pattern: "They are a very troublesome lot & I don't think they will ever do one much good." While Gordon goes on to describe the death of Bundhoo's child (apparently from heat exhaustion) in the next paragraph, he quickly concludes that "I maid a Deposition the next day to the Magistrate of the Umgeni Devision & he told one he would send the District Surgeon to the hospitel & through an interpreter explained to the Father who said he knew the boy was very sick before cumming hear."[31] For Gordon, the boy's death is a practical problem to be solved, as is the problem of what to do with Bundhoo and his wife: "If you would be so good as to transfer them to someone else it would be a great relief to one."[32]

In the final letter in this collection, we again hear from Gordon, having now clearly enlisted the aid of a lawyer:

> I have the honor to acknowledge receipt of your letters of date 5th. And in reply, beg to say that I have called at the Magistrate's office (Umgeni Division) and he is gone out to the country on official Business & subsequently I cannot obtain his signature to Schedule D Law 12. 1872, but having seen clerk to Attorney General (where my Deposition relative to the death of the Coolie Child) made on the 21st December 1876 is now deposited and who has promised to me that he will lend you a copy accompanied with this letter by tomorrow's post (Medical certificate).[33]

Gordon is now fluent in the language of the law ("Schedule D Law 12," "Medical certificates," "Depositions"). Bundhoo and his family have been transferred under the terms of the indenture contract, and Gordon is confident that he "should hear no more of them."[34] This set of documents reinforces the indentured laborer's relative silencing before the law, underscoring how emotional bonds are dismissed, and the language of law stresses documentation, dates, and the convenience of employers.

The language of the contract seeps into both Gordon's letter here, and also into the complaints by the indentured laborers discussed earlier. The form of these complaints and letters, which must be legible to the law, prohibits certain forms of sentimental writing. In the context of this book, which traces the deployment of sentiment in writings by and about marginalized subjects traveling across the Indian Ocean, the reader will have noticed that sentiment, initially legible to law and incorporated as evidence in Dutch eighteenth-century court cases, became a weapon used by both pro- and antislavery activists in the nineteenth century, when legal cases were increasingly stripped of sentiment. In the cases lodged by indentured laborers seen here, sentiment has been almost completely erased from these documents. Gandhi's *Green Pamphlet*, which can be compared to the writings of earlier abolitionists, demonstrates that he is aware of the conventions of sentimental writing (his depiction of the Balasundaram case in his *Autobiography*, which will be discussed in chapter five, renders the whole incident in far more sentimental tones), but also views his charge as convincing the reader through the depiction of material, rather than sentimental, grievances.

I turn now to another contemporaneous source, which offers a partial view of how indentured laborers framed their own experiences of indenture, this time expressed lyrically, in a folk song composed during the early days of indenture in Natal. Autobiographical writings by indentured laborers are rare, and folk songs like this one are valuable sources for scholars interested in indentured writings. For example, Lalbihari Sharma's *Damra Phag Bahar* (*Holi Songs of Demerara*), a book of songs to be sung during Holi in Demerara, published in 1915, is one of the few works of literature written by indentured laborers in the Caribbean. An anthology of folk songs from Suriname, collected in 1968 by Usharbudh Arya, is similarly useful for understanding both the continuities between Hindu communities in Suriname and South Asia, and the way this community in Suriname viewed itself.[35] My final source from Natal, a short song, stresses the practical aspects of indentured life:

> "Coolie" is the name given to you, "coolie" is the name given to you
> Sing the song of coming to Natal, brother
> *Cambu* in your hand, spade on your shoulder
> Let the foreigners go home.[36]

The song, collected by the linguist Rajend Mesthrie, is in the South African dialect of Bhojpuri: a North Indian language, closely related to Hindi, spoken predominantly in Bihar and Uttar Pradesh. The song is of unknown date and authorship, but Mesthrie suggests that it is of "relatively early composition, probably by an indentured or ex-indentured worker."[37] In the repeated refrain in the first line "*kuulii naam dharaayaa*" (coolie name is given), the passive verb form, to be given a certain name, stresses the passivity of the indentured laborer onto whom the name is bestowed by an unknown third party. This again centers the word *coolie* as shorthand for the experience of being indentured, as an identity that is temporarily imposed upon the bearer but affects every aspect of their life.

Mesthrie identifies three loanwords—*cambu*, a "container, pot," from South African Tamil; the place-name Natal; and *kuulii*, in the untitled song above. Loanwords have inflected the native language, Bhojpuri, spoken by a group of indentured immigrants in Natal. The name *coolie* that the group is given becomes integrated into the song, but also other loanwords stemming from the mixture of cultures that takes place in Natal. The final line, *pardesiyaa ghare jaaii*, where I have used Mesthrie's translation of "let the foreigners go home," is particularly challenging. It is left ambiguous who the "foreigner" is, and where "home" is—the incorporation of loanwords suggests that the line between the "foreign" and the "domestic" is no longer clearly delineated. *Pardesiyaa* is derived from the root, *desh*, a Sanskrit word meaning country (in this context, homeland). In the formulation *par-desi*, the prefix *par(a)*- stems from a shared Indo-European particle meaning besides, beyond, aside, or away from. *Desh* and *desi* usually refer to South Asia, but in this case, when it is deliberately left unclear which "country" is being referenced, the term itself becomes both an open question and a challenge. Do these laborers view themselves as foreigners in Natal, longing to go home to India? Or are they now par-desi in the sense of having become foreign to India, such that home is now Natal?

The ambiguity around home permeates the entire verse of "*kuulii naam dharaayaa*"—the tools carried by the addressee can be seen as signs of oppression, but also as signs of belonging: because you have claimed your place on the land using these tools, and as your language has incorporated the experience of indenture, you are no longer a "foreigner" who has to go home. The *bhajan* (devotional song) that the narrator instructs the others to sing (implicitly, this song itself) is not necessarily one of thanks, as Mesthrie's translation would suggest ("You've come to Natal, give thanks in song, brother").[38] It is simply a song of coming to Natal, one describing this experience. If a *bhajan* as a form is usually sung in religious contexts, the experience of indenture in Natal has affected the content of this song, which does not seem to be either making a particular plea to or praising any religious entity. If devotion is being expressed, it is left unclear what the content of the devotional act is: Working the land? A prayer to be allowed to return to India? Gratitude for the journey to Natal?

While the form of the *bhajan* is far distanced from the pleas written to the Office of the Protector of Immigrants, here, too, expressions of sentiment (as are often found in devotional songs) have been erased or suppressed. We do not know how these workers felt about coming to Natal, and it is not clear whether they now consider Natal to be their home, or whether they long for their homes in British India. They are given the name *coolie*, and the only glimpse we have of their lives is through their labor.

In these sources from the late nineteenth and early twentieth centuries, Gandhi's original impulse, to separate the coolie from the "Indian" while the former is under the indenture contract, is largely supported by other forms of documentation from this period. We are often forced to view the indentured laborer in the terms of the contract, as a laboring body. This is not to suggest that these immigrants did not have other dimensions to their lives: we can see glimpses of family life and other emotional connections even when overwritten by the language of the contract, of law and labor, of material grievances. In these sources, expressions of sentiment seem to be irreconcilable with the demands of form, whether that form is the pamphlet, the legal complaint, or the *bhajan*.

The Legacy of Abolitionist Sentiments: A "New System of Slavery"?

Indenture has been described through radically different frameworks, either as a "new system of slavery"—as the title of Hugh Tinker's influential 1974 study phrases it—or as a form of free labor migration that offered British Indian subjects opportunities to migrate and settle in other parts of the British Empire, much as British settlers could. The centenary of the abolition of indentured labor in the British Empire was celebrated in 2017 with a series of conferences, at which scholars sought, in the words of one of the participants, to "move from the indenture-as-slavery thesis to giving agency to the indentured and seeking to understand their motivations and initiatives in making new lives in the colonies."[39] Both characterizations, however, represent extremes that risk oversimplifying indenture. As Hershini Bhana Young explains, "Neither complete victimization nor sovereign voluntarism seems an adequate explanation for the experience of indenture."[40] Even as historians have been calling since at least the 1990s for more nuanced views of indenture, beyond simply agency or slavery, this dichotomy continues to shape the discourse around indenture.[41] This section traces the impact of the conflation of indenture and slavery, first in nineteenth-century debates and then in the contemporary moment.

Historian Madhavi Kale elaborates on these two views of indenture:

> Implicit in the "new system of slavery" narratives is the assumption that traditionally, in other words before British intervention, people in the recruiting regions were largely stationary, and that indentured emigration was just another facet of the ongoing displacement and immiseration precipitated by colonialism. Uprooted, these migrants to overseas colonies like Trinidad and British Guiana struggled to reproduce remembered village communities to the best of their abilities, the unpromising ground of local plantation conditions permitting. Implicit in the Whiggish "great escape" account of emigrants' motivations [on the other hand] is the functionalist and modernization notion that, freed from the heavy hand of custom, these Indian indentured migrants transplanted in their new worlds those cultural forms and features they valued, rejecting oppressive features of Indian society.[42]

Both frameworks thus relied upon essentialist assumptions about "traditional" society in India. Kale, in *Fragments of Empire: Capital, Slavery, and Indian Indentured Migration in the British Caribbean*, demonstrates the extent to which the antislavery movement and its legacies restricted the terms under which debate about indentured labor could take place: "From the mid-1830s and for the next seventy-odd years, opponents of the trade in Indian indentured labor were largely confined to making their various cases either by resurrecting the specter of slavery or by representing the Indian workers in question as particularly vulnerable to abuse.... Supporters of the system [indentured labor] would use the same images to their own ends."[43] The language of abolition, and its deployment of sentimental tropes around the enslaved, thus continued to limit the frameworks within which indentured labor could be imagined and discussed at the time it was implemented.

One influential early writer on indenture, for example, was John Scoble, a founding member of the British and Foreign Anti-Slavery Society, who after a trip to British Guiana wrote pamphlets that strongly resembled earlier antislavery writings like those of Pringle. In 1840, describing the indentured as variously "ignorant and wretched creatures," "wretched Coolies," and "ignorant and degraded beings," he alludes to his own interaction with some of the indentured on one of the plantations: "When in the presence of those they know to be their friends, and really interested in their welfare, they give full vent to their feelings, and exhibit their real sentiments, and with tears and clasped hands, and in broken English, entreat to be sent back to their native country and to their kindred from whom they have been wantonly separated."⁴⁴ He also cites several eyewitnesses "of the melancholy scene": "The spectacle... presented to the observer in the sick-house was heart-rending!... The squalid wretchedness of their appearance, their emaciated forms, and their intense sufferings from disease and sores, were enough to make the heart bleed!"⁴⁵ Scoble's rhetoric simply replicates earlier abolitionist writings, and he concludes by representing "the state of the Coolies as deplorably wretched, and their hardships and sufferings greater than those endured, even by the Negroes when slaves."⁴⁶ The figures of indentured laborers as wretched, ignorant, suffering, clasping their hands with tears in their eyes, are all very familiar, as is the figure of the benevolent observer with the bleeding heart. As Kale concludes, while these strategies, relying on a dichotomy between free and slave labor, were briefly successful in the 1840s in stopping the transport of indentured laborers to British Guiana and Mauritius, the same dichotomy "could be and was used to reopen the trade" in terms of representing indenture as a step away from slavery toward freedom.⁴⁷ Gandhi's recourse to the language of material grievances, and his focus on the importance of language and nomenclature in leading to material grievances, must be seen in the context of the failures of the sentimental tropes of abolitionist writers to improve the conditions of British Indian subjects abroad.

The conflation of slavery and indenture that originated in these early debates about the morality of indenture, however, did not end in the nineteenth century, but persists today. Perhaps the most well-known novel about indenture, Amitav Ghosh's 2008 *Sea of Poppies*, draws, I suggest, on some of these same sentimental abolitionist tropes. Ghosh's text, part of a trilogy (*Sea of Poppies, River of Smoke* [2011], and *Flood of Fire* [2015]) that was recently termed "one of the most significant works of historical fiction of our times" by the editorial board of *The American Historical Review*, is very deliberately inscribed into this historical tradition of tracing the continuities between slavery and indenture, as Ghosh has his indentured characters travel on the *Ibis*, a refitted blackbirder originally used to illegally transport enslaved persons.⁴⁸ In these novels, Ghosh traces the itineraries of both subaltern and elite characters as they travel between Africa, India, and China, featuring vivid descriptions of an opium factory in northern India, the port cities of Calcutta, Hong Kong, and Canton, and the island of Mauritius.

Sea of Poppies charts the movement of the protagonist, Deeti, from her first husband's overleveraged poppy fields in Bihar to the *Ibis*, a ship traveling from Calcutta to Mauritius, where she and her second husband, Kalua, are contracted to work as indentured laborers. The novel opens with her having a vision of the *Ibis* while harvesting poppies and ends with Kalua's dramatic escape from the *Ibis*, along with a Chinese opium addict, a lascar, and a Bengali nobleman who has lost his extensive landholdings and been convicted of fraud in a British colonial court. The trilogy thus deals with two highly profitable yet ethically dubious exports from British India: "thugs and drugs—or opium and coolies as some would have it."[49] In writing about "opium and coolies," Ghosh is explicitly concerned with resurrecting previously marginal figures, such as lascars, indentured laborers, and transported convicts, from the historiography of India, and allowing them the fictional space to tell their own stories. Ghosh's novel demonstrates that the question of representation—who can speak for indentured laborers, and what form that speech takes—is still relevant today.

Sea of Poppies has been discussed in many ways: as history from below, as oceanic literature, as migrant literature, as a neo-Victorian novel, and more.[50] While the connection Ghosh makes between the Atlantic Ocean history of enslavement and the trade in "thugs and drugs" has been lauded as representing historical Global South solidarities, I would rather suggest that Ghosh falls into the trap of not adequately grappling with the difference between these two forms of trade, that of "opium and coolies," and treating indentured labor as a commodity that can be bought and sold, like opium, or slave labor. The first mate on the *Ibis* is Zachary Reid, the son of a Maryland freedwoman who joins the *Ibis* in Baltimore as a novice sailor and rapidly advances through the ranks while also being tutored by one of the lascars, unknowingly at first, to pass as white. Reid's transformation partially mirrors that of the *Ibis* herself: a former "blackbirder" or illegal slave transport, this schooner has been refitted to transport opium and indentured labor between British India, Mauritius, and Canton.[51] This fictional ship rather neatly brings together the forced migration networks of slavery, indentured labor, and penal transportation. As Clare Anderson writes of the *Ibis* trilogy, "It is the juxtaposition of the related unfreedoms of the enslaved, convicted, and indentured, and of color, caste, and gender, that makes a key intervention in the representation of the political economy of the East India Company."[52] Gaurav Desai, too, lauds Ghosh's determination to link the Atlantic, Indian, and Pacific Oceans in the trilogy, going beyond the oceanic provincialism of focusing on just one ocean as isolated from larger oceanic networks.[53]

However, even though *Sea of Poppies* is ostensibly a novel about indenture, we never see the protagonists perform any indentured labor. The novel ends before Deeti's arrival in Mauritius, and its sequel, *River of Smoke*, picks up the story years later, when, presumably, the indenture contract under which Deeti initially arrived on Mauritius has long expired. Instead, it almost seems as if the sugar plantations in Mauritius have been replaced in the text by descriptions of the poppy fields in Bihar, and labor in the opium factory, which Ghosh depicts in extravagant detail. The understanding of indenture as a "new system of slavery" does not allow for some aspects of the indenture contract to be represented. Ghosh's desire to connect the system of indenture (in this case, in the Indian Ocean) with the earlier Atlantic Ocean system of slavery parallels not only earlier critics of indenture, who used the language of abolition to frame their critiques, but also contemporary theorists' interests in connecting different oceans. Greg Forter, in *Critique and Utopia in Postcolonial Historical Fiction: Atlantic and Other Worlds*, reads *Sea of Poppies* alongside Barry Unsworth's 1992 novel about the Atlantic slave trade, *Sacred Hunger*, arguing that both texts present supranational and interoceanic perspectives that echo "what we might term the oceanic turn" in literary studies.[54] Each text, in this reading, links the Indian and Atlantic Oceans while focusing specifically on one, gesturing toward the "larger, transoceanic story" that cannot be told within its pages.[55] This is similar to the argument Desai makes in "The Novelist as Linkister" that the centrality of slave descendant Zachary to the *Ibis* trilogy "will ensure that readers of the trilogy will always bear in mind the linkages between vast oceanic spaces."[56]

I would add, however, that *Sea of Poppies* also tells a cautionary tale about the oceanic turn, in that too much transoceanic comparison (in this case, between Atlantic slavery and Indian Ocean indenture) can overwhelm the specificity of the experience of indenture (Richard B. Allen, citing historian Edward Alpers, calls this the "tyranny of the Atlantic").[57] Ghosh balances many different narratives and experiences in the *Ibis* trilogy, and it is perhaps understandable that Deeti and her fellow indentured laborers on Mauritius do not remain the focus of attention—but the elision of the laboring, contracted body that featured so prominently in the other sources I examine in this chapter is worth noting.

We do not have many sources, literary or autobiographical, written by indentured laborers themselves, though their descendants have enriched the literary canon of the briny South. Vijay Mishra, for example, identifies what he calls a "*girmit* ideology" within the literatures emerging out of South Asian indenture, which focuses on mourning (and the impossibility of mourning), travel and translation, and trauma.[58] In a more positive vein, Mauritian poet Khal Torabully coins the term *coolitude* as a creative blending of *négritude* and *créolité*, writing that "it is impossible to understand the essence of coolitude without charting the coolies' voyage across the seas. That decisive experience, that coolie odyssey, left an indelible stamp on the imaginary landscape of coolitude."[59] Such a transoceanic indenture canon would include the autobiographical writings, originally in Hindi, of Totaram Sanadhya (*My Twenty-One Years in the Fiji Islands* [*Fiji Mein Mere Ekkis Varsh*]) and Munshi Rahman Khan (*Jeevan Prakash: Autobiography of an Indian Indentured Labourer*) about Fiji and Suriname, respectively, and Lalbihari Sharma's *Holi Songs of Demerara*, as well as fiction by Jan Shinebourne (Guyana), David Dabydeen (Guyana), V. S. Naipaul (Trinidad), Deepchand Beeharry (Mauritius), Satendra Nandan (Fiji), Sam Selvon (Trinidad), and others.[60] These concepts suggest the importance of thinking about indenture beyond a simple framework of slavery or agency. As one artist recently phrased it, Torabully's concept of *coolitude* "insists that what binds indenture descendants is not some biological essence or overstated point of geographic origin but the *experience of indentureship*."[61] While Ghosh's *Sea of Poppies* spends a lot of time with indentured laborers at their port of embarkation, Calcutta, the rest of the experience of indentureship is rendered invisible.

In a poem by Torabully, "[Coolitude: petites mains des colonies]" (1992), the speaker reflects: "Coolitude: because I am Creole by my rigging, I am Indian by my mast, I am European by the yardarm, I am Mauritian by my quest and French by my exile. / I can only be elsewhere within myself because I can only imagine my native land. My native lands?"[62] This final questioning note reflects one of the central themes animating creative works about indenture: how to negotiate multiple or conflicting sources of identity. Torabully's poem suggests a sense of belonging originating not in autochthony or a rootedness in the soil, but in the oceanic journey itself, naming the various parts of the ship, and its ambiguous purpose (quest or exile?), as the parts making up a sense of self. This resonates with the folk song from Natal, in which the nature of foreignness, and thus of belonging, are called into question. The various tools named in that song—the *cambu* (water pot) and the spade—perform a similar function as the list of the parts of the ship does in Torabully's poem, except that the focus is shifted to the land, and the labor performed on the land. Kumar compares the agricultural production cultures of North India and the various sugar plantations, suggesting that "the culture of North Indian societies is tied to an agricultural calendar, but in the colonies, it was not."[63] He expands: "On the plantation, agricultural time did not belong to the 'coolie'—every moment of the working day was governed by the clock, every movement was dictated by a manual."[64] The invocation of the *cambu* and the spade thus, perhaps, speaks to the new rhythm of life in Natal, adding another dimension to the experience of indenture beyond the centrality of the voyage as envisioned by Torabully.

The first few poems/songs in Lalbihari Sharma's book of songs intended to be sung during Holi in Demerara (Guyana) also refer more specifically to the experience of the indentured laborers. In a *chaupai*, or narrative poem, Sharma writes:

> I want to write a little
> of Demerara's customs. Listen,
> this is a country of infinite ills,
> where wisdom is scarce.
>
> I left my home and came to Demerara,
> my name penned as "Coolie."
> Forsaking bhajans, forsaking dharma,
> the Vedas I abandoned, to my disgrace.
>
> Of the routines of this Demerara life,
> I write these kavitt, these verses.[65]

These poems, written down and published as a songbook by Sharma in 1915, are also written partly in Bhojpuri. It is intriguing to compare Sharma's reaction to the nomenclature of coolie with that of the Natal song. Here, too, the passiveness of the recipient is stressed: "My name penned as Coolie," आपन नाम सो कुली लिखाय/*aapan nam so kuli likhai*.[66] The word Rajiv Mohabir translates as "penned" is the same as Sharma uses in both the first and last verses, *likhana*, to write. Writing is important in Sharma's poems: another *kavitt*, or rhythmic poem, starts, "Bearing a book, the sardar reaches / the coolies. Inspecting the cane field, / he accounts their work."[67] The power to write, to account, to bear the book (बुक/*buk* in the original, a loanword from English) is shown to be as important an "instrument of punishment" as the whip, as Gaiutra Bahadur writes.[68] However, crucially, Sharma seems to suggest that this power of writing can be reclaimed—by framing the writing of the name as *coolie* between the speaker's two acts of writing, the passivity of the naming is counteracted. In this light, we can also read the Natal *bhajan* as reflecting two acts of speaking: the name of *coolie* that is given to the laborer, but also the act of speaking/singing this *bhajan*, which implicitly responds to that violent naming.

The legacy of the abolitionist tendency to erase the difference between slavery and indenture and use the same sentimental tropes to speak for and silence indentured laborers as had previously been used in antislavery discourse lives on in different forms in a work like *Sea of Poppies*, which, while creating the narrative space for subaltern voices to be heard, still stages the experience of indenture as simply a new version of enslavement. Concepts like Mishra's *girmit* ideology and Torabully's *coolitude* allow for a different approach that both encourages transoceanic comparisons while remaining focused on the specificity of indenture as distinguished from slavery, as my brief comparative reading of sources from Natal, Demerara, Suriname, and Mauritius here begins to suggest. Gandhi's complex balancing act, in speaking for indentured laborers while both using them as a metonym for the broader experience of subjects of British India in South Africa and seeking to distance his own position from that of an indentured laborer, bespeaks some of the challenges these histories pose.

I will return to Gandhi briefly in chapter five, when I read his autobiography (written after he left Natal) as typical of South African Indian writings seeking specifically to distance the author from the legal language of the indenture contract. To understand what happens in South Africa as the territory changes from British and Boer colonial settlements to a unified British colony to racialized minority rule under apartheid, however, we need to turn once again to the Indian Ocean as a space of displacement. Examining the writings of Boer war prisoners, transported to British India during the second South African War (1899–1902), I show that while these men were fighting an anti-imperial war in South Africa, they are also able to frame their war memoirs as travel literature, inscribing these texts into a long tradition of imperial travelogues, albeit as rather belated exemplars. The next chapter thus builds on Gandhi's attempts to inhabit a certain position of privilege—that of the British imperial subject—to render his grievances legible to British authorities. While Gandhi's writings on indentured laborers can be compared to those of Pringle on the enslaved, Gandhi cannot draw on the racial privilege that allows Pringle to identify with his objects of sentiment with no risk of being conflated with them. The Boer prisoners of war, on the other hand, are able in their memoirs to both occupy and satirize the subject position desired by Gandhi, that of imperial subject. Moving from the writings of Thomas Pringle to Mohandas K. Gandhi to war prisoner J. N. Brink thus allows for an ongoing meditation on issues of representation, self-representation, and racial authority that underlie the question of who can speak, and how, in these briny South narratives of displacement.

4. A SENTIMENTAL EDUCATION IN BOER WAR IMPRISONMENT CAMPS IN SOUTH ASIA, 1899–1902

J. N. Brink, burgher of the Orange Free State and Boer war prisoner, marveled at the natural beauty of the island of Ceylon: "Instead of marshes and palms, we now see mountains, the sides of which are covered with tea-plantations, forests, and shrubs while here and there mighty precipices are visible. Indeed," he adds, "a railway journey from Colombo to Diyatalawa is really worth the trouble, provided one has a return-ticket."[1] This is the problem, however: while Brink describes train travel in Ceylon as enthusiastically as any other tourist, he was not in possession of a return ticket, or any ticket at all. In fact, he traveled as the unwilling guest of the British Empire. Brink was not on a sightseeing excursion, but traveling to the internment camp, Diyatalawa, where he would spend the next year and a half. And yet, listen to his excitement: "What is that brownish object, lying in the mud? It is a buffalo, which, like a pig, wallows in the dirt, and those two things there? Those are tame buffaloes, drawing a somewhat queerlooking implement, which is here called a plough.... What is up now? Nothing, only a station" (50). He describes, step by step, all the sights he encounters along the trip, educating the absent reader about the buffalo, its appearance, behavior, and uses. While Brink's memoir *Ceylon en de Bannelingen/Recollection of a Boer Prisoner-of-War at Ceylon* (the text is published simultaneously in English and Dutch in Amsterdam in 1904) also contains passages about his capture in South Africa and experiences in the camp, the undisputed star of the text is the island of Ceylon, "the pearl of the Indian Ocean" (1). The same trend appears in other prisoner-of-war memoirs published immediately following the second South African War (1899–1902): these authors focus more on their travel adventures than on deprivation and suffering. They seem to see no contradiction in enjoying the fruits of empire—servants, trains, tea plantations—abroad, while fighting a war against the British Empire at home.

To understand the form taken by the writings of Brink and his fellow former war prisoners, and specifically the muting of expressions of mourning, loss, or nostalgia in these belated imperial travelogues, we need to understand circumstances in the camps themselves. The British Colonial Office (in charge of the administration of the camps) attempted a sentimental education of these prisoners in order to turn them from rebellious Boer fighters to contented British subjects, using the tools at their disposal: education, censorship of news from home, and physical confinement. British documents related to the administration of these camps demonstrate that the control and manipulation of the sentiments of war prisoners were central to the British vision for the camps. At the same time, camp newssheets demonstrate how prisoners reacted to attempts at a sentimental education. In these camp newssheets, the prisoners satirize imperial subjecthood in response to British censorship. The memoirs published immediately after the war, however, are written by former war prisoners who seem comfortable occupying the position of imperial "seeing-men" (in Mary Louise Pratt's formula).[2] While the camp newssheets can be read as resisting the sentimental education imposed in the camps, the memoirs suggest that perhaps this education has succeeded, as sentiment for the lost Boer Republics is reconciled with an imperial imaginary built on traveling and cultural exchange.

In the previous chapters I focused largely on expressions of sentiment as they were deployed strategically, in pro- and antislavery propaganda, political pamphlets, and even legal complaints. This chapter shifts focus to less explicitly political forms of writing, such as family letters, camp newssheets, and memoirs, to ask what happens to expressions of sentiment in these seemingly more personal forms of writing. The dangers of expressions of sentiment become increasingly visible in this chapter: in the camps, war prisoners were punished for expressing, in their personal letters, the wrong kinds of sentiment—sentiments that marked them as less amenable future British subjects. However, the shift in sentiments expressed by former prisoners in memoirs from immediately following the war to later, apartheid-era writing is even more ominous: as Afrikaner memoirists became increasingly invested in creating tales of suffering and martyrdom, these sentimental claims became instrumental, as I will develop in the next chapter, in justifying oppressive minority rule. Examining the complex briny South contact zone established between these Boer war prisoners and their fellow colonial subjects, South Asian inhabitants of British India and Ceylon, reveals shifting racial power hierarchies and uneasy solidarities, which are erased in later Afrikaner nationalist renderings of these interactions.

Tensions between Dutch settlers and their descendants, who became known as the Boere (farmers), and English-speaking British settlers were simmering at the Cape even before the British occupation of 1795 and resulted in the so-called Great Trek that began in 1835, when many Dutch-speaking settlers moved to occupy the interior of South Africa, beyond the territory occupied by the British.[3] By the end of the nineteenth century, this conflict between the British and Boer settlements in southern Africa had escalated, resulting in the two South African Wars, 1880–1881 and 1899–1902, the latter a far more serious conflict. The second South African War involved a confrontation between British colonial powers, settled in Natal and the Cape Colony, and the Boer Republics of the Orange Free State (Oranje Vrijstaat) and the South African Republic (Zuid-Afrikaansche Republiek). The conflict rapidly turned into a form of guerrilla war, with Boer fighters using their knowledge of the local terrain to inflict unexpected damage upon the much larger and better-armed British forces. Lord Kitchener, the British commander, and his military strategists would eventually turn to a scorched earth policy, under which Boer farms and potential sources of supplies were burnt or confiscated, and Boer women and children, and Africans, were confined in internal concentration camps in British-controlled territories.[4] More than forty-five camps for Boers and sixty camps for Africans were established in South Africa, and this was one of the earliest uses of the term *concentration camp*.[5] Mortality rates in these camps were extremely high.[6]

The British Army in South Africa was confronted with a difficult problem in dealing with captured Boer fighters—attempting to keep them in internment camps in South Africa resulted in multiple escapes, with escapees going straight *Terug na Kommando* (back to commando), as one escape narrative is titled.[7] Thus the British Army turned to "the empire as gulag," as Isabel Hofmeyr phrases it.[8] During the course of the second South African War, the British military authorities transported more than twenty-four thousand war prisoners to different parts of the empire. Using islands within the empire (Bermuda, Ceylon, and St. Helena), and the mainland of India, to house these war internment camps can be seen as a natural extension of penal deportation.[9] Between August 1900 and May 1901, 5,127 war prisoners were transported to five different camps in Ceylon. From April 1901, 9,131 prisoners of war were transported to India, where they were kept in fifteen different camps in the Punjab, Bengal, Madras, and Bombay Commands.[10] A separate group of 1,443 Boer war prisoners, captured by the Portuguese in Mozambique, were transported to Portugal and held in six Portuguese camps.[11] Prisoners were allowed to return to South Africa at the conclusion of the war on May 31, 1902, if they agreed to take an oath or sign a declaration of allegiance to the British crown. A few refused to sign. These *bittereinders* (bitter-enders) were eventually resettled elsewhere in the Empire, in British India, Ceylon, Malaya, or northern Borneo.

South African historiography has been skewed, often with a nationalistic agenda, toward studying the Boer war–era concentration camps for women and children internal to South Africa, with Afrikaans literature following suit.[12] As Hofmeyr points out, "Within the massive scholarship on the South African War, the POWs occupy a marginal space, players offstage, not central to the major business of the war."[13] However, during the 1930s and 1940s, as the National Party comes to power on a platform stressing Afrikaner martyrdom and sacrifice during the war, the Boer war prisoners were rediscovered as romantic suffering figures in exile—this period features the publication of a number of war imprisonment memoirs, edited and translated into Afrikaans, as well as numerous magazine articles on the overseas internment camps. In 1983, a statue to the war prisoners (Die Banneling [The Exile] by Danie de Jager) was added to the grounds of the Anglo-Boer War Museum in Bloemfontein, South Africa, off to the side from the famous Vrouemonument (Women's Memorial), erected in 1913. In 1989, the first season of an Afrikaans TV show, *Arende (Cape Rebel)*, was set in the St. Helena war internment camp.[14] While remaining marginal to the enterprise of commemorating the war throughout the years of Afrikaner nationalism, the war prisoners were increasingly remembered alongside other martyr figures from the war.

This chapter shows how the war prisoners' expressions of sentiment regarding both the Boer Republics and the British Empire change over time: from letters written from Diyatalawa to memoirs published immediately following the war to later memoirs and accounts published as Afrikaner nationalism was consolidating power, leading to the institution of the apartheid regime, during the 1930s and 1940s. Sentiments could, to a certain extent, be trained: overt expressions of homesickness and loyalty to the Boer Republics were punished in the camps and countered by a project of anglicization, or British subject formation. Postwar memoirs reflect a sense of comfort with the identity of the war prisoner as a global traveler, reporting back on the (re)discovered island of Ceylon to a South African audience imagined as newly interested in the global dimensions of empire. By the 1930s, however, the Afrikaner patriot has emerged, and a nationalist agenda shapes the writers' expressions of sentiment.

A "Cheap, Healthy Resort": Sentiment and Censorship in Diyatalawa Camp

Diyatalawa was one of five camps in Ceylon, the others being Ragama, Mount Lavinia, Hambantota, and Urugasmanhandiya.[15] The three main camp newssheets from Diyatalawa were titled *De Prikkeldraad* (*Barbed Wire*), the *Diyatalawa Dum-Dum*, almost immediately renamed the *Camp Lyre*, and *De Krijgsgevangene* (*The War Prisoner*). The prisoners wrote these by hand and reproduced them through an early version of the mimeograph, the cyclostyle.[16] *De Prikkeldraad* (figure 4.1) was the more serious of the three camp newssheets, dedicating closely written pages to detailing war news (section entitled "De Brandwacht," or "The Sentry"), news from the rest of the world ("L'echo du monde vivant," or "Echoes from the Living World"), news from the camp itself ("Among the Bungalows"), and retold episodes from the war ("Van de Kopjes," or "From the Hills"). These news sections are interspersed with advertisements for goods and services in the camp (photography, carved souvenirs, French and German lessons) and jokes, cartoons, and poems. The newssheets featured articles written in English, Dutch, Afrikaans, French, and German, with the majority of the articles in English and Dutch.

The following poem appears in *De Prikkeldraad*, in 1900:

Diyatalawa
This place is full of little charms,
And forms a happy home.
Just, trust "Old Bobs,"[17] lay down your arms,
And you are sure to come.

This is a chance for a cheap sea-trip
Finest place for taking a holiday.

They speak of Paris, Rome and Naples
And places known of yore.
But there are none which ever rivalled
With this cheap healthy resort.

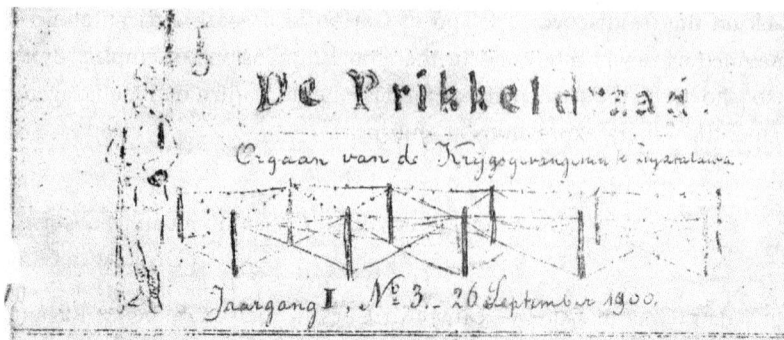

FIGURE 4.1. *De Prikkeldraad* 1, no. 3 (September 26, 1900). Acquisition no. 03079/00019. War Museum of the Boer Republics, Bloemfontein, South Africa.

This is the last opportunity
Offered to the public.

Roll up and take your chances. Look out for the camp, Diyatalawa, Ceylon! You are sure to like it. Home for incurable sympathizers with the Transvaal and O.V.S. [Oranje Vrystaat; Orange Free State]. Board, lodging, and police supervision free of charge. Treatment in accordance with the principles of Temperance Societies and rules of modern warfare. Rhodes's dream verified; no Uitlander grievances. There is equal right for every white man inside the wire fence. No gratuities to be given! Sticks, dogs and better halves to be left outside the wire fence (the gatekeeper will take care of them). Care is taken to supply the latest news as late as possible. Visitors are requested not to tease or feed inmates. We have here the finest collection.[18]

In this poem from the third issue of the newssheet, a prisoner satirically depicts the war prisoners as tourists, taking a "cheap sea-trip" abroad. By the third stanza, however, Diyatalawa has become a "cheap healthy resort." There is some truth to this statement as Diyatalawa, originally a military barracks, was located amid several hill stations, with a cooler mountain climate.[19] The phrase *healthy resort* suggests that these holidaymakers may be traveling for their health, but we are still unsure what ails these travelers. The long final paragraph (in which the author turns to prose) answers the question: they are "incurable sympathizers with the Transvaal and the O.V.S." (Orange Free State). The holidaymakers thus become patients—their disease, sympathy for the Transvaal and the Free State. In the final two sentences of the poem, the involuntary nature of their confinement is revealed as they change from patients to "inmates," which, when combined with the medical imagery of the preceding lines, perhaps suggests an asylum rather than a prison.

This little prose poem allows me to discuss the "treatment" of these inmates, and their "incurable sympathies" for the Boer Republics. Correspondence exchanged between camp officials and the Colonial Office reveals great interest on the part of British officials in the care and management of the sympathies of war prisoners. In a letter dated December 31, 1901, from Governor Ridgeway in Kandy, Ceylon, to the secretary of state for war in London, Ridgeway writes: "The Burgher Prisoners have certainly benefited from their internment, as regards cleanliness of person and discipline, and we are now able to influence their education much more than formerly.... The boys under 17, of whom there are nearly 90, have now been placed in separate huts, apart from the other Prisoners, under suitable guardians, and English is taught for longer hours."[20] Later, speaking of a separate group of "loyalists" who have agreed to take an oath of allegiance to Britain, he writes that they are "becoming rapidly more anglicised in feeling."[21] Ridgeway also sends a monthly report on the sentiments of the Boer and other prisoners back to London, based on details collected from letters sent and received in the camps. In an earlier letter, Ridgeway states, "I have little doubt that when peace is restored nearly all the Boer prisoners of war in Diyatalawa will settle down as peaceable subjects of the Crown."[22]

Both through the censorship of letters, which meant that anti-British sentiment needed to be repressed, and through the structures in place in the camp, including schools, workshops, and organized entertainment, the British camp officials and their supervisors in the War and Colonial Offices in London saw themselves as anglicizing the feelings of the Boer war prisoners, teaching the appropriate sentiments for "peaceable subjects of the Crown."[23] In a report compiled after the war, the Colonial Office, in regard to the question of education in camps in Ceylon, is summarized as saying "apart from the question of education proper they were in favour of explaining to prisoners by means of pamphlets, &c, the true causes of the war, teaching them English, and, if possible, modifying their prejudices and making them fitter for their future positions as British subjects without forcing books or learning on them."[24] The educational system in the camp is designed to produce future loyal subjects of the British Empire.[25] Beyond loyalty to the British Empire, though, this project of anglicization is also imagined as a civilizing effort: "cleanliness of person and discipline," as Ridgeway phrases it.

To return to how the prisoners viewed the "discipline" provided in the camp, as the "Diyatalawa" poem states, "Care is taken to supply the latest news as late as possible." The supply of news, and the timing of that supply, is also part of the "care" provided for these "incurable" patients. This is managed through censorship of newspapers and letters entering and leaving the camp. The "Censor's Report on the South African Correspondence" from November 1901 states that during the month of November, 15,824 letters, parcels, photos, and papers were sent from the camp, and 18,723 letters, photos, papers, and parcels received, just to give an idea of the sheer volume of correspondence.[26] In Ceylon, the censors were F. R. N. Findlay and Otto Hansen, who read, translated, and sent key excerpts from the correspondence entering and leaving the camp to the commandant for prisoners of war in Ceylon, who in turn passed it along to the War Office and Colonial Office in Britain. Each month, the censors would include a short summary of the general tone of the letters: "moderate," "satisfactory," "a bitter strain pervades in most of the letters," and so forth.[27] Negative sentiments and critiques of the British, in both incoming and outgoing letters, were censored. Some of these examples include the following: "When I think of the blood of my brother shed upon the earth then I would rather die in Ceylon than to do aught against my country and people. I will remain an Africander" (J. J. Vander Watt, October 19, 1901), and "Through all this that the poor gutless women have to endure, our hatred grows daily greater" (C. L. du Plessis, October 19, 1901).[28] In cases where prisoners or their family members continue to write negatively about the British, their entire correspondence could be halted, as was the case for one family: the censor notes that "the correspondence of this family is most rabid; 14 letters have been stopped quite recently, and when the S[outh] A[frican] authorities receive same all future correspondence should be suppressed. The correspondence between P. O. W. P. J. E. Erasmus and J.G. Opperman with this family must in future be stopped."[29]

In the letters collected, this strain of anti-British sentiment is balanced by several letters praising the British: "Our camp is surrounded by wire similar to the camp at Waterval in which the English prisoners were placed, but it is much better, for it is clean; it is cleaned even day and everything is neat, so you see we are well treated by the English government" (H. Nothling, November 19, 1901).[30] Another prisoner writes, "Mother says I must try and love the British; to tell mother the truth I am become a Britisher through and through, and the Boer I simply hate them. What, if I could get a chance I would have a hit of revenge for our home they (the Boers) destroyed" (Chas. J. Stevens, November 23, 1901).[31] Some of the women writing to the prisoners echo these sentiments: "The dear British are far the best" (Mrs. K. E. Pitcher, November 3, 1901), and "A nation who can treat you her prisoners like England treats you must be one in a thousand" (Edith, October 23, 1901).[32] One father, J. C. Mergenrood, in Urugasmanhandiya camp in Ceylon (the camp in which the most pro-British prisoners were kept), writes to his son John in Diyatalawa camp: "I am working for the government. I am getting my rupee every day besides other work, and we are treated very kindly, we have no guards to take care of us, only we must be in the huts at roll call. . . . Why don't you write English letters. I don't see that you are improving" (March 3, 1902).[33]

These extracts suggest two things—first, that expressions of sentiment (whether nostalgia, anger, or happiness) are explicitly considered as politically relevant in the camps, with the censors in Ceylon carefully marking each extract as either "favourable" or "unfavourable" toward the British, and second, that prisoners, aware of the censorship of letters, may have used this as an opportunity to prove their loyalty toward the British. Throughout these letters, one can see the anglicization of the prisoners at work, in the mention of English classes, better treatment for those expressing their loyalty toward the British, and their reticence to express anti-British sentiment.

The camp newssheets also demonstrate an awareness of censorship, and the way it affects the possibility of communication and receiving news within the camps. The first edition of *De Prikkeldraad*, for example, has a whole section on "The Situation" (De Toestand) crossed out (although in other surviving versions of the same paper, the article, on the progression of the war in South Africa, has not been censored), and in another, right above a bilingual section containing news about the Boxer Rebellion, a section is titled "England," followed by the word "Censor" underlined twice and the laconic lines "It is rainy weather here/*Het is hier regenachtig*."[34] While these newssheets were published with the knowledge and approval of the authorities, and were part of the regime of the censors, prisoners still used these as means of resistance and subversion. In the poem "Diyatalawa," for example, the poet satirizes the position of the war prisoners as tourists or sea-trippers. The camp newssheets suggest that war internees commonly thought, and even joked about, the journey to Ceylon in relation to tourism and exploration. Furthermore, one map from this period, a popular souvenir from the camps, printed in Colombo, is titled *Onze Reis naar Ceylon* (*Our Trip to Ceylon*) (figure 4.2). This map visually reimagines the deportation of these individuals as a trip, the word *reis* suggesting a voluntary rather than forced journey. In the memoirs published after the war, these jokes transform into reality, as the memoirists convey a sense of imperial entitlement in traveling, and writing about their travels, as tourists rather than prisoners.

"The Pearl of the Indian Ocean": War Prisoners as Imperial Travel Writers

Relatively few war internment memoirs were published following the war: three in the Netherlands (a pamphlet in 1901, and two books in 1904), one in Berlin (1903), and one in Pretoria (1905).[35] While the newssheets poke fun at the idea of war prisoners as imperial tourists, memoirs published immediately following the war suggest that this idea had been internalized. The sentiments expressed in war prisoners' memoirs suggest that they are quite comfortable depicting themselves as cosmopolitan world travelers. These

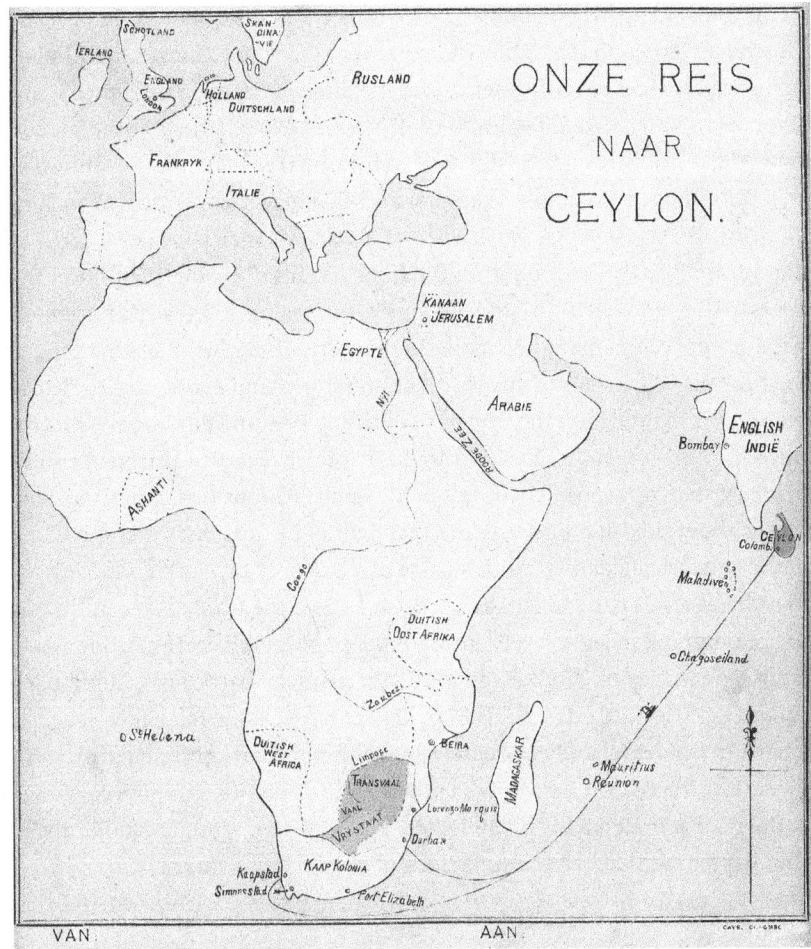

FIGURE 4.2. *Onze Reis naar Ceylon* (Our Journey to Ceylon). Acquisition no. 02016/00002. War Museum of the Boer Republics, Bloemfontein, South Africa.

texts employ the language and conventions of travel and adventure narratives, rather than those associated with prison or deportation memoirs.

The preface to J. N. Brink's *Recollections of a Boer Prisoner-of-War in Ceylon* reads, for example: "I have tried to give in this little book a short sketch of the history of the island of Ceylon—the pearl of the Indian Ocean—, and to that I have added a description of some of the natural scenery of the island, in order to give the reader a faint idea of a place, which may be considered as an unknown country to the Africander."[36] Brink's authority as narrator stems, then, from his position as war prisoner: the titles of both English and Dutch texts stress that his ability to write about Ceylon is inextricably linked to his experiences as a prisoner of war (in English) or exile (in Dutch). At a time when tourism had begun to routinize the exotic (the first Indian edition of the publisher John Murray's well-known *Handbooks for Travellers* was published in 1859, for example, and in 1892, it expanded to include Ceylon), Brink's unusual experience as a war prisoner provides a sense of adventure. Brink's description of the book as "little" (using the diminutive *boekske* in Dutch) is thus strategic: he is not trying to create, or compete with, an encyclopedic guidebook. At the same time, Brink claims that, at least for the "Africander," this is still an unknown and exotic space. He can take on the mantle (and the tropes) of both explorer and educator. While the novelty of the text might derive from his experience as war prisoner, Brink's primary stated purpose is not to tell his readers about this experience, but rather about the island itself. More than half of his text describes the island and its historical context, while his life as a prisoner of war comes across as peripheral to his experiences as a tourist. Even if the frontispiece of his text is a photograph of a graveyard, most of the photographs Brink includes—"a landscape in Ceylon," "a Banyan tree," "the artificial harbor of Colombo," "a catamaran with little divers," "a Sinhalese lady," to name but a few—suggest a narrative of travel and exploration, not suffering and confinement.

Part of the reason for Brink's enthusiasm for Ceylon, and his eagerness to describe it in detail for his audience, is a persistent sense of familiarity. In the chapter entitled "First Impressions of a Prisoner," Brink writes:

> Ceylon! As a youngster I would sing:
> "Even if a cool wind blows
> From Ceylon's fragrant land"
> Ceylon! As a lad I had learnt: Ceylon–Colombo on the coast. But that was it![37]

Brink would have learned about Ceylon as a child because the island had once been a governorate of the Vereenigde Oost-Indische Compagnie, the same company that originally established a trading post at the Cape of Good Hope to restock the ships making the trip between Europe and Asia. Ceylon thus became a familiar name within Dutch-speaking territories, with certain tropes for describing the island readily available to these travelers. This moment in the text recalls circulation within an earlier trade empire. The first imperial forced migrants between these two geographic regions had been the enslaved persons brought over from parts of South Asia (Dutch India) and Southeast Asia (Dutch East Indies) under the auspices of the VOC, discussed in chapter one. When Brink arrives at Ceylon in 1901, he is thus revisiting an earlier history of imperial displacement. *Ceylon* is a familiar and evocative term to a boy growing up in South Africa. The imperial gaze of the Boer war prisoners is a complex outcome of briny South imperial networks: South Africa, Ceylon, and India are doubly bound, by Dutch and British imperial projects. Pratt explains how eighteenth- and nineteenth-century "travel books . . . gave European reading publics a sense of ownership, entitlement and familiarity with respect to the distant parts of the world that were being explored, invaded, invested in, and colonized."[38] Brink and his fellow POWs in Ceylon do not have expansionist intentions, or any proprietary stake in the landscape they describe, and yet they are only there because of this imperial history. Here we see how this sense of familiarity also manifests between fellow colonies, such that a part of the world initially described as unknown to the Afrikaner is shown to be uncannily familiar, to the extent of returning Brink to his childhood.

Critical writings on imperial and colonial travel narratives have largely focused on the unequal power relations embedded in travel writing: the imperial traveler as possessed of the means and authority to both travel and narrate his (it is most often his) experiences.[39] Paul Smethurst, in the introduction to *Travel Writing, Form, and Empire*, describes the most significant of the "ideologically informed asymmetrical relationships" upon which travel writing is constructed as the divisions into "traveller/travellee, observer/observed, and narrator/narrated."[40] The typical travel writer in these texts embodies the covetous colonial gaze, seeing, and writing, with "imperial eyes," in Pratt's phrase.

Other theorists have called for a more nuanced reading of the power relations embedded in imperial and colonial travel writing, moving beyond the idea of a monolithic Eurocentrism, or for an expansion of the kinds of texts read as travel writing.[41] For example, Stephen Keck argues that soldiers' memoirs from colonial Burma can be considered as travel writing, "partly because soldiers often participate in some of the same activities (such as 'sightseeing') as tourists."[42] Simonti Sen examines the same interplay between nation and empire I identify in the war prisoners' writings in travel writing by Bengali authors who traveled to Europe between 1870 and 1910.[43] Another unconventional travel narrative would be Thakur Gadadhar Singh's *Chīn Me Terah Mās* or *Thirteen Months in China*, an account of Singh's experiences in the British Army in China during the Boxer Rebellion written and published in Hindi in 1902. In the introduction to Singh's narrative,

Anand Yang stresses that "the sheer breadth of topics he writes about, based on his first-hand experiences and his follow-up research, speak volumes about his intellectual curiosity and the uniqueness of the book as a travelogue and a historical account of China."[44] Singh is, interestingly enough, influenced by narratives about the second South African War. He writes that he knows that the reading public in India are interested in "war stories": "I have seen in Calcutta that, at the beginning of the battle of Transvaal (the Boer War in South Africa), hundreds and thousands of copies of newspapers were sold in a short span of time. They were sold only for the war stories."[45]

The South African war prisoners are in a comparable position to soldiers like Singh writing travelogues, in that they also traverse new countries—as such, their observations will necessarily be written from a tourist perspective. Unlike these soldiers, however, the war prisoners are the conquered, not the conquerors. When they sightsee, they do so at the mercy of the British Army or having escaped the camps. In order to find more analogues for this kind of writing, we have to go back to the seventeenth and eighteenth centuries, and the captivity narrative. Earlier captivity narratives frequently included descriptive passages that aimed to educate the reader about a new part of the world, while also recounting the harrowing experiences of the captive. Brink's memoir thus bears a striking resemblance to an earlier captivity narrative set in Ceylon, that of Robert Knox. Knox's *An Historical Relation of the Island Ceylon* was published in 1681 and tells the story of how he was shipwrecked, along with his father and other Englishmen, and taken captive by the king of Kandy. He remained in captivity on the island for twenty years before managing to escape, but during that time, he lived in relative freedom, able to buy land, cultivate fruit trees, corn, and goats, establish a small money-lending business, and employ a number of Ceylonese servants. Daniel Defoe's character of Robinson Crusoe was based, in part, on Knox's narrative, which is also one of an Englishman making a home for himself on distant shores (though Knox had several English companions with him on the island, including other prisoners held by the king of Kandy).[46] Knox's text is filled with observations on the landscape and the Ceylonese inhabitants of the island: the first three parts of the narrative are descriptive and ethnographic, and only part four deals with his own experiences. The narrative also includes several woodcut illustrations, showing, for example, "the manner of their ploughing," "the manner of their sheltering themselves from the rain by the Taliput leaf," "an execution by an elephant," "Rajah Singah the King of Ceylon," "one impaled on a stake," and depictions of typical inhabitants, as well as a list of proverbs and their explanations.[47]

While it is possible that Brink consulted Knox's narrative in writing his own (Knox's text was republished in 1817 as an appendix to *A History of Ceylon*, an influential text on the subject), it is important to question why, more than two hundred years later, he chooses to take a similar approach to structuring his narrative, as one that is equal parts travelogue, ethnography, and personal memoir. As twentieth-century "belated travelers," in Ali Behdad's phrase, the Boer war prisoner memoirists' choice to actively employ tropes, narrative structures, and expressions of sentiment from earlier periods of European exploration invites investigation.[48] The memoirs by Brink and his contemporaries read more like these seventeenth- and eighteenth-century captivity narratives than the more contemporaneous prisoner-of-war memoirs from the American Civil War, published in the 1860s, for example.[49]

Knox starts his narrative by explaining that "my design being to relate such things only that are new and unknown unto these European nations. It is the in-land country, therefore, I chiefly intend to write of, which is yet an hidden land even to the Dutch themselves, that inhabit upon the Island."[50] Knox is thus aware of his position as writing of a place as-yet unexplored by Europeans. When Brink begins his narrative, he has to appeal to the imagined ignorance of his audience of "Africanders," positioning them as new to the project of imperial exploration. He is thus reinventing the genre of the captivity/exploration/travel narrative for an audience newly imagined as interested in the global. It is not hard to connect this style of writing to the anglicization described in the camps themselves: the project of educating the Boer prisoners of war to see themselves as British subjects, part of a larger British empire. If, in the camp newsletters I examine earlier, we see the prisoners satirizing this position (and the idea of transportation as a "cheap sea-trip"), the postwar memoirs suggest that the sentimental education in the camps may have been successful in affecting the way the prisoners saw themselves, and their audience at home, as newly international or imperial.

However, even as Brink envisions himself as an imperial tourist, his narrative is complicated by references to the Boer Republics left behind. Brink's text begins with the history of European conquest: "Ceylon visited by the Nations of Europe," where Brink writes that Ceylon deserves the title, the "pearl of the Indian Ocean," as "not only does its shape resemble that of a pearl, but its riches, its precious stones, and above all, its beautiful scenery, entitle it to that name."[51] His history of Ceylon starts with occupation by the "Cingalese [*sic*]" and the "Malabars" (Tamils). He then proceeds: "These two Indian tribes were, indeed, like two dogs fighting for a bone; other nations successively ran away with the coveted prize. These nations were, in the proper order of succession, the Portuguese, the Dutch, and the English" (1). Brink tells the story of the conquest of Ceylon by implicitly creating parallels between the Sinhalese and the Boers as early, effective occupiers, with the British and Portuguese as outsiders, and fairly incompetent ones at that. The Sinhalese, in resisting the Portuguese, are depicted as "inferior in armament to the invaders, their mode of fighting consisted in employing stratagems rather than actual force." They are "an observant and ingenious race"; "united, full of patriotism, and well-protected behind their mountain-ramparts, they proved a very dangerous enemy to the Portuguese" (4). The parallels to the Boer Republics in South Africa, resisting the British through guerilla warfare, are hard to miss. This positive view of the Sinhalese, however, does not extend into the author's present—Brink sees them as a degenerated people whose prime lies far in the past. "It is a sad idea, that a nation, once so mighty and powerful, should have sunk so deeply, after having once lost its energy, and should now fall into a state of absolute apathy," he opines later (40). While this sense of former greatness reduced to current indolence is typical of Orientalist narratives, in Brink's case, it has a more urgent implication: to Brink, this is a warning to Afrikaners about their possible fate, following defeat by the British. Brink's retelling of the history of Ceylon is thus not simply neutral background information, as would be provided in most itineraries and guidebooks. He is interested, not in the history and customs of the people of Ceylon for their own sake, but in deducing what the history of Ceylon predicts for the future of South Africa. Brink's residual loyalty to the Boer Republics thus infiltrates the travel narrative, in a similar way that the fact that he travels without a return ticket affects his initial appreciation of the Ceylonese countryside.

Analyzing the early war internment memoirs, the authors' descriptions of their experiences in India suggest that, at that historic juncture, they could reconcile patriotism for the Boer Republics with a more cosmopolitan, nomadic identity as offered by empire. These two identities, affiliated with the nation and with empire, were not opposed in the minds of the war prisoners. Manu Goswami, writing a sociohistoric genealogy of nationalism, reminds us that "the era of the late nineteenth- and early twentieth-centuries was defined by a structured dynamic between high nationalism and high imperialism; it was an age simultaneously of empire and nation."[52] Even though later forms of nationalism would cast these two forms as mutually exclusive, this "structured dynamic" was experienced in more unsettled ways at the time.

Another of the postwar memoirists, J. L. de Villiers, narrows the focus of his narrative to his escape from one of the camps, Trichinopoly, in South

India. This allows him to foreground the sense of adventure and risk involved in the endeavor. In the preface of de Villiers's 1904 *Hoe Ik Ontsnapte: Verhaal van een Merkwaardige Ontsnapping van een Boer uit Engelsch-Indie* (How I Escaped: Tale of a Remarkable Escape of a Boer from British India), he writes, "'Tis no war book, but a simple true tale of what I experienced. Were the reading of this to give the reader as much pleasure as the escape caused me anxiety and suspense, I would be satisfied indeed."[53] By depicting himself as a daring traveler in a foreign land, rather than a victim of British imperial power, de Villiers rewrites his own narrative: the two authorial identities—loyal burgher of the Boer Republics and imperial travel writer—are here reconciled through the narrative of escape. De Villiers escapes to the French territory of Pondicherry: "The rest of the information about the exact location of Pondicherry, the distance from Villupuram to the border, and the description of Pondicherry, I mostly got out of a book, a kind of travel guide to India, which also contained a map. We had obtained this book on board our ship" (36–37). De Villiers here literally becomes a tourist with a guidebook in hand!

The narrative strategy of former war prisoners in these camps in British India and Ceylon thus relied upon instilling a certain sense of glamor onto their experiences as prisoners by focusing on the exotic locales they experienced, thus framing themselves as tourists and travel writers, even as the backdrop of the South African War keeps intruding on the narrative. The tropes and sentiments of the travel writer—novelty, excitement, a desire to educate the reader—thus largely displace the sentiments of mourning and nostalgia from these texts.

De Villiers's escape attempt was based on the somewhat far-fetched idea of disguising himself as an Indian by blacking his face and exposed skin with burnt cork. In this, we can perhaps see shades of Richard F. Burton, who famously infiltrated a pilgrimage to Mecca disguised as an Afghan born in India. De Villiers would leave the camp with the group of Indian employees who manned the small store in the camp. Boer officers were treated graciously in the camps, and were usually assigned servants. In order to gain the necessary local knowledge, de Villiers has to quiz his servant on which class Indians generally travel on trains. He also needs to learn how to pronounce the name of the station he wants to go to, Villupuram, like a local: "The stations in India have, as we see it at least, barbaric names, not even to mention the way in which they are pronounced, or rather expelled, by the local population" (34–35). Even though de Villiers's attitude remains dismissive toward the local population throughout, his escape attempt does force him to become better acquainted with his servant. For example, he quickly learns that folding his turban correctly is much more difficult than he imagined, and he has to get his servant to fold the turban for him. He observes that most Indians either go barefoot or wear light shoes without socks, so he has to leave his socks behind, causing him severe discomfort. De Villiers thus receives a visceral education in the physical experiences of the local inhabitants. As he says, while the war prisoners would visit nearby towns while on parole, "in general we were completely in the dark about all habits and customs of the Indian population" (32). In order to carry out his escape, de Villiers needs this local knowledge.

The interactions between de Villiers and his manservant, Brink's attitude toward the Sinhalese as a formerly great nation, and other descriptions of interactions between the Boer war prisoners and the local population more broadly shed light on the racial dimension of this "contact zone," as Pratt names the "social spaces where disparate cultures meet, clash, and grapple with each other, often in highly asymmetric relations of domination and subordination."[54] In Ceylon, the local newspaper, the *Ceylon Observer*, documents a fascinating encounter in Diyatalawa, the nawab of Bhalwalpur's visit to the camp:

> Seeing the immense impression so many thousands stalwart prisoners in our midst (carried some thousands of miles from their own land across the ocean) has made on our own Kandyans and their Chiefs, we can conceive that it would be an admirable object-lesson for any dubious or recalcitrant Indian ruler or Chief if such were induced to visit Diyatalawa. Not that the Indian Nawab, we have referred to, is of that class. On the contrary he is as loyal as he is intelligent and well-educated, and will, we expect, make an admirable ruler in his important State.[55]

Here the Boer prisoners, and the fact that they have been transported "some thousands of miles," become an "object-lesson" to local rulers, serving both to impress and to enforce obedience. The contact zone in which the war prisoners, the British colonial government, the Ceylonese, and the nawab (ruler) of Bhalwalpur (a princely state in northern India) encounter each other is defined by racial and class complexity. The nawab is "loyal, intelligent, and well-educated": depicted here as superior to both "our own Kandyans" and, even the Boer prisoners, whom he can observe. Displaying the Boer war prisoners as abject victims of British might becomes part of the pageantry of the British strategy of divide and rule.

As we see in Brink's account, the war prisoners evinced great interest in local history and religion. A former Boer war internee, J. L. P. Erasmus, published a series of articles following the war on Hindu epics and Indian history in *Indian Opinion*, a newspaper founded by Mohandas K. Gandhi in South Africa.[56] Brink also includes a short description of a version of the Hindu epic, the *Ramayana*, in his memoir. However, the attitude evinced by the South African prisoners toward the South Asians they encountered remained tinged with racial condescension: while de Villiers acknowledges the importance of learning local "habits and customs," he does so by in the same breath complaining about the "barbaric names" that are "expelled" (*uitgestooten*) rather than pronounced. As Brink's narrative suggests, the authors distinguish between what they perceive as the rich cultural heritage and the contemporary state of the people they encounter. These authors thus view themselves as superior to the local population, who can, however, be co-opted into resisting the shared imperial yoke of the British.

"Our Beloved Fatherland": Turning the Tourist into a Nationalist

Twentieth-century Afrikaner nationalism would elevate the war, and particularly the suffering of women and children, to the foundational moment in the myth of the Afrikaans *volk*. There are notable differences between war memoirs published in the immediate aftermath of the war and later publications, such that one can clearly see a myth-making impulse at work. As Antjie Krog writes in "A Hundred Years of Attitude" (an article published in the newspaper *Mail & Guardian* in 1999 in order to reflect on the ways in which the second South African War has been processed and historicized), "What is notable about most Afrikaner Anglo-Boer War information is that the sacrifice and the bravery formed part of an official history written by the Afrikaners, while the betrayal, the failures, the exceptions, the real gruesome testimony often formed part only of the oral history, or of other neglected sources of information."[57] Thus "an exclusive myth" of the Afrikaner emerges from the war narratives.[58] The war prisoners, at least initially, fit poorly into this narrative—they formed part of the "failures and exceptions" that Krog sees as being shunted to the margins of history. Beginning in the 1930s, however, the war prisoners are rewritten back into the "bravery and sacrifice" of the "official history" of the Afrikaner. In these later narratives, the figure of the war prisoner as tourist is erased, while the nascent nationalist impulse is brought to the fore.

The 1930s and 1940s mark the consolidation of power by the National Party, the party that would formally instate the system of racial segregation known as apartheid, in South Africa (cemented in their decisive 1948 electoral victory).[59] Their platform stressed the suffering and forbearance of the Afrikaner people, both during the Great Trek and the South African Wars. In addition to a great number of Afrikaans magazine articles about the war internment camps that are published in the 1940s,[60] four memoirs are published in the 1930s in South Africa and five in the 1940s.[61] These include a memoir by Gustav S. Preller (*Ons Parool: Dae uit die dagboek van 'n Krygsgevangene* [Our Parole: Days from the Journal of a War Prisoner]), a nationalist historian who would profoundly influence Afrikaner historiography and myth making.[62]

One of these publications is A. P. Burger's *Worsteljare: Herinneringe van Ds. A. P. Burger, Veldprediker by die Republikeinse Magte tydens die Tweede Vryheidsoorlog* (Years of Struggle: Memories of Rev. A.P. Burger, Chaplain of the Republican Forces during the Second Freedom War). The memoir, based on a journal kept by Burger during the war, was published in 1936. It was edited by his son, A. J. V. Burger, who describes his editing process as part translation, part reworking. A. P. Burger was a Dutch Reformed minister who was a chaplain attached to the Boer forces during the war, before being captured in February 1902. He was sent to camps in Shahjahanpur and, eventually, Bhimtal, both in India. His memoir is self-consciously framed as providing a retrospective view on the war, showing how it fits into the grand narrative of the Afrikaner nation: "He who controls the fate of nations apparently used the war as a means in His hand to unite the Afrikaner people and to build a greater nation [*volk*] for South Africa."[63] The text regularly incorporates similar editorializing comments (probably added by his son), such that one has a sense of two temporal viewpoints being combined: one, a day-by-day perspective of life in the camp, and the second, a retrospective, God's-eye view in which the immediate suffering of the Afrikaner people makes sense as part of a longer historic narrative arc.

Hofmeyr, in "Building a Nation from Words: Afrikaans Language, Literature and Ethnic Identity, 1902–1924," investigates the concerted effort with which Afrikaans was standardized in the postwar moment, which she describes as the "'invention' of Afrikaner nationalism."[64] Discussing much of the work that has been done on the literature from this period, she argues that "the story of Afrikaans literature during these years has been told many times before in books of meticulous scholarship. But, like so many texts on Afrikaner history, they package these developments into a tight nationalism.

This set of ideas is generally predicated on a deeply rooted organic 'Afrikaner identity' which rumbles through South African history and mysteriously unites all Afrikaners into a monolithic *volk*."[65] The early prisoner-of-war memoirs, generally published in Dutch, undercut this Afrikaner identity and "tight nationalism" by depicting the Boer war prisoners as imperial wanderers and travelers, rather than patiently suffering Afrikaners.

In Burger's text, the landscape is described as beautiful, but then quickly dismissed:

> A lovelier environment for a prisoner-of-war is hard to imagine. But this beauty was not a gift from the enemy to us; it was the silver lining that the Almighty allowed to shine through our dark clouds. This natural beauty only made us long more for sunny South Africa, our beloved fatherland.... No, rather place me in the charcoal-grey old Karoo or on the dry flatlands of my old Transvaal and let me there long for more beautiful parts of the world, but just don't let me again wither away in the paradise of nature as an exile in a Khaki-camp.[66]

Compared to the earlier published accounts, where the landscape is described as if the reader will one day visit it, or at least wants to take a vicarious trip there, here we see a retrospective corrective glance: the foreign landscape only serves to remind the exile of "our beloved fatherland." The more beautiful the scenery is, the stronger his longing to return to the "charcoal-grey old Karoo or dry flatlands of my old Transvaal." J. M. Coetzee, in *White Writing*, stresses the task laid upon Afrikaans poets in the early decades of the twentieth century to "find evidence of a 'natural' bond between *volk* and *land*, that is to say, to naturalize the *volk*'s possession of the land."[67] Burger appeals to this "natural" bond, increasingly well established by the 1930s, in his rejection of the "paradise of nature" for the "charcoal-grey old Karoo." The imperial tourist has been fully recast as the sentimental patriot in exile, imagining a collective identity for the "us" longing for "our beloved fatherland."

We can trace the resurgence of the prisoner-of-war narrative in Afrikaans culture by studying the sudden preponderance of journalistic accounts and memoir extracts published in the popular magazine *Die Huisgenoot* in the 1940s. Starting at the end of 1939, *Die Huisgenoot* published a number of accounts emerging out of the prisoner-of-war camps in St. Helena and South Asia, as well as some from South African transportation camps at Green Point, Bloemfontein, and other parts of South Africa, where war internees were held en route to transportation abroad. These are short tales, but even so, their tone is different to the earlier published memoirs. In one case, for example, a young English farmer who had been living in the South African Republic at the time war broke out, and whose family is described as being "true to the country they had made their Fatherland," makes a dramatic escape from a camp in Bloemfontein: "'The injustice, the injustice done to such a young *volk*,' flashes repeatedly through his brain. 'Indeed, I shall escape tonight, with these other five; we shall avenge the injustice and fight to the bitter end.'"[68] The melodramatic tone of this account, a "tale of a true event," is typical to the *Huisgenoot* genre, in which the drama of the escapes, the tense moments and heroism, are more important to the writers than the precise descriptions of landscapes and scenery were to the previously discussed escapees.[69] Even this brief extract demonstrates conclusively how the war prisoner narratives were adapted to serve more explicitly nationalistic goals: fatherland, *volk*, injustice, vengeance—these are the terms in which the second South African War (in this text, called the Second Freedom War, of course) was rewritten. Even the reference to "bitter end" (*bitter einde*) brings to mind the *bittereinders*, the war prisoners who refused to sign the oath of allegiance and were therefore exiled permanently from South Africa: ironically, though their actions prevented them from returning to South Africa, they become the ultimate model for the staunch South African patriot, refusing to bow the neck to the English yoke.

This reveals the success of the process, described by Hofmeyr, of "stitch[ing] together an 'Afrikaner' history which could become a myth of national origin."[70] By the 1930s one can refer to an "old" Transvaal or an "old" Karoo without that seeming like a contradiction: the myth of national origin has been extended back in time to an undefined earlier moment. As Hofmeyr elaborates, "Together these works established a semiotics of Afrikaner history involving key events of 'black barbarism' and 'British perfidy,' personified in great, strong men whose names could be invoked like talismans."[71] This semiotics of Afrikaner history lends itself quite comfortably to a rewriting of the second South African War, and specifically the Boer prisoner-of-war experience, as clear examples of "British perfidy," while the local inhabitants of Ceylon, for example, become subsumed under the heading of "black barbarism," even though in the earlier accounts I studied they were cast as co-conspirators or educational native informants.

Here, just briefly, is a description of a South Asian man in an escape narrative published in *Die Huisgenoot*: "Slowly they crouch down, but behind them, the bushes are stirring. A yellow face with bright black eyes is spying on them. For a moment, the coolie grasps at his knife, but then he changes his mind. Softly, like a hyena that has spotted his prey but is too cowardly to attack it alone, he disappears into the bushes. He has gone to fetch the soldiers."[72] The animalization of the man here is impossible to miss, as are the exaggerated racial characterizations (yellow face, black eyes). The "cowardly" "coolie" is allied with the Britons, united in their clear determination to destroy the nascent Afrikaner *volk*. Thus we can see that, in order to fit into the mythology of the Afrikaner *volk*, the itinerant imperial wanderer figure of the Boer prisoner of war had to be erased, and the ambivalent briny South solidarities discussed earlier had to be turned into binaries of white civilization and Black barbarism.

This chapter, especially when read in conjunction with the one that follows, suggests the paradoxical nature of sentiment as a means of resistance. While the censorship of expressions of positive sentiment (regarding the Boer Republics) and negative sentiment (regarding the British) in the internment camps frames sentiment as a potential form of resistance, the reappropriation, and power, of patriotic sentimental tropes by apartheid-era writers reveal that sentiment functions much more effectively when wielded by those in power. In the following chapter, examining the writing of apartheid intellectual Geoffrey Cronjé reveals how the trope of a natural affinity or love between the Afrikaner and the land will be used to deny South Asian would-be settlers the claim to belonging ascribed to Afrikaners in South Africa.

5. SENTIMENT AND THE LAW IN EARLY SOUTH AFRICAN INDIAN WRITING, 1893–1960

"Don't you feel... the aura of mystery, the sanctity, the precious meaning of our home, of their home—the very pulse that keeps people together, that protects men and women with the children from the world of harshness, from the changeable forces of nature?"[1] These words are uttered by the protagonist of South African Indian author Ansuyah R. Singh's 1960 novel *Behold the Earth Mourns*, published in Cape Town, as the title page informs us, "on the centenary of the arrival of the Indians in this country."[2] This chapter examines the role sentiment plays in staking imaginative claims to belonging in South Africa, highlighting the dangers of sentiment when deployed by the powerful, and its ambivalence as a weapon of resistance in the writings of the dispossessed. Continuing the narrative of the Afrikaner deployment of sentiment as a means of claiming the land that I started in the previous chapter, here I also return to the story of indentured laborers, and sentimental grievances, which began in chapter three. These narratives collide in two competing claims to belonging examined here—that of Singh, and other early South African Indian writers, and that of apartheid legal theorist Geoffrey Cronjé, whose writing crystallizes how sentiment functioned in the Afrikaner ideologies that attempted to displace and expel nonwhite inhabitants of the South African land. In the latter part of the chapter, I revisit Mohandas K. Gandhi's writing on indentured labor in his *Autobiography, or the Story of my Experiments with Truth* (*Satya Na Prayogo*), reading it as a type of settler narrative typical of early South African Indian authors. These authors attempt to distance themselves from the essentially transient figure of the indentured laborer by drawing on the sentiment of love for the new land familiar from other forms of settler writing. However, the specter of the indenture contract introduces the rhetoric of law into these works, at odds with the sentimental language associated with settler narratives. The legal and affective afterlife of indenture is, then, a lingering sense of precarity and marginalization.

Gandhi witnessed many changes during his sojourn in South Africa: when he arrives in 1893, South Africa as a colony does not yet exist. The four territories—the Cape and Natal Colonies and the two Boer Republics, the Orange Free State and the South African Republic—are still separate. Gandhi participates in the second of the two South African Wars, 1899 to 1902, by founding the Voluntary Ambulance Corps.[3] After the defeat of the Boer Republics in 1902, they are renamed as the Orange River Colony and the Transvaal Colony, respectively, and in 1910 all four colonies are unified into the Union of South Africa (a British dominion). The year 1911 marks the official end of the indenture program in South Africa, although some indentured laborers will continue to serve out their contracts until 1915. The Union of South Africa was governed successively by the South African Party (SAP) (1910–1924); a coalition between the National and Labour Parties (1924–1934); the United Party, a coalition between the SAP and the National Party (1934–1948); and the Reunited National Party (Herenigde Nasionale Party), soon called just the National Party, from 1948 onward. It is this latter, radicalized Afrikaner party that introduced the system of segregationist policies known as apartheid.

In the first chapter of Singh's *Behold the Earth Mourns*, the Nirvani family have just received a letter informing them that they will have to vacate their house on the outskirts of Durban soon because of racial zoning laws—most likely the Group Areas Act (1950). The two brothers, Srenika and Krishnadutt, react very differently. Krishnadutt, the elder, is a pragmatist: "We will have to apply our minds to this matter carefully. It needs a great deal of thought and perhaps it will not be so bad. Perhaps if we come to some compromise about the lands.... Incoherent emotionalism does not get us anywhere. We have to obey the rules and live on."[4] Krishnadutt is invested in following the letter of the law. In contrast to this, his younger brother, Srenika, reacts with so-called "incoherent emotionalism": "Don't you feel... the aura of mystery, the sanctity, the precious meaning of our home, of their home—the very pulse that keeps people together, that protects men and women with the children from the world of harshness, from the changeable forces of nature?"[5] Although dismissed by his brother as "incoherent emotionalism," Srenika's stance allies his claim closely with that of typical settler narratives, where the family's deep bond to the land is seen as legitimating their ownership. The "precious meaning of home" is stable and timeless, opposed to the "changeable forces of nature." This is at first glance an unusual comparison—the time of nature is usually seen as stable, the referent against which to compare manmade rhythms. Srenika here extends the implicit conflict envisioned in the description of their typical settler house: nature is "raw, unbuilt" until the settlers tame it, such that the settlers impose order and stability onto the land. This comparison already suggests a certain chronotope: one that is invested in erasing the history of the now-settled land and superimposing the history of a specific family onto it. As J. M. Coetzee writes of South African farm narratives, "The farms [the founding fathers] carved out of the wilds . . . become the seats to which their lineages are mystically bound, so that the loss of a farm assumes the scale of the fall of an ancient house, the end of a dynasty."[6] Krishnadutt's argument, that "we have to obey the rules and live on," however, introduces an unexpected and atypical note to what seems to be a typical settler narrative, as it suggests that the ownership claim on the land is contingent upon rules and laws, not an emotional bond, and that these claims, and the meaning of home, can change. The sentimental rhetoric of the settler novel, invested in this notion of a stable, unchangeable relationship between one family and the land, is undercut—I argue, deliberately—by Singh's use of legalistic language throughout the text.

Though a significant canon of South African Indian fiction now exists, most of these texts were written during the final years of apartheid and after the 1994 democratic election.[7] *Behold the Earth Mourns* is the first novel published by a South African Indian. Singh (1917–1978) was born in Natal, studied medicine in Edinburgh, Scotland, and practiced medicine in the United States and South Africa. She is also the author of several other works of fiction, including two plays, *Cobwebs in the Garden* (1963) and *A Tomb for Thy Kingdom* (1966), and an anthology of poems, short stories, and essays, *Summer Moonbeams on the Lake* (1970). Devarakshanam Govinden, in her text *Sister Outsiders: The Representation of Identity and Difference in Selected Writings by South African Indian Women*, places Singh's novel in the "benign, liberal tradition" of protest writing, pointing out the "striking similarity" between the title of this novel, *Behold the Earth Mourns*, and *Cry, the Beloved Country* (1948), by the more famous liberal critic of apartheid, Alan Paton.[8]

Singh's novel, which can be seen as inaugurating South African Indian fictional writing, is also unique in that, under apartheid, subsequent South

African Indian authors turn to the short story, rather than the novel, as a vehicle for expressing what Pallavi Rastogi calls the "contradictory impulses—of collectivity versus specificity" that animate the South African Indian community under apartheid.[9] These short stories appear after 1975, and it is only in the 1990s, with the democratization of South African society, that South African Indian writers return to the novel.[10] Rastogi presents an elegant analysis of the turn to the short story form in South African Indian writing, diagnosing a set of community-specific anxieties that found their best expression in this form: "The neuroses engendered by their erasure from the public imagination and the alienation bred by racial, religious, cultural, and linguistic difference."[11] In examining *Behold the Earth Mourns* as a novel that *fails* to inspire a tradition of antiapartheid South African Indian novel writing, I complement Rastogi's analysis by stepping back in time to examine how the novel predicts its own failure as a literary progenitor.

Behold the Earth Mourns is structured by the introduction of two discriminatory laws in South Africa following the National Party's electoral victory in 1948. While there were several laws passed before 1950 that limited the areas within which South African Indians could live and conduct business, the displacement with which the novel starts seems to take place as a result of the introduction of the 1950 Group Areas Act, one of the keystones of apartheid lawmaking, which divided cities into racially segregated areas, reserved for either white, native, or colored groups, and which resulted in the forced relocation of enormous numbers of people in South Africa. The second piece of legislation shaping the narrative is the 1953 Immigration Regulation Amendment Act, which legislated that, contrary to the practices in place at the time, wives of South African Indians born outside of South Africa were no longer allowed to move to and reside in South Africa after their marriages.

Singh's novel begins by introducing the Nirvani family, focalized on Krishnadutt Nirvani: "His children were the third generation of settlers in this southern land of sunshine and adventure. His father Nirvani had come out as a virile young trader accompanied by an inexperienced wife.... In the years of their life together she could have been strengthened by adversity, success and excitement—the trials and heartaches that they were faced with in a new country, undeveloped, raw, and unbuilt."[12] By explicitly identifying her characters as "settlers," and in her descriptions, both of the landscape and the people "settling" it, Singh conforms to much of typical colonial writing. South Africa is described as "this southern land of sunshine and adventure," "a new country, undeveloped, raw and unbuilt." The new settlers are heroic, bravely confronting "trials and heartaches that they were faced with in a new country." Even the architecture of the house Nirvani builds is recognizably colonial: "Several porticos and verandahs supported by thick white columns surrounded the inner rambling house," while the garden consisted of "carpet-like lawns, orchards of mango, figs and citrus groves."[13] There is no indication of who performed the labor to establish these orchards, or acknowledgment that mangos were not originally indigenous to South Africa. The obfuscation of the question of who works the land is central to traditional settler writing: In *White Writing: On the Culture of Letters in South Africa*, J. M. Coetzee comments on the necessary "occlusion of black labour from the scene"[14] of white pastoral literature: "To satisfy the critics of rural retreat, it must portray labour; to satisfy the critics of colonialism, it must portray white labour."[15] Black labor is erased from early South African literature, a "shadowy presence flitting across the stage now and then to hold a horse or serve a meal."[16] In Singh's description, and her novel in general, no mention is made of any labor taking place on the sugar cane farm owned by the Nirvanis at all—both Black labor and, crucially, indentured South Asian labor are effaced.[17]

The interior decoration of the house is also noteworthy: "The lounge was airy with the soft evening light streaming over the cream and white walls, decorated with oil paintings of beautiful landmarks of South Africa—the Montagu Pass, the Drakensberg covered with snow gleaming in the winter sunshine."[18] These landscape paintings represent a certain way of viewing the land, one which stresses the sublimity of the landscape by firstly emptying it of people and secondly focusing on mountains, features that were more readily accommodated within preexisting European ideas of the sublime. As Coetzee argues, "In European art the sublime is far more often associated with the vertical than the horizontal, with mountains than with plains. . . . The language of the sublime is easily enough transported to the mountains of South Africa."[19] This landscape art adds to the impression that the owner looks at the South African landscape through the framework of European artistic conventions. To understand Singh's ostensible embrace of the settler narrative here, a detour into South African legal history is paramount.

In South African legal history, the period between 1902 and 1936 involved the development and consolidation of a pluralistic common law legal system: one for whites, or "Europeans," which followed the Roman-Dutch model heavily influenced by English common law, and another for the Black inhabitants of the territory, which was supposedly modeled on traditional or customary practices, but as filtered through the understanding of white lawmakers who often chose to interpret customary practice in the way most convenient to them. The main challenge that faced South African lawmakers was the need to maintain a facade of impartial justice and the rule of law, when, in practice, they were implementing extremely discriminatory racial policies. The existence of South African Indians troubled this dichotomy of African customary law and Roman-Dutch law. As the colonial legal historian Martin Chanock explains, "Because Asians could not, like Africans, be relegated to a different legal regime, but had to be discriminated against within and by the ordinary law, they posed many of the most difficult problems to South Africa's lawyers."[20]

While individuals who had migrated under indenture contracts were governed, during the period of their contract, by laws specifically designed for this purpose, once the period of indenture expired, legal authorities had to pass new laws to maintain the difference between these would-be settlers and the white settlers. The practice of transporting indentured laborers to South Africa was curtailed in 1910, and so, by the end of 1915 (when the last of the five-year indenture contracts had come to an end), the laws written for indentured laborers were no longer relevant. Even before 1910, however, one can see discriminatory laws against nonindentured Indian immigrants coming into force, beginning with the 1895 £3 Law (a tax on former indentured laborers who chose to remain in South Africa rather than be repatriated) and the 1897 Immigration Restriction Act of Natal, implicitly designed to prevent South Asians from entering the colony. These laws, I argue, can be traced to the desire, on the behalf of the British rulers of the South African colonies, to return South Asian would-be settlers in South Africa to the control of the indenture contract. For example, the 1907 Asiatic Registration Act (with its focus on fingerprints and passes) likens the South Asian immigrant to the precarious position of an indentured laborer, who could not legally be more than a mile from his or her place of employment without a signed pass from an employer. When writers of South Asian descent turn to the sentimental tropes of colonial settler writing, they are thus explicitly seeking ways to resist laws and statutes that make it impossible for them to settle permanently in South Africa.

A text by an influential apartheid thinker, the sociologist Geoffrey Cronjé, on the "Asiatic Question," shows how racist ideologues viewed the presence of Indian settlers in South Africa. Published in 1946, Cronjé's treatise *Afrika sonder die Asiaat: Die blywende oplossing van Suid Afrika se Asiatevraagstuk* (Africa without the Asiatic: The Lasting Solution to South Africa's Asiatic Question) is intended as a supplement to his earlier text *'n Tuiste vir die nageslag* (A Home for the Posterity), which introduces Cronjé's plans for total race segregation, but without touching on the so-called "Asiatic Question" (i.e., the presence of South Asians in South Africa). In *Afrika sonder die Asiaat*, Cronjé sums up some of the problems the presence of South African Indians causes for race-based policy making:

> This is indeed a complicated and "slippery" ["*glibberige*"] question that differs completely from any other race-question.... When we discussed the native and Colored questions elsewhere, those questions were considered on the one hand from the point of view of the whites, but on the other hand also from the point of view of the natives and the Colored people respectively because they are indigenous and won't find a homeland other than on this continent. When we get to the Asiatic or Indian question, however, we are dealing with a racial group that is alien and will remain alien.[21]

Cronjé's argument ultimately concludes with an ambitious total repatriation scheme, after evaluating the more modest alternatives of local segregation (within South Africa) and total segregation (giving South Asians their own "homeland" elsewhere in sub-Saharan Africa) and concluding that these latter two would be just short-term solutions to the problem. We can see that Cronjé's argument depends upon this key point: that South African Indians are *alien and will remain alien*.

J. M. Coetzee, in an article entitled "The Mind of Apartheid: Geoffrey Cronjé (1907–)," argues that, in reading Cronjé, "above all, we must be sensitive to his language."[22] Cronjé's use of the adjective *slippery* (*glibberig*) in *Afrika sonder die Asiaat* is telling. Coetzee does not address this appendix to *'n Tuiste vir die nageslag* in his analysis, but he points us to certain imagery that Cronjé is fond of using. Noteworthy in this context is Cronjé's use of the term *insypel* or *to seep in*: "'Seep . . . in' (Afr. *insypel*, *insyfer*) is another key term for Cronjé's imagination: variable in form in Afrikaans as in Dutch (*sijpelen, zijpelen, siepelen, sieperen*), he uses it in contexts where it easily changes places with its rhyme-word *insluip*, steal in: the secret bastard who tries to find a place in the white community, and the bed of a white woman, is 'die sluwe in-sluiper,' the sly stealer-in (77). The semantic nexus evoked is one of dark and treacherous fluidity."[23] *Glibberig* falls within this same semantic nexus, of "dark and treacherous fluidity." The word can be applied to the Indian immigrant as Cronjé sees him, who slips (*glip*) into the country from outside, and who is slippery in his careful evasion or misuse of the law. Chanock, writing on the legal position of Indians in South

Africa, describes the frustrations of lawmakers when Indian lawyers learn to negotiate within the law and even use it against the intentions of the lawmakers. "These people are continually creeping beyond the intention of the law," one authority complains.[24] Another says, "They may have acted within the four corners of the law, but anyone will admit that what they did was done by means of subterfuge."[25] "Creeping beyond" belongs to this same set of vocabulary generated by the presence of Indians in South Africa. In Act 1 of 1897 in Natal, the Immigration Restriction Act that provided the "Natal Formula," persons who could not prove their written proficiency in "any European language" are classed along with prostitutes, pimps, felons, the insane, and, crucially, "anyone suffering from a loathsome or a dangerous contagious disease" as undesirable immigrants.[26] The language of contagion is key here. *Glibberig* is etymologically related to the English word *glib* (which is Germanic in origin), a term also used by a magistrate to describe the arguments made in court by Gandhi: "I'm afraid it [intimidation] will continue so long as your friends are permitted to do what you so glibly term 'watching.'"[27] "Slippery," "glib," and contagious, "creeping beyond" the boundaries imposed by law, we can see how Indian would-be settlers were semantically constructed as insidiously threatening through the use of emotionally charged language.

Cronjé seems unaware of the irony of arguing for the repatriation of South African Indians because they are not indigenous to South Africa while at the same time taking for granted the position of white South Africans within South Africa. In this text, he doesn't acknowledge the fact that whites do not have the same claim to indigeneity as "natives" and "coloreds" are accorded in the passage I quote above. Later in *Afrika sonder die Asiaat*, we read, "As concerns the white race, the 'contribution' of the Indian comes down to slowly but surely uprooting [*ontbodem*, or de-earthing][28] him. This must be prevented. When the white race relinquishes its intimate bond with the earth of the Fatherland [*Vaderlandse bodem*], it will surely and definitely be one of the causes leading to his downfall in this country."[29] This passage reveals Cronjé's anxieties. While ostensibly he is simply talking about South African Indians becoming successful farmers in South Africa at this point in the text, his language returns to this image of Indians as a force that will, "slowly but surely," creep or slip in and force Afrikaners to release their hold on the land. The "intimate bond" with the *bodem* (earth or soil), so central to the Afrikaner myth of belonging, is revealed to be reversible, one can be de-earthed (*ontbodem*), one's claim on the land lost to the "alien"—implicitly revealed here as a *fellow* alien—South Asian settler.

Cronjé wants to stress the difference between South Asian would-be settlers and Afrikaners, who at that point wanted to see themselves not as settlers but as a *volk* having evolved in Africa. As Rita Barnard writes on the use of the language of pastoral intimacy to justify the large-scale resettlement schemes of apartheid, "It is important to recognize that the function of pastoral ideology in South Africa (sentimentally expressed in *Blut und Boden* songs like "O Boereplaas, geboortegrond!") was not so much to assert positive values like rootedness, simplicity, and tradition as to signify racial difference."[30] Tellingly, Cronjé focuses his argument on indentured Indians and their descendants, asking whether there was a need to use indentured laborers in the first place. His model for South Asians in South Africa is the indenture contract: a brief, legally controlled interlude, after which they are supposed to return to British India. Indians would thus never really become a legitimate presence in South Africa—Cronjé wistfully quotes a report by the Indian Immigration Commission in 1909, which (unsuccessfully) recommended that "indentures or contracts of Indians, whether first or subsequent, shall in future terminate in India or upon the high seas."[31] In order to make this argument in which the Indian never actually becomes a settler, Cronjé switches between legal language and claims (demonstrating an encyclopedic knowledge of laws and reports on Indians in South Africa) and sentimental rhetoric, as we have seen in his stress on the "intimate bond" the Afrikaner has with the soil, for example. He argues that South Asians lack this intimate relationship with the land: "What makes the Indians stick [*vaskleef*] to South Africa, is not their love for this land *as Fatherland*, but the economic prosperity and economic promise they enjoy here, in contrast to that offered by India, their actual home."[32] *Vaskleef*, or to stick or cling tightly, again partakes of the language of contagion, of insidious, viscous forces that, once settled, are impossible to uproot.

Cronjé's argument, that it was unnecessary to use indentured labor to begin with, relies on a strong indictment of British imperialism. Both his rhetoric of intimacy with the soil and his renunciation of imperialism originate in the ideology of Afrikaner suffering and resilience that emerged in the wake of the second South African War (1899–1902), as discussed in the previous chapter. "The Indian question was deeply rooted [*het diep aarde gevind*] in the imperial context, within which it would grow to a problem that claimed a colony as casualty," he writes, claiming, for example, that "out of imperialistic considerations, the interests and favorable attitudes of the Asiatics (that is, India) weighed more heavily on the British government than the interests and feelings of the Transvaal and its white population."[33] The "Indian question" is associated with the history of British imperialism. The Afrikaners are framed as still engaged with clearing up the growing, invasive aftereffects of British imperialism—a continuation of the war that they lost in 1901. Cronjé's treatise exemplifies the dangers of sentiment when deployed by a man tasked with shaping the policies of a white supremacist state: the rhetoric of the intimate bond of love for the soil was used with devastating effect to displace, oppress, and, in some cases, expel the nonwhite residents of South Africa.[34]

In *Behold the Earth Mourns*, Singh tells a different story about the origins of South Asians in South Africa, emphasizing that her protagonists are the descendants, not of indentured laborers, but of traders who built their own shops and developed their own land. However, the specter of the indenture contract and its legal language intrudes into the settler narrative she initially seems to embrace, such that the language of her characters often reflects that of laws regulating the presence of South Asians in South Africa. Yagesvari, Srenika's wife, who was born in India, is not legally allowed to move to South Africa after the passing of the 1953 Immigration Regulation Amendment Act. When talking to the clerk selling air tickets who asks her for an "entry permit" for South Africa, she replies that "but my husband was born in South Africa and his parents were domiciled there."[35] Usually, one would simply say his parents "lived" or "resided" in South Africa. However, the earlier Immigrants Regulation Act (1913), under which she would have been allowed to relocate to South Africa after her marriage, uses the word *domiciled* repeatedly when speaking about permissible immigrants: "Any person born in any place after the commencement of this Act whose parents were at the time of his birth domiciled in any part of South Africa included in the Union, f) any person domiciled in any Province who is not such a person as is described in paragraph (e) or (f)."[36] Singh portrays Yagesvari as attempting to echo the language of the law when confronted with a figure of authority.

Singh thus seems to be aware of the problem of mutually contaminating legal and sentimental rhetoric and even builds it into the text itself, as we saw in the debate she stages between the two brothers, Srenika and Krishnadutt. This is why the ending to this novel is particularly interesting. Initially, it seems like Singh's text wants to frame itself within the chronotope of the traditional settler novel, which is one of genealogical or dynastic descent—the *nageslag* (posterity) referred to by Cronjé—one generation succeeding the other and inheriting the land. This chronotope of genealogical descent in the traditional sense is denied to Singh's characters, however, by the imposition of apartheid legislation, which tears the family from their home and disrupts the imagined endless time of generation succeeding generation into the future.

Thus the dynastic chronotope is abandoned—but Singh stakes a different kind of filiative claim toward the end of the novel. Yagesvari comes back to the house following her stay in jail for returning to the country illegally and sees her daughter, Malini, in the arms of her Black nanny, Anna: "Reluctantly Malini went to her mother almost sensing a strangeness. Yagesvari had neither the strength of emotion nor the energy of the body to receive the dearest creature of her heart. She smiled in half thankfulness that there was an attachment—that there should be Anna for her little one. At this moment it was all she could convey to Anna and she understood it. Anna took her new child and went into the house, hiding from her the thoughts that passed deep in her mind."[37] The novel ends shortly afterward with the death of Yagesvari, leaving the suggestion open that the future of the family lies in this adoption of Malini by her African nurse, who recedes enigmatically, hiding her thoughts. This is a strange end to the novel, dedicated "to South Africa on the centenary of the arrival of the Indians in the country."[38] Is Singh implying that South Africa should be abandoned, given up on as a home for South African Indians? Or is she hinting at the possibility of a new kind of voluntary affiliation, or even filiation, between Black and Indian? Crossing racial boundaries that had seemed inviolable, this end traces a dramatic divergence from both the genealogical association with the soil and the language of law and possession that we have seen to be operative in Singh's and Cronjé's texts.[39]

Another section of the novel suggests a possible reason for this divergence. Yagesvari, soon upon her initial arrival in South Africa, attempts to have a conversation with Anna while sketching her portrait:

"Oh Anna. I feel sad. Can I come and see your home?"

"You have to get a paper to come to the farm. The land does not belong to us."

"Then who does it belong to?"

"That is a long story Yagesvari."

"Why did your husband leave you, Anna?"

"This place grow big, big like this."

"Keep your hands down please, Anna."

"I show you all right. More chimneys come, more smoke, and more husbands leave wives."

"But why did he leave you behind?"

"He can't bring me. He find another woman."

Yagesvari was exasperated. She could not understand. Well she would try another time and went on with her drawing.[40]

In both these last passages, Anna remains opaque—she "hid[es] . . . the thoughts that pass deep in her mind" and here refuses to explain herself clearly to Yagesvari. In her article "'Every Secret Thing?' Racial Politics in Ansuyah R. Singh's *Behold the Earth Mourns*," Antoinette Burton describes this scene by saying that "Yagesvari clearly doesn't know about, let alone understand, the township system or the pass laws."[41] While she is right in describing Yagesvari's complete inability to understand or connect with Anna here, I would like to add that the system of which she is completely ignorant is not just the pass laws or the township system, but the system of migrant labor in force in South Africa at the time. Starting in the 1870s, African men were recruited to work primarily in mining compounds but later also in factories on short-term contracts.[42] Crucially, they could not bring their families with them, and lived in large compounds in hostels close to their place of work. Between contracts they would return to their families who usually lived in the so-called Native Reserves. The migrant labor system was incredibly disruptive to the family lives of these migrant laborers. The question that Yagesvari doesn't understand, why Anna's husband left her, is thus a reference to the fact that he was most likely one of these migrant laborers. "He can't bring me. He find another woman," Anna says—a common fate when migrant laborers spent the vast majority of their time away from their families. Notice also that the "farm" does not belong to Anna's family anymore either. The same fate that assails the Nirvani family at the beginning of the novel, the loss of the farm, has happened to Anna's a generation earlier. But this exchange also hints at something Singh seems to disavow in her novel— the parallels between internal migrant labor in South Africa and the system of indentured labor that brought so many South Asians to South Africa.

While at first glance this conversation between Anna and Yagesvari seems merely patronizing, both in its content but also in the broken English Singh ascribes to Anna, there is more at stake here. If indentured labor is written out of Singh's narrative, these covert references to migrant labor, and the fact that Yagesvari hands over Malini to Anna at the end of the novel, may be a way to read indenture back into the novel. The filial connection Yagesvari makes with Anna by having her adopt her child could also be an acknowledgment of this alternative history of Indians in South Africa. Traces of briny South entanglements haunt this text, manifested in this uneasy contested contact zone between would-be settlers of South Asian descent in South Africa and the "also-colonized other," Black South Africans.[43]

This returns us to the question of Singh's novel as a literary progenitor. While the system of apartheid resulted in a rich body of resistance literature by Black South Africans, the relative paucity of South African Indian fiction in this canon is noticeable.[44] Singh's novel, in its ambiguous ending, signals its own failure as a model or progenitor of a literary tradition. While this novel could have served as the origin for a tradition of South African Indian novel writing under apartheid, by partly drawing on the settler novel mode, as well as the white liberal mode associated with Alan Paton's *Cry, the Beloved Country,* Singh's novel does not inaugurate a new tradition, but rather self-consciously stages the failure of this sentimental form. The lack of a robust canon of South African Indian writing under apartheid is thus linked to the essential precarity or liminality of this population, linked, in the mind of apartheid thinkers like Cronjé, to the indenture contract.[45]

Other South African Indians, like the memoirist Dr. Goonam, attempt to resist this precarity in their life-writing. Goonam, the author of *Coolie Doctor: An Autobiography*, was born Kesaveloo Goonaruthnum Naidoo in 1906 in Durban. As she explains, "That made me African, but not quite, for my father had immigrated from South India and my mother from Mauritius."[46] Like Singh, she moved to Edinburgh to study medicine, returning to Durban to practice. She lived in South Africa, South India, England, Australia, and Zimbabwe, suffering under oppressive apartheid legislation that forced both her family out of their childhood home and, at a later point, her out of her own house. She began writing her autobiography in 1979 but didn't publish it until 1991.

Goonam's descriptions of her childhood home are particularly fascinating to look at alongside Singh's text: "There was a flower garden at the entrance and a large shady tree beneath which my father often sat with his visitors, sipping tea.... My father also purchased a farm about this time.... I came to love the farm, set against the rolling Natal hills with its sugar cane, and eucalyptus groves, and dipping into the Umgeni River through wooded thickets, slashed red with hibiscus and the amatingula fruit."[47] The sugar cane on the rolling Natal hills is naturalized, along with the uncultivated eucalyptus groves, hibiscus, and amatingula fruit, so that it seems like all of these things occur without human intervention. This, of course, obscures the question of labor—who established those sugar cane fields, and who harvests them? The members of the family sip tea and entertain visitors, but we don't see who maintains the garden, and who makes the tea. Later in the text Goonam is slightly more forthcoming: "Our attendants were as extra-ordinary as our animals,"[48] she says, going on to name Periyar, Narain, and Fakir Chacha as the farm attendants. The only workers named thus seem to be of South Asian descent. As the purchase of the farm takes place around 1927, Periyar, Narain, and Fakir Chacha could no longer be under indenture contracts, but the odds are that they had come over to South Africa as indentured laborers. As Gandhi's biographer, Joseph Lelyveld, points out, South Asians did on occasion employ indentured laborers: "At least one of [Gandhi's] patrons, a land and property owner named Dawad Mahomed, employed indentured laborers, presumably on the same exploitative terms as their white masters."[49] Even as the Indian laborers eclipse Black labor on the farm, Goonam also carefully avoids going into the political and economic circumstances that brought them to South Africa. By comparing them to the farm animals ("our attendants were as extraordinary as our animals"), Goonam is doing the same thing as she does with the sugar cane fields in her description of the farm: the presence of these former indentured laborers is naturalized. Like the farm animals, they simply belong on the farm. Even in this quick comparison between Dr. Goonam's text and Singh's novel, we can see that indenture and the chronotope of the contract play an important, though unacknowledged, role, haunting the text in distorted forms even as the writers try to erase them from the narrative.

As a counterpoint to this erasure of the history of indenture in South Africa, a fragmentary set of documents from the archives allows us a glimpse into the life of a former indentured laborer who stayed in South Africa after the expiry of his contract. Studying a series of receipts documenting the purchase of a piece of land outside Ladysmith by one Shingolam/Sewgolam juxtaposes a different kind of contract with the indenture contract: "Memorandum of Agreement made this 26th day of February 1906 between Bhola, Free Indian,[50] of Ladysmith (hereinafter called the seller) of the one part and Shi-ngolam, Free Indian, no. 56934 and Joykandani, his wife, (hereinafter called the purchasers) of the other part."[51] In this document, formerly indentured laborers become, legally, "sellers" and "purchasers" of land: a reclassification that upsets the idea, held up by Cronjé, that these laborers are defined purely by the terms of the indenture contract. The contract includes the stipulation that the land ("in extent two acres, less a ten feet right of way on the boundary of Lot 81, and being a subdivision of Lot 82 of the Townlands of Ladysmith") is to be paid off in installments, due on specific dates.[52] Here we thus see a different contract, and legal relationship, supplanting the indenture contract. At the conclusion of the timeframe specified by this contract, Shingolam/Sewgolam can become the new "seller" of the piece of land. The rest of this set of documents is a series of receipts, demonstrating that Sewgolam/Shingolam did finish paying for the land. It is this kind of transaction, and the legal redefinitions implied by it, that the increasingly restrictive and discriminatory statute law of the Union and Republic of South Africa would attempt to render impossible. Goonam's autobiography and Singh's novel are silent on the subject of indentured laborers, seeming to erase the history of the indenture contract and its time limits from the tale of South Asian settlers in South Africa such that this history has to be read between the lines. It is not until Praba Moodley's *The Heart Knows No Colour*, a historical novel published in 2003, that the indenture experience in South Africa is explicitly narrativized in fiction.[53] Shingolam/Sewgolam's contract thus offers us a rare glimpse of an alternative narrative, a story in which formerly indentured laborers play the main role—*and* in which they become legally recognized settlers.

"The Coolie Barrister"

> I have said that Balasundaram entered my office, head-gear in hand. There was a peculiar pathos about the circumstance which also showed our humiliation. I have already narrated the incident when I was asked to take off my turban. A practice had been forced upon every indentured labourer and every Indian stranger to take off his head-gear when visiting a European.... Balasundaram thought that he should follow the practice even with me.... I felt humiliated and asked him to tie up his scarf. He did so, not without a certain hesitation, but I could perceive the pleasure on his face.[54]

An earlier example of what could be called precursor South African Indian writing, Gandhi's *Autobiography, or the Story of My Experiments with Truth* (written starting in 1925) covers the period from his birth up to 1921, when he says that "it therefore seems to me to be my plain duty to close this narrative here. In fact my pen instinctively refuses to proceed further" (768). All autobiography is retrospective, and in Gandhi's case, many years had gone by between the actual events detailed in his autobiography and the time when he recalls them. These events have thus been shaped into a narrative, given a specific meaning within the context of Gandhi's life experiences. Gandhi initially wrote his autobiography in weekly installments, published in *Navajivan*, a Gujarati newspaper which he founded in India in 1919. While his metaphor, that of his pen "instinctively refusing" to write, suggests a kind of spontaneous and "instinctive" act of writing, like all autobiography this text has been constructed to convey a certain message, both deliberately and through the erasures and modifications involved in all acts of recall.

In this part of his autobiography, Gandhi revisits his encounter with the indentured laborer Balasundaram, described in the *Green Pamphlet* and discussed in chapter three. Gandhi links Balasundaram's appearance with his own experience of having to remove his turban and transposes his feeling of humiliation from that encounter onto this one. He also reads Balasundaram's face to perceive an expression of pleasure. Gandhi's narrative of this encounter, which marks the moment when he first starts legal work on behalf of indentured Indians, is part of a longer narrative of self-invention in which various turning points in Gandhi's life are rehearsed and repeated. The link between Balasundaram's removal of his headgear and Gandhi's experience of having to remove his turban is typical of the affective narrative links Gandhi creates between different moments. Throughout his autobiographical writings on his time in South Africa, Gandhi evinces a desire to distance himself from indentured laborers—here reflected in the way Balasundaram's behavior reminds him of his own humiliation—in tension with a reparative drive to help indentured laborers, also stemming from his own personal traumas.

Gandhi's writings about his time in South Africa echo some of the rhetoric of the settler narrative that we see in the beginning of Singh's novel and in Goonam's autobiography. Gandhi's legacy, and especially his writings on race, has increasingly come under fire from various different directions.[55] His South African writings have been carefully examined by Ashwin Desai and Goolam Vahed in *The South African Gandhi: Stretcher-Bearer of Empire*, in which they conclude that "he not only rendered African exploitation and oppression invisible, but was, on occasion, a willing part of their subjugation and racist stereotyping."[56] Gandhi's writings on indenture, however, have not received the same amount of critical attention.[57] As discussed in chapter three, Gandhi's initial reaction to the term *coolie* in South Africa involved carefully distinguishing between indentured laborers and other South Asians in South Africa: "The word Coolie is a term of contempt when applied to those who have not come under the Immigration Act, and it is a pity that every coloured man passes generally for a Coolie. It will have been seen that no Indian is a Coolie by birth. Any Indian is a Coolie who has come under the Immigration Act, and ceases to be one when he has finished his agreement."[58] Gandhi's biographer Lelyveld claims that the final ten months Gandhi spent in South Africa, the period in which he first mobilized Indian indentured laborers to take part in his passive resistance campaigns, "transformed his sense of what was possible for him and those he led."[59] If this attitude shift regarding formerly indentured laborers is as crucial to his development into someone perceived as a "spiritual pilgrim and secular saint"[60] as Lelyveld suggests, it is worth studying this "conversion narrative" as it unfolds in his autobiography, written thirty years after his arrival in South Africa.

Gandhi the young lawyer comes to South Africa at the behest of a wealthy firm, a "Meman firm from Porbander."[61] He initially views his sojourn in South Africa as temporally bounded—he is contracted for "not more than a year. We will pay you a first class return fare and a sum of £105, all round," he is told in India (195). I use the term *contracted* deliberately here, though Gandhi makes no specific mention of signing a contract with his new employers. I want to suggest that the time frame of Gandhi's stay in South Africa is perhaps not so different from the time frame of the indentured laborer—a limited temporal and geographic displacement. Gandhi himself says of his initial trip: "This was hardly going there as a barrister. It was going as a *servant* of the firm" (195).[62] His anxiety is reiterated when he arrives in South Africa and meets his new employer: "He read the papers his brother had sent through me, and felt more puzzled. He thought his brother had sent him a white elephant" (200). Gandhi is "sent" over accompanied by "papers" supposedly legitimizing his presence. Gandhi's attitude toward indentured laborers, as evidenced by the letter in the *Transvaal Advertiser*, goes beyond simple class prejudice: he is anxious about his proximity to the indentured. His objection is that the term *coolie* is applied indiscriminately to "all coloured men" rather than its proper object, the indentured laborer.

Gandhi writes in his autobiography: "I was hence known as a 'coolie barrister.' The merchants were known as 'coolie merchants.' The original meaning of the word 'coolie' was thus forgotten, and it became a common appellation for all Indians" (203). A later chapter in Gandhi's autobiography, "What it is to be a 'Coolie'" (229), is about his experiences with racial discrimination. Important to note, however, is that all the incidents described in this chapter highlight the distance between Gandhi and a typical indentured laborer, rather than their closeness. In the first case, Gandhi explains how his friend,

Mr. Coates, with whom he would frequently be walking around after the start of a curfew imposed on nonwhites, felt uncomfortable "issuing" him a pass as he did for his servants. Rather than do this, he takes Gandhi to the attorney general, a Dr. Krause. As it happens, "we turned out to be barristers of the same Inn. . . . Instead of ordering for me a pass, he gave me a letter authorizing me to be out of doors at all hours without police interference" (231).[63] In the second case, Gandhi is accosted by a policeman for being too close to the house of the president of the South African Republic. His friend Mr. Coates passes by right at that moment and reprimands the policeman: "I could not follow their talk, as it was in Dutch, the policeman being a Boer. But he apologized to me, for which there was no need. I had already forgiven him" (233). Both of these incidents thus stress Gandhi's status as educated lawyer and his friendship with men who could shield him from the worst excesses of the discriminatory laws. The chapter heading thus becomes ironic, as he never becomes a *coolie*, except through mistaken identity. Gandhi concludes this chapter by writing that "the incident deepened my feeling for the Indian settlers" (233). His choice to use the term *settlers* here emphasizes the difference between *coolies* and *Indian settlers*, and reveals his desire to identify with the latter.

Gandhi's autobiography, however, also imagines a moment of reconciliation between Gandhi and the indentured laborers. While the disdain toward indentured laborers that we see in his letter to the editor of the *Transvaal Advertiser* is never apparent in the autobiography, indentured laborers initially play no part in his circle of acquaintances. In order to find the source or origin of Gandhi's conversion narrative, I argue, one has to go back to a much earlier passage in the text, when Gandhi describes the death of his father:

> It was 10:30 or 11 p.m. I was giving the massage [to his father]. My uncle offered to relieve me. I was glad and went straight to the bedroom. My wife, poor thing, was fast asleep. But how could she sleep when I was there? I woke her up. In five or six minutes, however, the servant knocked at the door. . . . "Father is no more." So all was over! . . . I saw that, had animal passion not blinded me, I should have been spared the torture of separation from my father during his last moments. I should have been massaging him, and he would have died in my arms. . . . The shame, to which I have referred in a foregoing chapter, was this shame of my carnal desire even at the critical hour of my father's death, which demanded wakeful service. It is a blot I have

never been able to efface or forget.... Before I close this chapter of my double shame, I may mention that the poor mite that was born to my wife scarcely breathed for more than three or four days. Nothing else could be expected. (91–93)

This is a very far cry from the genealogical model Singh's novel initially seems to espouse. Gandhi's autobiography refuses the cyclical time of reproduction: he is punished for his lust by the death of his child. The intergenerational momentum, in which the living child succeeds and, in a sense, replaces the dead grandfather, is cut short—"nothing else could be expected." Instead, Gandhi's life arguably becomes a constant attempt to atone for that moment in which he held his wife in his arms, rather than his dying father—a desire to repeat and repair a moment that is past: "It is a blot I have never been able to efface or forget."

Much has been written about Gandhi's celibacy, by himself as much as by others, and I am not the first to read this moment in his adolescence as one of the roots of his vow of celibacy, as he indeed implicitly does himself in this passage.[64] This description, however, also suggests that while every act of lust repeats the act by which he chose to love his wife rather than his father, every act of "nursing" represents Gandhi's reparation for his earlier failure. This repetition can be seen, for example, in the following. The young Gandhi describes his duties to his dying father as follows: "I had the duties of a *nurse*, which mainly consisted in dressing the wound, giving my father his medicine, and compounding drugs."[65] In later life, Gandhi writes: "I was fond of nursing people, whether friends or strangers" (293). On a trip to India, he becomes nurse to his brother-in-law: "I put my brother-in-law in my room and remained with him night and day. I was obliged to keep awake part of the night.... Ultimately, however, the patient died, but it was a great consolation to me that I had had an opportunity to nurse him during his last days" (295). Here Gandhi puts the patient in his own room, and stays with him "night and day"—reversing his actions at his father's bedside. Gandhi repeats the scene of his father's death, but this time, he gets it right: he is by the patient's side when he dies.

Gandhi comments on this incident: "My aptitude ["hobby" in the original] for nursing gradually developed into a passion, so much so that it often led me to neglect my work, and on occasion I engaged not only my wife but the whole household in such service" (295). His "animal passion" for his wife has been replaced by a passion for nursing. I began this section by examining how Gandhi contextualizes his encounter with the indentured laborer

Balasundaram by referring to his own humiliation in having to remove his turban. Returning to the way in which Gandhi writes about that incident suggests that his newfound interest in advocating for the indentured stems from a personal source as well.

Gandhi writes:

> I had put in scarcely three or four months' practice, and the Congress also was still in its infancy, when a Tamil man in tattered clothes, headgear in hand, two front teeth broken and his mouth bleeding, stood before me trembling and weeping. He had been heavily belaboured by his master. I learnt all about him from my clerk, who was a Tamilian.[66] Balasundaram, as that was the visitor's name, was serving his indenture under a well-known European resident of Durban. The master, getting angry with him, had lost self-control, and had beaten Balasundaram severely, breaking two of his teeth (265).

I don't think it too far-fetched to see in this incident an opportunity for Gandhi to exercise his "passion" for nursing. A wounded man comes to the Congress office, "still in its infancy," for help—and this time, Gandhi can help him. The child nurses the father, rather than abandoning him. Subsequently, Gandhi describes how "Balasundaram's case reached the ears of every indentured labourer, and I came to be regarded as their friend" (266). Gandhi's turn to and eventual championing of indentured laborers can thus be read, not only as a politically strategic move, but also as a moment of reparation within his own developmental arc. This personal, even filial, connection allowed Gandhi to care for and help Balasundaram and other indentured laborers without sacrificing his claim to a settler identity, which, as we have seen, was still so important to him at the time of writing his autobiography. Gandhi's encounter with Balasundaram thus allows him to work through earlier experiences of trauma or humiliation, but from a position of power.

It will not be until 1913, however, that indentured laborers would be included in Gandhi's passive resistance campaigns. When Gandhi first appears in what will become his iconic outfit of a "lungi and knee-long kurta with his hair and moustache shaved off"[67] in 1913, he writes to the *Natal Mercury* that "with some modification in deference to the feelings of his European friends, he had adopted the dress similar to that of an indentured Indian."[68] Even at this moment, Gandhi maintains a certain distance: he references his "European friends" and makes it clear that he has only "adopted the dress similar to" indentured laborers. Gandhi's affective stance toward indentured laborers remains poised between kinship and disavowal, as he attempts to negotiate his own position in racially divided South Africa.

In *Commerce with the Universe*, Desai recognizes a "family resemblance" between the narratives he studies, which he traces to the "mythological charter that often accompanies Indian claims about the community's contributions to East African modernity," a charter that makes the generic switch to "reading commerce as romance rather than conflict."[69] I have argued that we can see the family of writing, both fictional and autobiographical, by writers of South Asian descent living in South Africa, as bearing the traces of a different history: that of indenture. These are texts that seek to erase the history of the indenture contract from their claims to legitimate residency and, crucially, landownership in reaction to legal statutes that seek to restore the essential conditions of indenture: precarity and impermanence. The genre, and expressions of sentiment, these writers subsequently adopt in their narratives are those of the settler narrative—however, they cannot comfortably inhabit this genre, as the texts are repeatedly unsettled by reminders of the indenture contract.

In chapter three, I read Gandhi's earlier *Green Pamphlet* (1896) to show how he represses so-called "sentimental grievances" in favor of material demonstrations of harm to the South African Indian community. Writing his *Autobiography* (1925) after his departure from South Africa, Gandhi is able to frame his advocacy in more explicitly sentimental terms, referring frequently to his own feelings and those of other South African Indians. I thus have traced a deeply personal arc in Gandhi's life, starting with his father's death, which intersects with his political arc in the moment when Balasundaram enters the offices of the Indian Congress in Durban. This encounter, described both in the *Green Pamphlet* and in his autobiography, marks a point of inflection in the course of his life that is both personal and political. Gandhi's political advocacy on behalf of South African Indians, and particularly his understanding of the symbolic dangers of the indenture contract, anticipates and predicts the writings of legal theorists like Geoffrey Cronjé. Cronjé is eager, in *Afrika sonder die Asiaat* (1946), to deny the difference Gandhi seeks to underscore between former indentured laborers and other South Asian would-be immigrants, using the figure of the indenture contract as a means of framing the presence of all South Asians as permanently "alien." In doing so, Cronjé draws upon sentimental imagery depicting a close bond between the Afrikaner and the soil—the kind of nationalistic sentiment that also emerges, as I discuss in chapter four, in contemporaneous revisions of Boer prisoner-of-war memoirs, edited and published in the 1930s and

1940s. Singh's novel *Behold the Earth Mourns* (1960) is explicitly in dialogue with both these sentimental settler tropes, as well as the segregationist laws inspired by the writings of Cronjé and others. Attempting to use the language of love for the soil that we also see in Cronjé's writings to establish a natural link between South African Indians and the land they own, Singh also seems to be aware of the limitations of this approach, when deployed by the disempowered. Her novel, I suggest, seems to both predict and deliberately stage its own failure as a literary progenitor, denying the possibility of posterity. South African Indian fictional writing, furthermore, will remain unable to acknowledge the importance of indenture to the community's existence until well after the end of apartheid.

CODA

No Human Footprints

The legacy of empire in the Indian Ocean world has recently come into sharp relief in a legal battle about the Chagos Archipelago, a series of coralline islands in the middle of the Indian Ocean, halfway between Ethiopia and Indonesia. Here, the sun has not yet set on the British Empire. In spite of intense international pressure to hand over jurisdiction of the Chagos Archipelago to Mauritius, the United Kingdom still claims the island group as the British Indian Ocean Territory (BIOT). Fifty years ago, the United Kingdom agreed to lease these islands to the United States for use as a military base, displacing the inhabitants of the islands, the Chagossians, most of whom moved to Mauritius and the Seychelles. The exiled Chagossians have been challenging their eviction since 1973. In September 2018, Mauritius challenged the United Kingdom's right to sovereignty over these islands in front of the International Court of Justice in the Hague. The court's decision, which was purely advisory, was handed down in February 2019, at which time they found that "the process of decolonization of Mauritius was not lawfully completed when that country acceded to independence in 1968, following the separation of the Chagos Archipelago" and that "the United Kingdom is under an obligation to bring to an end its administration of the Chagos Archipelago as rapidly as possible."[1] In May 2019, the United Nations General Assembly voted 116 to 6 in favor of a six-month deadline for Britain to withdraw from the Chagos Archipelago and for the Chagos Islands to be reunified with Mauritius, which would allow for exiled

Chagossians to return. At the time of writing, the United Kingdom has not relinquished its control of the group of islands.

In a cable from 2009, published on Wikileaks, Colin Roberts, the Foreign and Commonwealth Office's (FCO) director, is described discussing the plans (implemented in 2010) to make the Chagos Archipelago into the world's largest marine preserve as a means to prevent the resettlement claims of the Chagossians: "Roberts stated that, according to the HGM,s [sic—HMG's] current thinking on a reserve, there would be 'no human footprints' or 'Man Fridays' on the BIOT's uninhabited islands. He asserted that establishing a marine park would, in effect, put paid to resettlement claims of the archipelago's former residents."[2]

All the forced imperial displacements discussed in this book come together on this island chain: slavery, internment, and indenture. Roberts's remarks, and the longer history of invoking Daniel Defoe's 1719 novel in referring to the Chagos Archipelago, foregrounds specifically the legal and bureaucratic imagination of these displacements: What stories do imperial administrators tell about forced migration? The reappearance of Friday, Robinson Crusoe's "man"—the reincarnation of this imagined ideal imperial subject from the eighteenth century in the twenty-first century—suggests that the legal, administrative narratives of imperialism coexist with certain aesthetic forms. Fictional imperial narratives respond to but also shape legal imperial narratives. Friday and his fictional history haunt the real-life history of the Chagos Archipelago: a ghost that the United Kingdom hopes, in vain, to lay to rest.

While the archipelago was uninhabited when first discovered by the Portuguese in the sixteenth century, the French, upon claiming the islands in the 1770s, established coconut plantations worked by slaves. These slaves came from Portuguese East Africa, Mauritius, Madagascar, and the Seychelles. Great Britain captured Mauritius (then called Isle de France) during the Napoleonic wars in 1810, and in 1814, Mauritius and its dependencies (including the Chagos Archipelago) were formally ceded to the United Kingdom. When slavery was abolished in Mauritius and its dependencies in the 1830s, former slaves remained on the island under apprenticeship contracts, and in 1835, when indentured laborers from South Asia were first transported to Mauritius, some of them were sent to the Chagos Islands to work on coconut plantations. Between 1815 and 1837, convicts were also transported to Mauritius (including the Chagos Islands) from South Asia under the auspices of the East India Company. By the beginning of the twentieth century, the Chagos Archipelago housed a society of about one thousand people of African,

South Asian, and European descent speaking Chagos Kreol, a language related to the Kreols in Mauritius and the Seychelles.[3] Starting in 1960, the US Navy entered into secret negotiations with the British government to secure Diego Garcia, the largest of the Chagos Islands, as a US military base, and in 1966, an agreement was signed between the US and UK governments to deport the Chagossians and grant the United States access to Diego Garcia for a fifty-year term with the possibility of a twenty-year extension. In 1971, the BIOT commissioner enacted immigration ordinances that made it illegal for someone to be in the BIOT without a permit.[4] By 1973, the expulsion and resettlement of more than two thousand Chagossians to Mauritius and the Seychelles was complete. This briny South community was thus created by imperial displacements to provide labor, but then expelled and resettled partly because they could not claim any rights that indigeneity may have offered them. The cycle of oceanic displacement seems inescapable here.

More recently, public interest in Diego Garcia, the largest of the Chagos Islands, has been fueled by ongoing allegations that the military base is being used as a prison camp for terror suspects, a so-called CIA "black site" where prisoners are held and interrogated.[5] While these allegations were never officially confirmed, the UK government had confirmed that, on at least two "extraordinary rendition" flights (extrajudicial flights to transport terror suspects arrested on foreign soil to a non-US territory), planes did refuel on Diego Garcia.[6] The legacies of slavery, indenture, and war internment thus intersect on this small group of islands in the middle of the Indian Ocean.

During the 2013 court case contesting the establishment of the Marine Protected Area in front of the UK High Court, which featured the leaked cable cited above (though the cables were eventually ruled out as forms of evidence), "[Roberts] adamantly denied making any reference to 'Man Fridays' for reasons which he explained: it was a quote from a colonial official from the 1960s," though he did admit referring to a human footprint or "words to that effect."[7] Roberts's defense thus leads us to a colonial official from the 1960s, and the longer history of comparing Diego Garcia to Defoe's island. The 1966 exchange between the permanent undersecretary of the foreign office and another official, D. A. Greenhill, reads: "The object of the exercise was to get some rocks which will remain *ours*; there will be no indigenous population except seagulls who have not yet got a Committee (the Status of Women Committee does *not* cover the rights of Birds)."[8] To which Greenhill replied, in a handwritten note, "Unfortunately along with the Birds go some few Tarzans or Men Fridays whose origins are obscure, and who are being hopefully wished on to Mauritius etc. When this has been done I agree we must be very tough and a submission is being done accordingly."⁹

These references to Daniel Defoe's *The Life and Strange Surprising Adventures of Robinson Crusoe* suggest that the officials attempting to regulate and control this archipelago (and its surrounding waters) are sensitive to the narratives generated in the public imagination by islands: stories of original inhabitants and their claims to the land. The "human footprint" marks the land as already occupied, and the appeal to pristine, uninhabited nature—the marine preserve—seeks to rewrite the narrative, erasing the traces of the Chagossians, who, as the descendants of slaves, penal transportees, and indentured laborers, cannot claim rights of indigeneity.

The character of Crusoe was inspired by several real-world figures, including Alexander Selkirk, a Scottish sailor who was stranded on the Juan Fernandez Islands in the South Pacific for four years (one of the islands is now named Robinson Crusoe Island). However, a key inspiration for Crusoe, as I discuss in chapter four, was Robert Knox, a British sea captain who, along with his father and crew, was shipwrecked on the island then known as Ceylon and held captive there for nineteen years. Knox's manuscript *An Historical Relation of the Island Ceylon* was published in 1681 and served as one of the historical sources for Crusoe.[10] By figuring Robinson Crusoe and his "servant" Friday as inhabitants of the Chagos Archipelago, the Foreign Office is thus returning Crusoe to one of his original homes in the Indian Ocean.

Here is the famous scene of Crusoe discovering the footprint:

> It happen'd one Day about Noon going towards my Boat, I was exceedingly surpriz'd with the Print of a Man's naked Foot on the Shore, which was very plain to be seen in the Sand: I stood like one Thunder-struck, or as if I had seen an Apparition; I listen'd, I look'd round me, I could hear nothing, nor see any Thing; I went up to a rising Ground to look farther. . . . I went to it again to see if there were any more, and to observe if it might not be my Fancy; but there was no Room for that, for there was exactly the very Print of a Foot, Toes, Heel, and every Part of a Foot; how it came thither, I knew not, nor could in the least imagine.[11]

The footprint is at once miraculous and mundane; an apparition or fancy and a plainly visible exact print of a single foot. Crusoe carefully deploys his empiricist reasoning to investigate the print—he listens, he looks, he dissects the print into its constitutive parts—in order to establish that impossible as it may seem, it is not a fancy or apparition. The footprint is hard evidence: a sign that he is not alone on the island, that the island has a human history that predates his arrival. This is both surprising and terrifying. Crusoe cannot "in the least imagine" where the footprint came from—the idea of other humans on the island is unthinkable within the isolated island narrative he had previously been living in. When Roberts of the FCO attempts to wipe the narrative of the Chagos Archipelago free of the footprint, he appeals to the idea of islands as spaces without history, spaces of pure nature outside time: an island where Robinson Crusoe would not be interrupted by the appearance of that sole footprint. But Roberts's reference to *Robinson Crusoe* obscures the question of the observer of the footprint: who sees (or, in his formulation, does not have to see) a footprint? By what right does Robinson Crusoe inhabit the island, and what historical circumstances lead to him being there? By extension, who, on the Chagos Archipelago, will be spared the sight of this footprint?

It is the slave trade that brought Robinson Crusoe to his island, as it was slavery that allowed the Chagos Archipelago to be occupied and rendered productive in the first place. Roberts's comments invoke thus not only the cannibals who leave the famous footprint, or Crusoe's faithful servant Friday, but also the easily forgotten figure of Xury, the boy who helps Crusoe escape the North African enslavers who first capture him, whom Crusoe promptly sells into slavery upon reaching Brazil. Crusoe explains: "I was very loath to sell the poor Boy's Liberty, who had assisted me so faithfully in procuring my own" so he obtains from the purchaser the agreement that "he would give the Boy an Obligation to set him free in ten Years, if he turn'd Christian; upon this, and Xury saying he was willing to go to him, I let the Captain have him."[12] The sale of Xury into a kind of indenture is in part what finances Crusoe's plantation in Brazil, and it is in search of slave labor for this plantation that he leaves Brazil for the coast of Guinea and is eventually shipwrecked somewhere in the Atlantic Ocean on the island where he spends twenty-eight years. The Colonial Office's tendency to refer to the Chagos Archipelago in terms of scenes and figures from *Robinson Crusoe* is thus uncannily apt and demonstrates the lasting imbrication of imperial fiction and imperial reality.

The question of speech and silence in the representation of subaltern characters is partly why Defoe's narrative remains so powerful. In Defoe's novel, both Xury and Friday can speak, but, like the slaves imagined by abolitionist Thomas Pringle I discuss in chapter three, they are represented as spouting sentiments of love for their "rescuer," Crusoe: "The Boy [Xury] answer'd with so much Affection that made me love him ever after. Says he,

If wild Mans come, they eat me, you go wey."[13] In the case of the man Crusoe names Friday, Crusoe is even the one who teaches him to speak English:

> At last he lays His Head flat upon the Ground, close to my Foot, and sets my other Foot upon his Head, as he had done before; and after this; made all the Signs to me of Subjection, Servitude, and Submission imaginable, to let me know, how he would serve me as long as he liv'd.... In a little Time I began to speak to him, and teach him to speak to me; and first I made him know his name should be Friday.... I likewise taught him to say Master, and then let him know, that was to be my Name.[14]

Once again, the foot plays a crucial part in the interpretive work Crusoe performs in translating signs from the empirical world into meaning: signs of subjection, servitude, and submission, which translate effortlessly into a language of subjection, servitude, and submission.[15] If Defoe's novel returns us to the eighteenth century, where this book began with Caesar van Madagascar, Colin Roberts's invocation of Friday and footprints on the beach should remind us that these issues—of speech and silence, presence or absence, settling and expulsion—are still very relevant today. Exiled Chagossians struggle to make their voices legally legible in the face of the remnants of British imperial might, and other minority voices are silenced by the conventions—legal and literary—that constrain the ways in which thoughts, emotions, and experiences can be expressed.

These forms of constraint include, as I have shown throughout this book, seemingly neutral conventions, like the conventions of legal verisimilitude I examined in eighteenth-century court records, or abolitionist use of sentimental tropes to make the case against slavery. Sentiment can also be explicitly weaponized, as in the case of settler narratives with sentimental claims to the land, where what seems to be a literary trope can infiltrate legal theorization (as we saw in the case of apartheid legal theory). Sentiment, in both fictional and legal documents, is a weapon easily mobilized by those in power, and hard to deploy as a form of resistance. The Indian Ocean as a briny South site of oppression and solidarity, speech and silence, can help us revisit or discover other connected histories of marginalization and displacement with this suspicion of sentiment firmly in place.

NOTES

INTRODUCTION

1 Worden and Groenewald, *Trials of Slavery*, 613. My translations throughout, with reference to the translations provided by Worden and Groenewald.
2 Simon Gikandi suggests that the challenge to scholars of the Black Atlantic is to "recover black subjectivity in bondage." Gikandi, "Rethinking the Archive of Enslavement," 91.
3 Worden and Groenwald, *Trials of Slavery*, 612–13.
4 For studies of Indian Ocean displacement, see, for example, Clare Anderson and Kerry Ward on convicts in the British and Dutch empires, respectively; Nira Wickramasinghe on slavery in British Ceylon; Megan Vaughan on slavery in Mauritius; Pier M. Larson on slavery in Madagascar; Marina Carter and Khal Torabully on indenture in Mauritius; and Robert Shell on slavery at the Cape. Anderson, *Subaltern Lives*; Ward, *Networks of Empire*; Wickramasinghe, *Slave in a Palanquin*; Vaughan, *Creating the Creole Island*; Larson, *History and Memory*; Carter and Torabully, *Coolitude*; Shell, *Children of Bondage*.
5 My understanding of these terms is influenced by the work of affect theorist Sianne Ngai, who summarizes the differences between *affect* and *emotion* in *Ugly Feelings*. Ngai, *Ugly Feelings*.
6 Lowe, *Intimacies of Four Continents*, 7.
7 Ann Laura Stoler points out that, far from separating reason from emotion, Dutch colonial governance was particularly interested in sentiment. She argues that "the 'political rationalities' of Dutch colonial authority—those strategically reasoned forms of administrative common sense informing policy and practice—were grounded in the management of such affective states, in assessing both appropriate sentiments and those that threatened to fly 'out of control.'" I draw on her understanding of sentiment and its role in governance and racialization in my analysis. Stoler, *Along the Archival Grain*, 59.
8 Gandhi, *The Grievances of the British Indians*, 361. I return to Gandhi's writings in chapter three.
9 Pringle, "Slavery at the Cape of Good Hope." I return to Pringle's writings in chapter two.

10 For a summary of developments in ocean studies, see Bystrom and Hofmeyr, "Oceanic Routes." For more on the Global South as a framework in literary studies, see Mahler, "Global South," and Armillas-Tiseyra and Mahler, "Introduction: New Critical Directions."

11 "briny, adj.1," OED Online, accessed June 1, 2020, https://www.oed.com/view/Entry/23400.

12 Regarding the nongeographic nature of the South in the Global South, Magalí Armillas-Tiseyra argues that a "non-locational understanding of 'Southness'" allows for "wide-ranging and flexible frameworks of association rooted in the identification of processes and shared experiences rather than location." Armillas-Tiseyra, *The Dictator Novel*, 20–21. For more on moving away from traditional geographic notions in ocean studies, see Cohen, "The Global Indies."

13 For other potential uses of the framework of the *briny South*, see Boer, "The Briny South."

14 For an overview of the Indian Ocean world, see Chaudhuri, *Asia before Europe*; Pearson, *The Indian Ocean*; and Bose, *A Hundred Horizons*. For more on early Indian Ocean systems of slavery and bondage, see the various case studies found in these edited volumes: Reid, *Slavery, Bondage*; Campbell, *Structure of Slavery*; Campbell and Stanziani, *Bonded Labour*; Chatterjee and Eaton, *Slavery and South Asian History*; and Alpers, Campbell, and Salman, *Slavery and Resistance*.

15 For more on the history of Indian Ocean slavery under European empires, see, especially, Allen, "Satisfying," and Schrikker and Wickramasinghe, *Being a Slave*. Marcus Vink, in an overview of Dutch slavery in the Indian Ocean in the seventeenth century, estimates that, in 1688, there were about four thousand company-enslaved persons and sixty-six thousand individuals enslaved by private slaveholders spread out in settlements across the Indian Ocean. The main overseas Dutch entrepots at the time were Batavia (Java) and Colombo in Ceylon. Vink, "The World's Oldest Trade," 167.

16 Crais and McClendon, "The Necessity of Slavery," 47–48.

17 For more historical background on nineteenth-century indenture, see Northrup, *Indentured Labor*; Tinker, *A New System of Slavery*; Jung, *Coolies and Cane*; and Shimpo et al., "Asian Indentured and Colonial Migration."

18 For a comprehensive bibliography of the second South African War, see van Hartesveldt, *The Boer War*.

19 War Office, *General Questions*, 4–5.

20 One very influential argument on connected histories is Subrahmanyam, "Connected Histories."

21 Lionnet and Shih, *Minor Transnationalism*.

22 Doyle, *Inter-Imperiality*, 4.

23 Stoler, *Along the Archival Grain*; Smallwood, "The Politics of the Archive," 125; Best, *None Like Us*, 25–26.

24 Spivak, "Can the Subaltern Speak?"

25 Berlant, "Intuitionists," 847.

26 Hartman, "Venus in Two Acts," 4.

27 Freeburg, *Counterlife*; Best, *None Like Us*, 15.
28 Jared Sexton and Frank Wilderson's work on Afropessimism as a philosophical worldview falls into this category, as does Christina Sharpe's compelling *In the Wake: On Blackness and Being*. Wilderson, *Afropessimism*; Sexton, "Afropessimism"; Sharpe, *In the Wake*.
29 Best, *The Fugitive's Properties*.
30 On the use of slavery as an allegory for apartheid in literature, see Johnson, "Representing Cape Slavery."
31 Gqola stresses the "ongoing entanglements" of the past with the present that produce what she calls the "cost of rememorying"—that "changes the present as well as conceptualisations of the past." Gqola, *What Is Slavery to Me?*, 19.

CHAPTER 1. REPRESENTING SPEECH IN BONDAGE IN THE COURT RECORDS OF THE DUTCH CABO DE GOEDE HOOP, 1652–1795

1 Cupido van Mallebaar, quoted in Worden and Groenewald, *Trials of Slavery*, 163. My translations throughout, with reference to the translations provided by Worden and Groenewald. Sequential quotations from *Trials of Slavery* are indicated by in-text parenthetical citations with the name of the person accused and year, as well as the page number from *Trials of Slavery*. In some cases I have consulted additional archival documents not published by Worden and Groenewald. These are indicated in the text by the abbreviation CJ (Council of Justice) and their archival reference number. While I have largely attempted to preserve the long sentences and convoluted references of the original, I have added quotation marks to instances of direct speech for ease of comprehension.
2 Gikandi, "Rethinking the Archive of Enslavement," 91, emphasis added.
3 Hartman, "Venus in Two Acts," 3.
4 For a discussion of the enslaved as represented in French legal systems in Mauritius and Louisiana, respectively, see Vaughan and White. Matthias van Rossum, Alexander Geelen, Bram van den Hout, and Merve Tosun have published a collection of court cases from Cochin on the Malabar Coast under the Dutch. Nira Wickramsinghe's *Slave in a Palanquin* looks at court cases from Ceylon, but in the period I study in the next chapter, after the British take over these Dutch colonies in 1795. Vaughan, *Creating the Creole Island*; White, *Voices of the Enslaved*; van Rossum et al., *Testimonies of Enslavement*; Wickramasinghe, *Slave in a Palanquin*.
5 Christopher Freeburg elaborates on these dichotomies and the historiography of slavery in the Black Atlantic. Freeburg, *Counterlife*.
6 Worden and Groenewald, *Trials of Slavery*, 163.
7 Lynn Festa charts the use of the term *sentimental* as well as the link between sentimental writing and sympathy as understood in the eighteenth century in Festa, *Sentimental Figures of Empire*.
8 Worden and Groenewald, *Trials of Slavery*, 163.
9 Festa, *Sentimental Figures of Empire*.

10 Diana Paton's analysis of the use of spectacular punishment for slaves in Jamaica is useful for understanding the role these forms of punishment play in colonial societies, as is Marisa J. Fuentes's reading of the punishment of female slaves in colonial Bridgetown, Barbados. Paton, "Punishment, Crime, and the Bodies of Slaves"; Fuentes, *Dispossessed Lives*.

11 Out of ninety-seven sentences of being broken on a cross in the eighteenth century, ninety-two were handed out to slaves and Khoisan servants. Among the free population of the Cape, including burghers, sailors, soldiers, and VOC servants, the death sentence was also handed out with great frequency, but usually involved hanging. Death by firing squad was reserved exclusively for free men, and drowning was the usual punishment for sodomy (a crime of which slaves and Khoi seemed not to have been accused). Other forms of punishment at the Cape included being executed with the murder weapon displayed above the head, having chunks of flesh pincered from the body with hot tongs, having hands chopped off, or being broken on the wheel. These punishments were almost exclusively used for the enslaved, excepting cases of unusual magnitude among the general population (such as large-scale insurrection against the VOC). Heese, *Reg en Onreg*.

12 Paton, writing on eighteenth-century Jamaica, states that very few legal records regarding slave crimes survive from Jamaica and other British Caribbean societies, since the slave courts failed to keep accurate day-to-day records, and newspaper accounts of court proceedings only start appearing in the 1780s. Her source for eighteenth-century Jamaica is a summary of the decisions of slave courts in St. Andrews between 1746 and 1782, made in 1834, which survived because it was apparently sent accidentally to London among unrelated documents. Paton, "Punishment, Crime, and the Bodies of Slaves."

13 Natalie Zemon Davis has produced an excellent description of legal pluralism in Dutch Suriname, which largely focuses on links between African justice systems and the enslaved experience of Dutch justice. Her work also gestures to the richness of the Dutch legal archives and, taking into account the differences between the VOC and the Dutch West India Company, is a very useful resource for understanding the workings of Dutch legal systems outside the metropole. Scholars such as Herman Bennett and Ana Hontanilla have also examined Spanish colonial legal records to understand the experience of slavery in the New World. Davis, "Judges, Masters, Diviners"; Bennett, *Africans in Colonial Mexico*; Hontanilla, "Sentiment and the Law."

14 The volumes in the National Archive in The Hague are copies of the records from the Cape sent back to the Netherlands.

15 Theal, *Records of the Cape Colony*, vol. 9, 153.

16 Theal, *Records of the Cape Colony*, vol. 9, 152.

17 See, for example, Böeseken, *Slaves and Free Blacks at the Cape*; Elphick and Giliomee, *The Shaping of South African Society*; Shell, *Children of Bondage*; Worden, *Slavery*; Loos, *Echoes of Slavery*; Penn, *Rogues, Rebels and Runaways*; Ross, *Cape of Torments*. Hershini Bhana Young performs an excellent literary analysis of

the afterlife of one of these court cases, that of Tryntie/Tryntjie van Madagascar, in historiography and fiction, in Young, *Illegible Will*. Authors that have used these sources as inspiration for their creative work include André P. Brink, Rayda Jacobs, Nadia Davids, Dalene Matthee, Karen Press, Karel Schoeman, Dan Sleigh, and Yvette Christiansë. *Cargo* (2007) is an innovative collaboratively written performance piece (directed by Mark Fleishman) incorporating the archives of slavery.

18   This approach is indebted to Natalie Zemon Davis's reading of sixteenth-century French pardon letters in *Fiction in the Archives*, as well as Ann Laura Stoler's readings of Dutch imperial records in *Along the Archival Grain*. While examining a different type of imperial subject in these Cape archives (Stoler largely focuses on colonial officers and their evolving epistemology of governance), I also focus on "archival form" as she describes it: "prose style, repetitive refrain, the arts of persuasion, affective strains that shape 'rational' response, categories of confidentiality and classification and not least, genres of documentation." Davis, *Fiction in the Archives*; Stoler, *Along the Archival Grain*, 20.

19   Festa, *Sentimental Figures of Empire*, 8.

20   Robert Shell estimates that, of the total foreign-born slave population at the Cape from 1652 to 1808, 26.4 percent came from East Africa (mostly Mozambique), 25.1 percent from Madagascar and the other Mascarene islands, 25.9 percent from South Asia, and 22.7 percent from Southeast Asia. Shell, *Children of Bondage*, 41. Nigel Worden gives a detailed breakdown of slave origins and numbers in Worden, "Indian Ocean Slaves in Cape Town." Linda Mbeki and Matthias van Rossum investigate the origins and networks of both the enslaved and enslavers at the Cape of Good Hope and Cochin (Mbeki and Van Rossum, "Private Slave Trade.")

21   Shell, *Children of Bondage*, 40–43. A further difference between the WIC and the VOC in relation to slavery is that, as Kerry Ward has it, "Unlike its smaller and more limited counterpart, the Dutch West India Company, the Dutch East India Company did not derive its main source of revenue from its trade in slaves. Its slave trade was used instead as a major source of labor." Ward, *Networks of Empire*, 81. For an overview of VOC slavery in the seventeenth century, see Vink, "The World's Oldest Trade."

22   The languages spoken in everyday contexts at the Cape in this period have been the cause of some debate, largely stemming from the reluctance felt by Afrikaner nationalists to admit to the creole origins of the Afrikaans language. For more on this, see Davids, *The Afrikaans of the Cape Muslims*; Hofmeyr, "Building a Nation from Words"; Franken, *Taalhistoriese Bydraes*; and Hoogervorst, "Kanala, Tamaaf, Tramkassie."

23   See, for example, Shell, "The Short Life"; Newton-King, "Family, Friendship, and Survival"; Shell and Dick, "Jan Smiesing"; Worden, "Cape Slaves"; and Glenn, "Eighteenth-Century Natural History."

24   This is not to suggest that eighteenth-century Cape society did not differentiate at all between the different ethnicities of the enslaved: Robert Shell documents

the changing notions of race, and racial stereotyping, of the enslaved at the Cape, though these notions only crystallize by the end of the century (see Shell, *Children of Bondage*, 49–58). The term *Black* is, of course, also not a stable referent in British eighteenth-century discourse. Roxann Wheeler writes on the instability of racial markers in *The Complexion of Race*.

25 For more on Southeast Asian exiles and convicts at the Cape, see Ward, *Networks of Empire*; Anderson, *Subaltern Lives*; and Jappie, "Many Makassars."

26 For more on nomenclature, see Carter and Wickramasinghe, "Forcing the Archive."

27 Some theorists of slavery at the Cape of Good Hope have suggested that the experiences of Khoisan peoples differed very little from those of the enslaved and thus refer to both enslaved persons and Khoisan laborers during this period as slaves. In this book, I hew to the distinction made in legal records between these two groups, while not seeking to deny the suffering of the indigenous peoples while employed in what was certainly a form of bondage. See Gqola and Abrahams for arguments on how the experience of the enslaved and the Khoisan servants at the Cape aligned as forms of slavery. Gqola, *What Is Slavery to Me?*; Abrahams, "Disempowered to Consent."

28 Since it is difficult to tell whether documentation from this period refers to either the Khoikhoi (or Khoekhoe) or the Sān peoples, I will use the compound name *Khoisan* throughout. For more on European representations of these indigenous groups, see Elphick and Malherbe, "The Khoisan to 1828," and Johnson, "Representing the Cape 'Hottentots.'" Mary Louise Pratt writes eloquently on early Cape travel narratives, and specifically the depiction of indigenous people in them, in "Chapter 3: Narrating the Anti-Conquest." Pratt, *Imperial Eyes*, 37–66.

29 Lauren A. Benton describes the changing legal jurisdiction over the Khoisan peoples under the Dutch and British in "Chapter Five: Subjects and Witnesses: Cultural and Legal Hierarchies in the Cape Colony and New South Wales." Benton, *Law and Colonial Cultures*, 167–209.

30 For instances of group desertion and community formation at the Cape, see Ulrich, "Journeying into Freedom."

31 See, for example, "1735 Varken, Toontje and Ruijter" in Worden and Groenewald, *Trials of Slavery*, 129–33.

32 One case that hinged on the testimony of an enslaved woman, accused of murdering a female slaveholder at the instigation of the woman's estranged husband, has received a lot of attention from scholars of slavery at the Cape. Tryntie van Madagascar's case is discussed in great detail by historian Nigel Penn and literary theorist Hershini Bhana Young, who performs a critical reading of Penn's microhistory of this case as reinforcing gendered stereotypes. Another intriguing case in which the testimony of an enslaved woman played a large role was that of Coenraad Appel in 1775—he was accused of having sex with his stepdaughter ("1775 Coenraad Appel," Worden and Groenewald, 460–68). Tryntie (Tryntjie, Trijntje) van Madagascar's Council of Justice records (CJ 782) are reprinted (in Dutch) in Heese, *Reg en Onreg*, 113–21. Penn, *Rogues, Rebels and Runaways*, 9–72; Young, *Illegible Will*, 73–107.

33 Catharina van Palliacatte, later known as Catharina van Bengal or Groote Catrijn (Big Catrijn), is a fascinating figure in the early history of the Cape, where she was eventually manumitted, married another freed slave, and became a slaveholder herself. See Upham, "*Groote Catrijn*."
34 Böeseken, *Uit die Raad van Justisie*.
35 De Wet, "Bestuurstinstellinge."
36 Ward describes the uneven and evolving system of governance that this multiplicity of legal sources of authority produced in *Networks of Empire*.
37 Theal, *Records of the Cape Colony*, vol. 9, 146.
38 Tannen, *Talking Voices*, 125.
39 For more on *amok*, see Bradlow, "Mental Illness."
40 Italics as in original. Kindersley, *Letters from the Island of Teneriffe*, 67. For more on the development of "Malay" as a racial identity during this period, see the special issue (vol. 32, no. 3 [October 2001]) of the *Journal of Southeast Asian Studies* on this topic, particularly the articles by Shamsul A. B. and Anthony Reid.
41 Sparrman, *A Voyage to the Cape of Good Hope*, 345. For more on Sparrman, see Pratt, *Imperial Eyes*, 48–56.
42 Worden and Groenewald, *Trials of Slavery*, 338.
43 Portuguese, the imperative form of *pegar* (to seize, nab). As explained in Worden and Groenewald, *Trials of Slavery*, 103, note 5.
44 The increased liveliness of the court records could perhaps be ascribed to the appointment of Adriaan van Kervel as fiscal in 1724. Earlier and later fiscals, however, also include direct speech in their claims. The cases I examine at length in this chapter are prosecuted by van Kervel (1724–1730), Daniel van den Henghel (1731–1741), and Baron Pieter van Reede van Oudtshoorn (1741–1760). See de Wet, Hatting, and Visagie, "Bylae 3: Fiskale aan die Kaap, 1652–1795."
45 Worden and Groenewald, *Trials of Slavery*, 203, 597.
46 Coetzee, "Realism," 4.
47 Barthes, "The Reality Effect," 142, 146.
48 Page, *Speech in the English Novel*, 11.
49 Page, *Speech in the English Novel*, 4.
50 Worden and Groenewald, *Trials of Slavery*, 169–70.
51 Page, *Speech in the English Novel*, 2.
52 Hunter, *Before Novels*, 193.
53 Hunter, *Before Novels*, 197.
54 Heinrich Heine is supposed to have said that if the world ended, he would want to move to the Netherlands, where everything happens fifty years later. In two instances that partly support this apocryphal aphorism, the first Dutch novel is published in 1782, sixty-three years after *Robinson Crusoe*, and abolition in the Dutch colonies happens in 1863, thirty years after the British Slavery Abolition Act is passed.
55 Barthes, "The Reality Effect," 148.
56 White, *Voices of the Enslaved*, 6.
57 White, *Voices of the Enslaved*, 11.

58   Vaughan, *Creating the Creole Island*, 82.
59   Vaughan, *Creating the Creole Island*, 82.
60   For a more detailed analysis of the power relations exemplified by the interrogation at this period in Europe, see Niehaus, *Mord, Geständnis, Widerruf*.
61   Worden and Groenewald, *Trials of Slavery*, 116.
62   Council of Justice Records (CJ), 1652–1843. Western Cape Archives and Records Services, Cape Town, South Africa. References in parentheses.
63   Worden and Groenewald, *Trials of Slavery*, 116.
64   For example, Claas van Bengalen threatens to "suck the blood" of his fellow slave, August van Malabar, and when the two come to grips, August says, "You said you wanted to suck my blood, now come!"—whereupon Claas bit him on the cheek (Claas van Bengalen 1744, Worden and Groenewald, *Trials of Slavery*, 234).
65   Worden and Groenewald, *Trials of Slavery*, 265.
66   Kazanjian, "Freedom's Surprise," 136.
67   Kazanjian, "Freedom's Surprise," 140.
68   Davis, *Fiction in the Archives*, 2.
69   Davis, *Fiction in the Archives*, 4.
70   Michel Foucault's reflections on the evolution of the inquisitory legal system and the necessity of the confession within it are pertinent to understanding the role of the confession in the Dutch legal system at the Cape. Foucault, *Wrong-doing, Truth-telling*.
71   Worden and Groenewald, *Trials of Slavery*, 264.
72   As Worden and Groenewald explain, "The *poolsche bok* was a way of tying somebody up: the hands are tied together and put over the drawn-up knees, after which a stick or something like it is inserted under the knees and across the arms, thereby rendering a person completely defenseless." *Trials of Slavery*, 267, note 4.
73   Walker, *Jamaica Ladies*, 23. For female violence against the enslaved, see specifically "Chapter Three: Plantations."
74   Worden and Groenewald, *Trials of Slavery*, 264.
75   Bakhtin, *The Dialogic Imagination*, 263.
76   Bakhtin, *The Dialogic Imagination*, 263.
77   Bakhtin, *The Dialogic Imagination*, 350. Bakhtin here specifically references (but does not develop) the potential for analysis offered by confession.
78   Hartman, "Venus in Two Acts," 2.
79   Hartman, *Scenes of Subjection*; Johnson, "On Agency"; Fuentes, *Dispossessed Lives*.
80   Freeburg, *Counterlife*, 18. Stephanie E. Smallwood, Stephen Best, and Walter Johnson provide more elaborate descriptions of the different stages of historiography on slavery in the Black Atlantic. Smallwood, "The Politics of the Archive"; Best, *None Like Us*; Johnson, "On Agency."
81   Hartman, "Venus in Two Acts," 5, 7.
82   Hartman, "Venus in Two Acts," 10.
83   Hartman, "Venus in Two Acts," 11.

84 Hartman, "Venus in Two Acts," 11.
85 Smallwood, "The Politics of the Archive," 125.
86 The next chapter of this book begins by looking at a similar case at the Cape Colony, where an 1825 slave insurrection is understood as being inspired by rumors of freedom.
87 Best, *None Like Us*, 115.
88 Best, *None Like Us*, 124.
89 Best, *None Like Us*, 126, citing Michel de Certeau, "Vocal Utopias: Glossolalias," *Representations* 56 (1996): 29–47.
90 Best, *None Like Us*, 128.
91 Worden and Groenewald, *Trials of Slavery*, 324–25. Jessica Murray examines this case in greater detail in Murray, "Gender and Violence."
92 Mbembe, "The Power of the Archive and Its Limits," 25.
93 Cited in Johnson, "Representing Cape Slavery," 511.
94 Christiansë, "Heartsore," n.p.
95 Pratt makes a related observation on the depiction of indigenous people at the Cape in travel narratives, when she identifies early travel writer Peter Kolb's narrative (published in 1719 in German) as "especially in comparison with subsequent ones, strikingly dialogic in character. Khoikhoi persons are often quoted (though never in their own language), or represented as speaking for themselves." As she adds, however, this same dialogism is entirely absent from Kolb's portrayals of the enslaved: "The dialogic dimension vanishes; it is not the words, but the silent non-screams of the tortured slaves that are recorded." This foreshadows the portrayals of the enslaved we will see in the next chapter. Pratt, *Imperial Eyes*, 43, 47.
96 Tannen, *Talking Voices*, 133.

CHAPTER 2. SILENCING THE ENSLAVED

1 Theal, *Records of the Cape Colony*, vol. 20, 188–341. The names of Galant's fellow accused are as follows: "Galant, formerly a Slave of the late W. N. van der Merwe, 2. Abel, Slave of B. van der Merwe, 3. Isaak Rooy, and 4. Isaak Thys, Hottentots in the service of the late W. N. van der Merwe, 5. Hendrik, a Hottentot in the service of Jan Dalree, 6. Klaas, Slave of Barend van der Merwe, 7. Achilles, and 8. Antony, formerly Slaves of the late W. N. van der Merwe, 9. Valentyn, and 10. Vlak, Hottentots formerly in the service of the late W. N. van der Merwe, 11. Adonis, Slave of J. A. du Plessis, 12. Pamela, formerly a Slave of the late W. N. van der Merwe, and 13. Petrus Josephus de Campher, Inhabitant." Theal, *Records of the Cape Colony*, vol. 20, 188.
2 For a historian's account of this uprising, see Ross, *Cape of Torments*, 96–166. For a heavily romanticized novelistic account, see André P. Brink, *A Chain of Voices*. Stephen Best's discussion of rumor, and specifically rumors regarding the emancipation of the enslaved, in the Caribbean archives of the nineteenth century offers a comparative lens through which to read this case. Best, *None Like Us*, 107–32.
3 Theal, *Records of the Cape Colony*, vol. 20, 194.

4   Theal, *Records of the Cape Colony*, vol. 20, 196–97. Testimony by other accused clarify that the "curse" that the fiscal censors is a moment in which Galant, confronting one of the slaveholders who was attempting to negotiate with the group, calls out "*Moerneuker* [Mother-fucker]! Do you still prate?" before getting his accomplice to fire on him. If we can believe the testimony as recorded, it is intriguing that in this instance, it is an enslaved man telling a slaveholder to stop talking—an evocative reversal of the silencing of the enslaved I discuss in this chapter. Theal, *Records of the Cape Colony*, vol. 20, 223.
5   Theal, *Records of the Cape Colony*, vol. 20, 199.
6   Theal, *Records of the Cape Colony*, vol. 20, 322.
7   Manjapra, *Colonialism in Global Perspective*, 10.
8   As Marisa J. Fuentes writes on debates on slavery in Britain, "Though constantly evoked in the Privy Council report, enslaved women (and men) are excluded from recounting their own violations except through the voices and interpretations of various classes of white men. This archival silence effectively mutes the very subjects of this inquiry and profoundly suppresses enslaved subjectivity, not only in the moment of its creation but also in its subsequent uses in histories of the abolition movement." In chapter five of *Slavery on Trial*, Jeanine Marie DeLombard elaborates on this effect of white advocacy in American abolitionist discourse through her discussion of Harriet Beecher Stowe's novel *Dred*, in which the legal representation of the enslaved forms the central theme. Fuentes, *Dispossessed Lives*, 129; DeLombard, *Slavery on Trial*, 151–76.
9   For more on abolition and antislavery activism in Britain, see Brown, *Moral Capital*; and Carey and Kitson, *Slavery and the Cultures of Abolition*.
10 "Questionnaire Relative to Slaves," 1–4.
11 Crais and McClendon, "The Necessity of Slavery," 47–48.
12 Mason, *Social Death and Resurrection*, 16–17.
13 Mason, *Social Death and Resurrection*, 17.
14 The authoritative social history on slavery in the Cape Colony during this period (1795–1835) is Mason, *Social Death and Resurrection*.
15 Hartman, *Scenes of Subjection*; Festa, *Sentimental Figures*; Fuentes, *Dispossessed Lives*; DeLombard, *Slavery on Trial*; Brown, *Moral Capital*.
16 Ogborn, "The Power of Speech," 121.
17 Cited in Ogborn, "The Power of Speech," 114–15.
18 Ogborn, "The Power of Speech," 116.
19 For more on the complexities of these laws across various states, see Morris, "Slaves and the Rules of Evidence."
20 For slavery in British Ceylon, see Wickramasinghe, *Slave in a Palanquin*.
21 For more on Cape Town as seen from both the Atlantic and the Indian Ocean, see Hofmeyr, "The Black Atlantic."
22 Travelers' accounts of eighteenth- and nineteenth-century Cape Town sometimes contained statements against slavery (including those of Lady Anne Barnard, Anders Sparrmann, John Barrow, and Cowper Rose), but mostly as part of descriptions of the customs and characters the travelers encountered, rather than

the more deliberately polemical writings of Thomas Pringle. For more on Cape abolitionist movements, see Voss, "The Slaves Must Be Heard."

23 Pringle, "Slavery at the Cape of Good Hope," 104. Page numbers henceforth cited as in-text parentheses.
24 For more on Pringle's life and work, see Vigne, *Thomas Pringle*; Masemola, "The Memory of Pringle as Prospero"; Coetzee, "The Poems of Thomas Pringle"; Shaw, "Thomas Pringle's Plantation"; and Voss, "The Personalities of Thomas Pringle." One of the most interesting sources on Pringle is Zoë Wicomb's novel *Still Life*.
25 Pringle, "Slavery at the Cape of Good Hope," 105–6.
26 Pringle, "Slavery at the Cape of Good Hope," 106.
27 Prince, *The History of Mary Prince*, 64.
28 Pringle, "Slavery at the Cape of Good Hope," 106.
29 See, for example, the cases of Cupido van Mallebaar and Jephta van Batavia discussed in the previous chapter.
30 Hartman, *Scenes of Subjection*, 4.
31 Pringle, "Slavery at the Cape of Good Hope," 108.
32 In the volume of Pringle's *South African Letters*, published in 2011, I failed to identify a likely correspondent (Pringle seems to have kept his work on the "Report on Slavery" quiet while still in South Africa). Pringle, *South African Letters*.
33 Pringle, "Slavery at the Cape of Good Hope," 111.
34 See Hartman, *Scenes of Subjection*, 36–42, on the auction block as a site of performance.
35 Here is the description in *The History of Mary Prince*: "I then saw my sisters led forth, and sold to different owners; so that we had not the sad satisfaction of being partners in bondage. When the sale was over, my mother hugged and kissed us, and mourned over us, begging of us to keep up a good heart, and do our duty to our new masters. It was a sad parting; one went one way, one another, and our poor mammy went home with nothing." Prince, *The History of Mary Prince*, 12.
36 For more on this, see Rauwerda, "Naming, Agency." For more on *The History of Mary Prince*, see Ferguson, *Subject to Others*; and Sharpe, "Something Akin to Freedom."
37 Pringle, "Slavery at the Cape of Good Hope," 111.
38 I will return to this question about the visual aesthetics of slavery, with a fuller discussion of the art of abolition, later in this chapter.
39 Pringle, "Slavery at the Cape of Good Hope," 111.
40 Pringle, "Slavery at the Cape of Good Hope," 108.
41 Coetzee, *White Writing*, 45.
42 Debbie Lee dates Romanticism from "somewhere in the 1780s (with Blake's publications) . . . [to] somewhere between 1832 (with the passing of the Reform Bill) and 1850 (with Wordsworth's death)." Lee, *Slavery and the Romantic Imagination*, 29.
43 Lee, *Slavery and the Romantic Imagination*, 29–30.
44 Discussions about Blake's *Visions of the Daughters of Albion* are legion. Some of the articles dealing specifically with slavery include Erdman, "Blake's Vision of Slavery"; Blake and Gruner, "Redeeming Captivity"; Welch, "Essence, Gender, Race"; and Bindman, "Blake's Vision of Slavery Revisited."

45 See Lee, *Slavery and the Romantic Imagination*; Thomas, *Romanticism and the Slave Narratives*; and Lively, *Masks*. Debbie Lee particularly dwells on the illustrations for *Visions of the Daughters of Albion*.
46 All subsequent quotations from Pringle, "The Bechuana Boy," reprinted in Prince, *The History of Mary Prince*, 89–93.
47 Letter to Leitch Ritchie, dated August 29, 1829, in Pringle, *The South African Letters of Thomas Pringle*, 322–23.
48 Pringle, *The South African Letters of Thomas Pringle*, x. See also Wicomb's novel *Still Life*, which is centrally concerned with this (unanswerable) question of the relationship between Hinza Marossi and the Pringles.
49 Pratt, *Imperial Eyes*, 84.
50 Blake, *The Complete Poetry and Prose*, 9.
51 Wicomb, *Still Life*, 108.
52 All subsequent quotations from Pringle, "The Slave Dealer," reprinted in Prince, *The History of Mary Prince*, 96–97.
53 These poems can be compared to other well-known abolitionist poems that confer a speaking voice onto an enslaved subject, like Thomas Day's "The Dying Negro" (1773) and William Cowper's "The Negro's Complaint" (1788). In Lynn Festa's reading of these two poems, Day's poem, by ventriloquizing a "dying" slave, stresses the futility of action regarding this particular slave and "defers the immediacy of any call to action," whereas Cowper's ballad is more effective in shifting the speaker from "victimized object to subject and agent"—a shift that is precluded to Pringle's Marossi. Festa, *Sentimental Figures of Empire*, 161–62.
54 Shell and Hudson, "Introduction to S.E. Hudson's 'Slaves,'" 46. Page numbers henceforth cited in in-text parentheses.
55 Shell and Hudson, "Introduction to S.E. Hudson's 'Slaves,'" 70, footnote 85.
56 "Negro," *Encyclopaedia Britannica*. This entry provides a snapshot of the scientific racism of the late eighteenth and nineteenth centuries and suggests why abolitionists were in some ways justified in basing their advocacy on simply attempting to prove the humanity of the enslaved.
57 Shell and Hudson, "Introduction to S.E. Hudson's 'Slaves,'" 47.
58 Lynn Festa makes a similar point when she argues that "acute sensibility and proslavery sentiments may go hand in hand; abolitionists did not possess a monopoly on sentimental feelings." Festa, *Sentimental Figures*, 178.
59 Shell and Hudson, "Introduction to S.E. Hudson's 'Slaves,'" 47.
60 Theal, *Records of the Cape Colony*, vol. 20, 317.
61 Shell and Hudson, "Introduction to S.E. Hudson's 'Slaves,'" 49.
62 Tara Menon, in a qualitative analysis of a representative sample of nineteenth-century British novels, found that on average, 36 percent of each novel consists of direct speech ("words, demarcated by quotation marks, that are conventionally understood to be the exact utterance of an individual character"). Menon, "Keeping Count," 161.
63 Christiansë, "Heartsore," n.p.
64 Christiansë, "Heartsore," n.p.

65 From the official court translation. The original reads: "Het storten van tranend te kennen gegeven, dat zy haar kind, Baro, genaamd uit hartzeer & verdriet hem [Baro] met een mes, het welk by ziy had, de keel had afgesneeden." Christiansë, "Heartsore," n.p.
66 For further reflections on *Unconfessed*, see Samuelson, "Lose Your Mother"; and Murray, "Gender and Violence."
67 Theal, *Records of the Cape Colony*, vol. 30, 43–44.
68 Theal, *Records of the Cape Colony*, vol. 30, 59.
69 Theal, *Records of the Cape Colony*, vol. 30, 71.
70 Theal, *Records of the Cape Colony*, vol. 30, 70.
71 Theal, *Records of the Cape Colony*, vol. 32, 63.
72 "Various Slave Returns, 1816–1834."
73 Smallwood, *Saltwater Slavery*, 98.
74 "Various Slave Returns, 1816–1834."
75 Gikandi, "Rethinking the Archive of Enslavement," 91.
76 McKittrick, "Mathematics Black Life," 16–17.
77 McKittrick, "Mathematics Black Life," 18.
78 Gikandi, *Slavery and the Culture of Taste*.
79 Festa, *Sentimental Figures of Empire*, 166.
80 Festa, *Sentimental Figures of Empire*, 166.
81 For more on the visual arts of abolition, see Wood, *Blind Memory*; Finley, *Committed to Memory*; and Thomas, *Witnessing Slavery*.
82 Burke, "Essay on the Sublime," 67. Both Immanuel Kant's *Critique of Judgment* [*Kritik der Urteilskraft*] (1790), which (among other things) attempts to define the difference between the picturesque, the beautiful, and the sublime, and Burke's writings on the beautiful and the sublime were very influential on Romantic poets and artists.
83 Burke, "Essay on the Sublime," 64–65.
84 The name of the ship was originally *Zorg*, which means "care" in Dutch. She was a Dutch slaver captured by the British in 1781. Philip, *Zong!*, 208, note 1.
85 Coetzee, "Review: African Poems of Thomas Pringle," 181–82.
86 Hartman, *Scenes of Subjection*, 52–53.
87 Baderoon, *Regarding Muslims*, 12.
88 Philip, *Zong!*, 193.
89 Philip, *Zong!*, 200.
90 Philip, *Zong!*, 204.
91 Sharpe, *Immaterial Archives*, 48. See also Shockley, "Going Overboard."
92 Sharpe, *Immaterial Archives*, 56.
93 Finley, *Committed to Memory*, 12.
94 Finley, *Committed to Memory*, 36.
95 Finley, *Committed to Memory*, 11.
96 One contemporary Atlantic example of what such artwork might look like would be British painter Lubaina Himid's *Cotton.com*, a series of eighty-four small, square, black-and-white patterned oil paintings, designed to replicate patterned

cotton samples. Art historian Anna Arabindan-Kesson argues that Himid "draws on the rhythmic repetition of the grid to establish a dynamic relationship between the places cotton moved." This work demonstrates how an abstract, utilitarian object associated with the slave trade (the cotton sample) can be reimagined today, embodying a critique of earlier art practices that aestheticized the enslaved body. As Arabindan-Kesson argues, "While eighteenth-century conversation pieces depict Black figures, those figures are shown as little more than objects, even as their labor underpins the wealth and status of the white families they serve. These paintings that hide Blackness in plain sight mirror the art-historical canon more broadly in their silencing of Black subjects. . . . *Cotton.com* overturns past conventions and disrupts their foundations." Arabindan-Kesson, *Black Bodies, White Gold*, 3, 117.
97 The suggestion of turning over the page to artists or poets to process came out of a conversation with M. NourbeSe Philip following an event—I am grateful to her for thinking through this question with me, and to Lawrence Ypil for organizing the event. M. NourbeSe Philip, *The Art of Erasure*, Yale-NUS College Writers' Centre (virtual event), January 29, 2021.
98 McKittrick, *Dear Science*, 3–4.
99 Sharpe, *Immaterial Archives*, 4.

CHAPTER 3. "GRIEVANCES MORE SENTIMENTAL THAN MATERIAL"

1 "indenture, n.," OED Online, accessed June 1, 2020, https://www.oed.com/view/Entry/94314.
2 For more historical background on nineteenth-century indenture, see Northrup, *Indentured Labor*; Tinker, *A New System of Slavery*; Jung, *Coolies and Cane*; and Kumar, *Coolies of the Empire*. For the Indian Ocean context, see Desai and Vahed, *Inside Indian Indenture*; Carter, *Servants, Sirdars and Settlers*; and Metcalf, *Imperial Connections*.
3 See Elphick and Malherbe, "The Khoisan to 1828."
4 See Allen, "Slaves, Convicts, Abolitionism," for references on these systems.
5 Anderson, "Convicts and Coolies," 104.
6 For more on the sugarcane plantations in Natal, see Richardson, "The Natal Sugar Industry."
7 For more demographic information on the indentured laborers who traveled to Natal, see Bhana, *Indentured Indians in Natal*. While this chapter focuses on South Asian indentured labor in Natal, the broader South African context also saw other forms of indentured and migrant labor. See, for example, Harries, "Slavery, Indenture," on migration from Mozambique during this same period; Richardson, "Chinese Indentured Labour," Kynoch, "Controlling the Coolies," and Ngai, *The Chinese Question*, on indentured labor from East Asia to Transvaal; and Moodie and Ndatshe, *Going for Gold*, on the experiences of African migrant laborers in South African mines.

8   For an extensive bibliography of writing on Mohandas K. Gandhi, see Pandiri, *Comprehensive, Annotated Bibliography*. Sukanya Banerjee's chapter "South Africa, Indentured Labor, and the Question of Credit" in *Becoming Imperial Citizens* sets Gandhi's writings on indentured labor in the context of the larger discourse on this issue in South Africa and India, while Goolam Vahed's 2019 article "'An Evil Thing': Gandhi and Indian Indentured Labour in South Africa, 1893–1914" summarizes and expands upon much of the research that has been done on Gandhi and the question of indentured labor in South Africa. Banerjee, *Becoming Imperial Citizens*, 75–115; Vahed, "An Evil Thing." For more on Gandhi's newspaper *Indian Opinion*, which he founded in South Africa, see Hofmeyr, *Gandhi's Printing Press*.
9   Gandhi, "Letter to the *Transvaal Advertiser*."
10 For more on the complexity of the Passenger Indian identity, see Dhupelia-Mesthrie, "The Passenger Indian as Worker."
11 Lowe, *The Intimacies of Four Continents*, 25.
12 The first Tamil-English dictionary, from 1862, translates the word கூலி (*kūli*) as follows:

    1. Hire, wages, pay; daily pay
    2. Fare freight
    3. Rent, commonly in composition
    4. A hired servant [for this fourth definition, it indicates that for this sense, kūli is usually followed by the word "karar" which mean a person who does some kind of work].

    Winslow, *Winslow's*. My thanks to Cecilia van Hollen for this reference. The *Oxford English Dictionary* describes the term as "of uncertain origin" ("coolie, n.," OED Online, accessed July 20, 2022, https://www.oed.com/view/Entry/40991). The earliest documented use in English is 1622, in Dutch, 1642, and in Portuguese, 1581. Hugh Tinker has an extensive discussion of the term *coolie* and adds a different potential etymology: "The term appears in Chinese in two characters *k'u* (bitter) and *li* (strength)," though the word is considered by lexicographers to be of foreign origin (41). For a longer discussion of the term, see Tinker, *A New System of Slavery*.
13 Worden and Groenewald, *Trials of Slavery*, 63, footnote 6.
14 Jung, *Coolies and Cane*, 5. Using data from one of the Natal newspapers, the *Mercury*, Kathryn Pillay discusses the emergence and solidification of *coolie* as a racial identity in public discourse in Natal in the time of indenture: Pillay, "The Coolies Here."
15 *Natal Ordinances*.
16 Stoler, "Colonial Archives and the Arts of Governance," 104–5.
17 *Report of Coolie Commission*, 14.
18 *Report of Coolie Commission*, 14.
19 Gandhi, *The Grievances of the British Indians*, 360. Page numbers henceforth cited with in-text parentheses.
20 Banerjee, *Becoming Imperial Citizens*, 76.

21 Gandhi, *The Grievances of the British Indians*, 361.
22 For example, "Genuine and Sentimental Grievances" in the editorial of the *Boston Medical and Surgical Journal*, November 1898, in which the board compared "fantastical" fault finding with "really just and proper criticisms" (478), or the distinction between "substantial" and "sentimental" grievances in "Summary of the Claims of the Medical Officers or the Army and Navy to Military Rewards and Distinctions," *The Lancet*, September 22, 1849. Anthony Trollope, in his 1873 volumes on Australia and New Zealand, contrasts "sentimental grievances" with "material advantages." Trollope, *Australia and New Zealand*, 75.
23 Gandhi, *The Grievances of the British Indians*, 361.
24 See Lynn Festa on the dangers of sentimental appeals in English parliamentary debates, for example, and Christopher Leslie Brown on the contingency of the moral prestige of the antislavery movement in Britain. See Madhavi Kale (discussed below) on the inefficacy of appeals to abolitionist sentiments in framing the debate on indenture in the nineteenth century. Lynn Festa, *Sentimental Figures of Empire*; Brown, *Moral Capital*; Kale, *Fragments of Empire*.
25 Gandhi, *The Grievances of the British Indians*, 373.
26 See Hartman, *Scenes of Subjection*.
27 Gandhi, *The Grievances of the British Indians*, 367.
28 Bhana and Pachai, "Charge of Assault against an Estate Manager."
29 Bhana and Pachai, "Complaint of Ill-Treatment on an Estate."
30 S. Bhana Collection, n.p.
31 S. Bhana Collection, n.p.
32 S. Bhana Collection, n.p.
33 S. Bhana Collection, n.p.
34 S. Bhana Collection, n.p.
35 Sharma, *I Even Regret Night*; Arya, *Ritual Songs and Folksongs*.
36 *kuulii naam dharaayaa kuulii naam dharaayaa*
    Natalwaa me aai ke bhajan karo bhayaa
    haath mee cambu kaandh mee kudaari
    pardesiyaa ghare jaaii (Mesthrie, "New Lights from Old Languages," 204; my translation).

    Meshtrie provides a slightly different translation:
    They've given you the name "coolie," they've given you the name "coolie"
    You've come to Natal, give thanks in song, brother
    With a cambu in your hand, and a hoe on your shoulder
    Let the foreigners go home

    My thanks to Ameeta Saini, Birendra Sinha, and Chitra Venkataramani for help with the translation.
37 Mesthrie, "New Lights from Old Languages," 204.
38 Mesthrie, "New Lights from Old Languages," 204. A *bhajan* is described as "a type of devotional song that does not have a set metrical structure. Bhajans often contain lyrics that praise deities and can be used as part of religious worship

ceremonies. Since they are written in the vernacular and not in Sanskrit, they are intended for use by lay people." Mohabir, "Translating," 195.
39 Vahed, "An Evil Thing," 655.
40 Young, *Illegible Will*, 161.
41 A 2003 BBC documentary, for example, was titled *Coolies: How Britain Reinvented Slavery* and begins, "Shipped under agreements they could neither read nor understand, they didn't know where they were going, and most of them never made it home." Ashutosh Kumar offers a more comprehensive historiography of the trends in scholarly discourse about indenture in Kumar, *Coolies of the Empire*.
42 Kale, "Capital Spectacles in British Frames," 131.
43 Kale, *Fragments of Empire*, 35–36.
44 Scoble, *British Guiana*, 3.
45 Scoble, *British Guiana*, 2.
46 Scoble, *British Guiana*, 3.
47 Kale, *Fragments of Empire*, 36.
48 "Introduction," 1521.
49 Ghosh, *Sea of Poppies*, 75.
50 See, for example, Frost, "Amitav Ghosh"; Anderson, "Empire and Exile"; Burton, "Amitav Ghosh's World Histories"; Ahuja, "Capital at Sea"; Arora, "The Sea Is History"; and Kent, "Ship-Siblings."
51 Ghosh, *Sea of Poppies*, 11.
52 Anderson, "Empire and Exile," 1529.
53 Desai, "The Novelist as Linkister."
54 Forter, *Critique and Utopia*, 30.
55 Forter, *Critique and Utopia*, 32.
56 Desai, "Novelist as Linkister," 1533.
57 Allen, "Slaves, Convicts, Abolitionism," 329.
58 Mishra, *Literature of the Indian Diaspora*, 22. *Girmitiya*, from agreement (*girmit*), was one of the terms by which indentured laborers became known.
59 Cited in Carter and Torabully, *Coolitude*, 11. In Mauritius, Torabully's voice is one among several creative writers reflecting on the experience and legacy of indenture, including Nathacha Appanah, Ananda Devi, and Amal Sewtohul. Theorists like Véronique Bragard, Françoise Lionnet, and Françoise Vergès take the literature of the Mascarenes as a starting point for theorizing diaspora and creolization. See, for example, Bragard, *Transoceanic Dialogues*; Lionnet, "Shipwrecks, Slavery"; and Vergès, *Monsters and Revolutionaries*.
60 Sanadhya, *My Twenty-One Years*; Khan, *Jeevan Prakash*. For comparative surveys of the literatures of indenture, see Mishra, *Literature of the Indian Diaspora*; Pirbhai, *Mythologies of Migration*; and Bragard, *Transoceanic Dialogues*.
61 Gosine, "After Indenture," 65 (emphasis added).
62 Carlson, "[Coolitude]," 286–87.
63 Kumar, *Coolies of the Empire*, 125.
64 Kumar, *Coolies of the Empire*, 150. Usharbudh Arya, who collected the songs of Hindus in Suriname in 1968, makes a similar observation regarding which

songs had been preserved from India and which lost: "Bārahmāsā songs, which describe the weather and attitudes towards the twelve months of the year, have not been heard in Surinam because the weather in Surinam is not divided into seasons." Arya, *Ritual Songs and Folksongs*, 3.

65 Sharma, *I Even Regret Night*, 35, Mohabir's translation. A *chaupai* is "the most common form used for narrative poetry." Mohabir, "Translating as a Practice," 195–96.

66 Sharma, *I Even Regret Night*, 34. This is the transliteration provided by Mohabir in the section titled "Transliteration for Chautal Singers," in Sharma, *I Even Regret Night*, 169.

67 Sharma, *I Even Regret Night*, 43. A *kavitt* is a "poem written in quatrains whose rhythm is meant to correspond with the movements of a kathak dancer." Mohabir, "Translating as a Practice," 196.

68 Bahadur, "Afterword," 182. Bahadur writes more extensively on this collection of songs in Bahadur, *Coolie Woman*.

CHAPTER 4. A SENTIMENTAL EDUCATION IN BOER WAR IMPRISONMENT CAMPS IN SOUTH ASIA, 1899–1902

1 Brink, *Recollections of a Boer Prisoner-of-War*, 51. Page numbers are henceforth cited with in-text parentheses. All citations are from the English translation unless noted otherwise.

2 Pratt, *Imperial Eyes*, 215.

3 For a detailed description of the evolution of the eighteenth-century Dutch (and other European) settlers at the Cape into the nineteenth-century Boers into the twentieth-century Afrikaners (to give a very rough periodization), see Giliomee, *The Afrikaners*.

4 For a comprehensive bibliography of the second South African War, see van Hartesveldt, *The Boer War*. Donal Lowry's 2000 edited volume *The South African War Reappraised* addresses many previously overlooked and marginalized perspectives. Lowry, *The South African War Reappraised*.

5 Smith and Stucki, "Colonial Development of Concentration Camps."

6 Jewell, "Using Barbaric Methods in South Africa"; Mangalo and du Pisani, "Victims."

7 Visagie, *Terug na Kommando*.

8 Hofmeyr, "South Africa's Indian Ocean," 365. The idea of transporting dissidents and prisoners across the ocean was not a new one for British functionaries. As Clare Anderson points out, "By the middle of the nineteenth century, the British colonial regime had set up a web of overseas penal settlements in Southeast Asia and the Indian Ocean." The East India Company deported numerous South Asian convicts to work in the Straits Settlements (Penang, Malacca, Singapore), Burma, Bencoolen, and Mauritius, and, following the 1857 Mutiny, the Andaman Islands. Anderson, "Convicts and Coolies," 95.

9 Anderson, "Convicts and Coolies." See also Yang, *Empire of Coolies*.

10 War Office, *General Questions*.
11 Ferreira, "Boeregeïnterneerdes in Portugal."
12 See, for example, Wessels, "Die Anglo-Boereoorlog." Most novels and short stories, at least until the 1990s, were concerned with either heroic battlefield experiences or the suffering of the women and children in the internment camps. See also Krebs, *Gender, Race*.
13 Hofmeyr, "South Africa's Indian Ocean," 367. André Wessels's *A Century of Postgraduate Anglo-Boer War (1899–1902) Studies* lists only two doctoral theses written in the period 1908–2008 on POWs, one of which focuses only on POWs in Portugal. See also Groenewald, *Bannelinge*; Wessels, *Bannelinge*; and Schoeman, *Vegter en Balling*.
14 *Arende*.
15 Diyatalawa was the largest, main camp. Ragama was the camp for the so-called troublemakers, and many of the foreign prisoners (from Europe, mostly) were held there. Mount Lavinia was used for convalescent prisoners, and Hambantota and Urugasmanhandiya were used to host prisoners who had already declared the oath of allegiance to the British king. Physical segregation into different camps was one of the techniques used by the British to reward prisoners prepared to be loyal to the British Empire and punish (and contain) ones who were seen as particularly rebellious.
16 The cyclostyle, patented in 1881, worked as follows (as described in an 1887 advert for one of these devices): "A sheet of the prepared Cyclostyle paper is fixed in printing frame. . . . The circular is then written on this sheet of paper with the Cyclostyle Pen, which consists of a wooden holder at the end of which is fixed on a pivot, a minute iridium wheel which revolves in the direction of the writing and perforates the Cyclostyle paper, making a perfect stencil composed of minute dots so close together as to appear a continuous line. In writing, you write freely and naturally. . . . The printing frame is now lifted, a sheet of ordinary paper placed under stencil, an inked roller passed over and a perfect copy obtained." "Advert for the Cyclostyle."
17 Lord Roberts, who took command of the British forces in South Africa on December 23, 1899.
18 *De Prikkeldraad: Orgaan van de Krijgsgevangenen te Diyatalawa* 1, no. 3, n.p.
19 One Reverend Bosmann writes from Diyatalawa on December 7, 1901: "But still I think this Diyatalawa climate is the best I have ever experienced. The health of the camp is simply excellent. People, in spite of the duration of this awful war, are bearing up remarkably too." "Extracts and Translations," *Correspondence (1901–1903)*, 100.
20 "No. 103 Governor Sir J. West Ridgeway (Ceylon) to the Secretary of State for War," *Correspondence (1901–1903)*, 96.
21 *Correspondence (1901–1903)*, 96.
22 "No. 82 War Office to Colonial Office," *Correspondence (1901–1903)*, 74.
23 A report on the two camps in St. Helena, for example, contains sections on "Discipline and Daily Routine," "Accommodation," "Rations," "Facilities for Exercise

and Parole," "Schools," "Church," "Clubs," "Workshops," "Voluntary Labour," "Gifts," "Health," and "Clothing," with exhaustive tables in the back detailing the exact rations, timetable for the school, and medical cases. "Report on Boer Prisoners-of-War."
24 War Office, *General Questions*, n.p.
25 Not all the internees in the camps were originally from South Africa, as the war attracted many other anti-imperial combatants. To give some sense of the different nationalities in the camp, I quote *De Prikkeldraad* from 1900: "In the camp there are currently 2152 prisoners: 1687 Free Staters, 261 Transvalers, 76 Dutchmen, 60 Germans, 14 Irishmen, 10 Frenchmen, 10 Americans, 8 Englishmen, 5 Austrians, 3 Belgians, 3 Danes, 2 Russians, 2 Italians, 2 Turks, 2 Greeks, 2 Swedes, 1 Australian." The foreigners, or *uitlanders*, were frequently the fiercest critics of the British Empire, and officials would often segregate them in separate camps to avoid interference with their imperial subject making. *De Prikkeldraad* 1, no. 1, my translation.
26 *Correspondence (1901–1903)*, 102.
27 *Correspondence (1901–1903)*, 102–9. Censors were occupied with the same task in other camps across the British Empire: from St. Helena, the Commandant of Prisoners of War writes on March 1, 1902, "The tone of the prisoners [sic] letters conveys nothing as to their political feelings, and there has been little to censor in out-going mails. The in-coming mails are mostly censored in South Africa, but the censors at this camp report the correspondence both ways to be quite temperate and mild." In Shajahanpur, the commander of the camp writes on November 5, 1901, that "as the letters are almost all in Dutch we have no means of censoring them." Findlay and Hansen seemed to have been the most diligent of the camp censors, as their reports contain far more detailed extracts, transcribed or translated from the prisoners' letters. *Correspondence (1901–1903)*, 148–49.
28 *Correspondence (1901–1903)*, 101.
29 *Correspondence (1901–1903)*, 152.
30 *Correspondence (1901–1903)*, 108.
31 *Correspondence (1901–1903)*, 109.
32 *Correspondence (1901–1903)*, 105.
33 *Correspondence (1901–1903)*, 179.
34 *De Prikkeldraad* 1, no. 1, my translation; *De Prikkeldraad* 1, no. 2, my translation.
35 Van der Hoeven, *Gevangen op Ceylon*; Von Braun, *Taktische Eindrucke*; de Villiers, *Hoe Ik Ontsnapte*; van der Watt, *Leven der Boeren-krijgsgevangenen*.
36 Brink, *Recollections of a Boer Prisoner-of-War*, n.p.
37 The English version leaves out the lyrics of the song, so I have translated this section from the Dutch version. J. N. Brink, *Ceylon en de Bannelingen*, 47.
38 Pratt, *Imperial Eyes*, 3.
39 For more on female travel writers, see Mills, *Discourses of Difference*.
40 Smethurst, "Introduction," 1.
41 For more on travel writing in the South Asian context, see Mohanty, *Travel Writing and the Empire*.

42 Keck, "Involuntary Sightseeing," 390.
43 Sen, *Travels to Europe*.
44 Yang, Sheel, and Sheel, *Thirteen Months in China*, 2.
45 Yang, Sheel, and Sheel, *Thirteen Months in China*, 56. For more on coverage of the war in Indian newspapers, see Datta, "The Interlocking Worlds."
46 See Frank, *Crusoe*, for more on Defoe and Knox.
47 Knox, *An Historical Relation of Ceylon*.
48 Behdad, *Belated Travelers*.
49 Ann Fabian, in her book *The Unvarnished Truth: Personal Narratives in Nineteenth-Century America*, dedicates a chapter to "Prisoners of War," discussing personal narratives published after the American Civil War (1861–1865) by United States (Union) authors. She writes on these narratives: "Concentrating on their sufferings in confinement, prisoners gave scant space either to the larger issues of the war." In the Boer war prisoner memoirs, "suffering in confinement" does not make up the majority of the narrative. Fabian, *The Unvarnished Truth*, 123.
50 Knox, *An Historical Relation of Ceylon*, 1–2.
51 Brink, *Recollections of a Boer Prisoner-of-War*, 1.
52 Goswami, "Rethinking the Modular Nation Form," 787.
53 De Villiers, *Hoe Ik Ontsnapte*, n.p. My translation throughout. Page numbers henceforth cited with in-text parentheses.
54 Pratt, *Imperial Eyes*, 4.
55 *Ceylon Observer*, Weekly Edition (September 14, 1900). *Readex World Newspaper Archive*, 1206.
56 Hofmeyr, "South Africa's Indian Ocean," 370. For more on *Indian Opinion*, see also Hofmeyr, *Gandhi's Printing Press*.
57 Krog, "A Hundred Years of Attitude," 28.
58 Krog, "A Hundred Years of Attitude," 29.
59 For more on the rise of the National Party, see Giliomee, *The Afrikaners*.
60 Some of the titles of stories appearing in *Die Huisgenoot*: "Mot Smith: Harlekyn in die kamp"; "Handwerk van die krygsgevangene: Hoe die Boer sy kierie versier het"; "Krygsgevangene as Joernalis"; "Letterkunde van die krygsgevangene"; "Mededelings van 'n gewese boerekrygsgevangene 1: Wil julle Boere sien wegloop?"; "Hoe krygsgevangenes ontsnap het. Uit die dagboek van De Graaf"; "Ontsnapping"; and "Ontsnapping uit Diyatalawa-kamp."
61 Preller, *Ons Parool*; Visagie, *Terug na Kommando*; Burger, *Worsteljare*; Brink, *Oorlog en Ballingskap* (the same author as *Recollection of a Boer Prisoner-of-War at Ceylon/Ceylon en de Bannelingen*) expanded to include descriptions of the war itself, with the section on Ceylon significantly shortened); Kotze, *My Ballingskap*; Nienaber, *Nag op St Helena*; Scholtemeijer, *Balling oor die See*; Van Blerk, *Op die Bermudas Beland*.
62 For more on Preller and his historical reenactments, see Hofmeyr, "Popularizing History."
63 Burger, *Worsteljare*, 1. My translation throughout.

64   Hofmeyr, "Building a Nation from Words," 95.
65   Hofmeyr, "Building a Nation from Words," 95.
66   Burger, *Worsteljare*, 149–50.
67   Coetzee, *White Writing*, 61.
68   P. M. R., "Die Ontsnapping," 69.
69   P. M. R., "Die Ontsnapping," 69.
70   Hofmeyr, "Building a Nation from Words," 109.
71   Hofmeyr, "Building a Nation from Words," 109–10.
72   Rörich, "Onstnapping uit Diyatalawa-Kamp," 31.

CHAPTER 5. SENTIMENT AND THE LAW IN EARLY SOUTH AFRICAN INDIAN WRITING, 1893–1960

1   Singh, *Behold the Earth Mourns*, 3.
2   Singh, *Behold the Earth Mourns*, n.p.
3   On the changes that have taken place in understandings of the idea of empire between Gandhi's time in South Africa and the time he writes his autobiography, see Sinha, "The Strange Death."
4   Singh, *Behold the Earth Mourns*, 2–3.
5   Singh, *Behold the Earth Mourns*, 3.
6   Coetzee, *White Writing*, 83.
7   For example, Ishtiyaq Shukri, Imraan Coovadia, Achmat Dangor, Shamin Sarif, Farida Karodia, Beverley Naidoo, Joanne Joseph, and other authors all publish novels and short stories in the postapartheid period. For a longer list of South African Indian authors, see Desai, "Asian African Literatures." Pallavi Rastogi's *Afrindian Fictions* examines South African Indian writing from the 1970s onward.
8   Govinden, *Sister Outsiders*, 145.
9   Rastogi, *Afrindian Fictions*, 26.
10 The short story form was popular for all kinds of resistance writing under apartheid, perhaps because of the importance of literary magazines like *Drum* and *Staffrider* in the antiapartheid movement. See Wicomb, "South African Short Fiction."
11 Rastogi, *Afrindian Fictions*, 26.
12 Singh, *Behold the Earth Mourns*, 3–4.
13 Singh, *Behold the Earth Mourns*, 5.
14 Coetzee, *White Writing*, 5.
15 Coetzee, *White Writing*, 5.
16 Coetzee, *White Writing*, 5.
17 Work on sugar cane plantations in South Africa indicates the centrality of indentured labor to the development of the industry. It is thus particularly interesting that Singh's fictional family would own specifically a sugar cane farm. See, for example, McMartin, "The Early Days," and Richardson, "The Natal Sugar Industry."

18 Singh, *Behold the Earth Mourns*, 7.
19 Coetzee, *White Writing*, 53.
20 Chanock, *Making of South African Legal Culture*, 19.
21 Cronjé, *Afrika sonder die Asiaat*, 4. My translation throughout.
22 Coetzee, "The Mind of Apartheid," 3.
23 Coetzee, "The Mind of Apartheid," 10, citing Cronje, *'n Tuiste vir die Nageslag*, 77.
24 Quoted in Chanock, *South African Legal Culture*, 493.
25 Quoted in Chanock, *South African Legal Culture*, 493.
26 "Act No. 1, 1897."
27 "Trial of the Naidoos and Others for Picketing," 9.
28 *ontbodem*: de-earth, used here not in the sense of uncovering but as a negative preposition before the term *earth* or *soil*. This is also an uncommon formulation in Afrikaans.
29 Cronjé, *Afrika sonder die Asiaat*, 164.
30 Barnard, *Apartheid and Beyond*, 74.
31 Quoted in Cronjé, *Afrika sonder die Asiaat*, 33.
32 Cronjé, *Afrika sonder die Asiaat*, 8.
33 Cronjé, *Afrika sonder die Asiaat*, 11, 25.
34 Looking forward into the 1970s, Barnard discusses how apartheid ideology (in this case, embodied in the Bantu Homeland Citizenship Act of 1970) sought to make the Black South Africans as precarious as the figure of the indenture contract made South African Indians. "The act would turn all black South Africans into migrant laborers, their status little different from, say, that of Turkish Gastarbeiters in Germany.... Forced removals could therefore be equated with the 'normal' deportation of undesirable foreign nationals." One could see this "legalistic fantasy," as Barnard terms it, as the logical outcome of Cronjé's rhetoric. Barnard, *Apartheid and Beyond*, 72.
35 Singh, *Behold the Earth Mourns*, 106.
36 "Act No. 22 of 1913," 226. On these anti-immigration laws in the British Empire, see Huttenback, "The British Empire."
37 Singh, *Behold the Earth Mourns*, 193.
38 Singh, *Behold the Earth Mourns*, title page.
39 Jon Soske investigates how the presence of the Indian diaspora in South Africa impacted debates within the African National Congress (ANC) about the nation and nationalism. While acknowledging fraught racial tensions between South Asians and Africans within South Africa, he also argues that "the problem of the also-colonized other drove the ANC's formulation of an inclusive, African nationalism." This can be compared to Cronjé's politics: "In direct opposition to apartheid's discourse of 'separateness' and its fantasy of coherent racial subjects [as imagined by Cronjé], this imagery located heterogeneity, entanglement, and an asymmetrical form of reciprocity at the center of a shared identity." Soske, *Internal Frontiers*, 24.
40 Singh, *Behold the Earth Mourns*, 146.
41 Burton, "Every Secret Thing," 76.

42 For more on the system of migrant labor that undergirded the South African mining industry, see Moodie and Ndatshe, *Going for Gold*, and Allen, *The History of Black Mineworkers*.
43 Soske, *Internal Frontiers*, 3.
44 Rastogi cautions that "literary publication often has little to do with literary proliferation," citing sources like the newspapers *Indian Opinion*, *Colonial News*, *Leader*, the *Graphic*, and *Indian Views* as outlets for writing by South African Indians. In a short chapter on the "Literature of South African Indians" published in 1949, journalist P. S. Joshi lists some of the early authors to contribute to this tradition, bemoaning the fact that "the distance of India from the Union and the difficulty of finance are largely responsible for non-publication of literary efforts by budding authors who stem largely from the Indian middle-class group." Joshi does expand our understanding of very early South African Indian writing, however, pointing to, for example, the poetry collection *The Black Coolie* by B. D. Lalla (1946), "a booklet of twelve poems depicting the Indian feeling towards colour." For more on Lalla, see also Sheik, "B D Lalla's *The Black Coolie*." Rastogi, *Afrindian Fictions*, 3; Joshi, "Literature of South African Indians," 612. See also Hofmeyr, *Gandhi's Printing Press*, for more on early publications by South African Indians.
45 In the canon of East African Indian writing (from Uganda, Kenya, and Tanzania), Gaurav Desai also identifies a rather late novel, M. G. Vassanji's *The Gunny Sack* (1989), as the inaugural novel in this tradition: "In many ways, Simon Gikandi's claims about the inaugural role of Chinua Achebe's *Things Fall Apart* in the tradition of the African novel finds a parallel in my reading of Vassanji's text within the East African Asian imagination." This suggests that the relatively late development of a tradition of novel writing by persons of South Asian descent in African postcolonial situations where "colonialism was necessarily structured not through the simple binary division between the 'settler' and the 'native' proposed by Franz Fanon, but through a rather more complex struggle between a variety of actors: the colonial authorities in England, the white settlers in East Africa (particularly Kenya), the 'Asians' of East Africa, the colonial Indian government in India, and the so-called 'natives' in the Fanonian framework, the black Africans of East Africa," as Desai describes it, is a question that may go beyond the apartheid state. As Desai also points out, the novel considered to be the first full-length anglophone novel written by an East African Asian is Bahadur Tejani's *Day after Tomorrow* (1971). Desai, *Commerce with the Universe*, 64, 172–73.
46 Goonam, *Coolie Doctor*, 11.
47 Goonam, *Coolie Doctor*, 17.
48 Goonam, *Coolie Doctor*, 19.
49 Lelyveld, *Great Soul*, 14.
50 In colonial parlance, "Free" Indians were those whose indenture contract had expired, "Passenger" Indians came over independently (not under indenture contracts), and "Colonial-born" Indians were those born in Natal.
51 "L. Sewgolam of Ladysmith," n.p.
52 "L. Sewgolam of Ladysmith," n.p.

53 See Rastogi, *Afrindian Fictions*, for a detailed analysis of this novel. Joanne Joseph's historical novel *Children of Sugarcane* (2021) also engages directly with the history of indenture in South Africa.
54 Gandhi, *An Autobiography*, 267. Page numbers henceforth cited in in-text parentheses.
55 A statue of Gandhi was removed from the campus of the University of Ghana in 2018 in response to a petition by university faculty. A recent piece on the controversy is Skaria, "What Gandhi's Racism Tells Us."
56 Desai and Vahed, *The South African Gandhi*, 22.
57 See Vahed, "An Evil Thing."
58 Gandhi, "Letter to the *Transvaal Advertiser*, September 5, 1893," 113–14.
59 Lelyveld, *Great Soul*, 22.
60 Lelyveld, *Great Soul*, xiii.
61 Gandhi, *An Autobiography*, 194.
62 Editor Tridip Suhrud clarifies that, in the original Gujarati, this reads as "This was hardly advocacy. It was employment."
63 Interestingly, the editor Suhrud says that Dr. Krause was not called to the bar from the Inns of Court in England (Gandhi, *An Autobiography*, 182). This suggests that Gandhi invented the Inn connection: perhaps through forgetfulness, or perhaps to strengthen the impression of the bond that he shared with Dr. Krause as fellow men of the law.
64 See, for example, "Chapter 6: Sex, Energy and Politics," in Parekh, *Colonialism, Tradition, and Reform*; Howard, *Gandhi's Ascetic Activism*; and Lal, "Nakedness, Nonviolence and Brahmacharya." Biographers of Gandhi such as William L. Shirer have also identified this, his father's death, as a key moment in Gandhi's psychobiography, shaping his relationship to sex and celibacy. Shirer, *Gandhi*.
65 Gandhi, *An Autobiography*, 89; emphasis added. The word *nurse* is specifically used in English even in the original.
66 Suhrud clarifies that in the Gujarati, this reads "knew Tamil." Gandhi, *An Autobiography*, 265.
67 Desai and Vahed, *South African Gandhi*, 245.
68 Quoted in Desai and Vahed, *South African Gandhi*, 245.
69 Desai, *Commerce with the Universe*, 122.

CODA

1 "Legal Consequences of the Separation," 13.
2 "HMG Floats Proposal," n.p.
3 Vine, *Island of Shame*, 29.
4 "R (on the application of Bancoult No 2) (Appellant) v Secretary of State," n.p.
5 "On two occasions former U.S. Army General Barry McCaffrey publicly named Diego Garcia as a detention facility. A Council of Europe report named the atoll, along with sites in Poland and Romania, as a secret prison." David Vine, *Island of Shame*, 9.

6 "UK Apology over Rendition Flights," n.p.
7 Cited in Jones and Motha, "A New Nomos Offshore," 257.
8 "Chagos Islanders v Attorney General," appendix A, paragraph 74. Emphasis in original.
9 "Chagos Islanders v Attorney General," appendix A, paragraph 74.
10 For more on Knox as an inspiration for Crusoe, see Frank, *Daniel Defoe*.
11 Defoe, *Robinson Crusoe*, 112.
12 Defoe, *Robinson Crusoe*, 26.
13 Defoe, *Robinson Crusoe*, 20.
14 Defoe, *Robinson Crusoe*, 149.
15 When J. M. Coetzee reimagines *Robinson Crusoe* in his novel *Foe*, he famously gives Friday no tongue: "'He has no tongue,' [the character Cruso] said. 'That is why he does not speak. They cut out his tongue.'" The novel revolves around Friday's silence: "It is for us to open Friday's mouth and hear what it holds: silence, perhaps, or a roar, like the roar of a seashell held to the ear," the narrator, Susan Barton, says to the fictionalized Defoe (Foe). Coetzee, *Foe*, 23, 142.

BIBLIOGRAPHY

Abrahams, Yvette. "Disempowered to Consent: Sara Bartman and Khoisan Slavery in the Nineteenth-Century Cape Colony and Britain." *South African Historical Journal* 35, no. 1 (November 1996): 89–114.
"Act No. 1, 1897." Immigration (Restricted). In *Statutes of Natal, 1845–1899*, vol. 1, edited by R. L. Hitchens and G. W. Sweeney, 1–3. Pietermaritzburg, South Africa: P. Davis and Sons, 1900.
"Act No. 22 of 1913, Immigrants Regulation Act." In *Statutes of the Union of South Africa 1913*, 214–50. Cape Town, South Africa: Printed under the Superintendence of the Government Printer, 1913.
"Advert for the Cyclostyle Duplicating Machine." 1887. Evan. 7309. Evanion Collection, British Library. Accessed July 22, 2022. https://www.bl.uk/catalogues/evanion/Record.aspx?EvanID=024-000005286&ImageIndex=0.
Ahuja, Ravi. "Capital at Sea, Shaitan Below Decks? A Note on Global Narratives, Narrow Spaces, and the Limits of Experience." *History of the Present* 2, no. 1 (Spring 2012): 78–85.
Allen, Richard B. "Satisfying the 'Want for Labouring People': European Slave Trading in the Indian Ocean, 1500–1850." *Journal of World History* 21, no. 1 (2010): 43–73.
Allen, Richard B. "Slaves, Convicts, Abolitionism and the Global Origins of the Post-Emancipation Indentured Labor System." *Slavery & Abolition* 35, no. 2 (2014): 328–48.
Allen, V. L. *The History of Black Mineworkers in South Africa*. Vol. 1–3. London: Moor Press and Merlin Press, 2005.
Alpers, Edward, Gwyn Campbell, and Michael Salman, eds. *Slavery and Resistance in Africa and Asia*. London: Routledge, 2005.
Anderson, Clare. "Convicts and Coolies: Rethinking Indentured Labour in the Nineteenth Century." *Slavery and Abolition* 30, no. 1 (March 2009): 104.
Anderson, Clare. "Empire and Exile: Reflections on the Ibis Trilogy." *The American Historical Review* 121, no. 5 (December 2016): 1523–30.
Anderson, Clare. *Subaltern Lives: Biographies of Colonialism in the Indian Ocean World, 1790–1920*. Cambridge: Cambridge University Press, 2012.
Arabindan-Kesson, Anna. *Black Bodies, White Gold: Art, Cotton, and Commerce in the Atlantic World*. Durham, NC: Duke University Press, 2021.
Arende. Directed by Dirk de Villiers. TV series. TV1, 1989–1994.

Armillas-Tiseyra, Magalí. *The Dictator Novel: Writers and Politics in the Global South*. Evanston, IL: Northwestern University Press, 2019.

Armillas-Tiseyra, Magalí, and Anne Garland Mahler. "Introduction: New Critical Directions in Global South Studies." *Comparative Literature Studies* 58, no. 3 (2021): 465–84.

Arora, Anupama. "'The Sea Is History': Opium, Colonialism, and Migration in Amitav Ghosh's *Sea of Poppies*." *Ariel: A Review of International English Literature* 42, no. 3–4 (2012): 21–42.

Arya, Usharbudh. *Ritual Songs and Folksongs of the Hindus of Surinam*. Leiden, The Netherlands: E. J. Brill, 1968.

Baderoon, Gabeba. *Regarding Muslims: From Slavery to Post-Apartheid*. Johannesburg: Wits University Press, 2018.

Bahadur, Gaiutra. "Afterword: Rescued from the Footnotes of History." In *I Even Regret Night: Holi Songs of Demerara*. Translated by Rajiv Mohabir, 176–89. Los Angeles: Kaya Press, 2019.

Bahadur, Gaiutra. *Coolie Woman: The Odyssey of Indenture*. Chicago: The University of Chicago Press, 2014.

Bakhtin, Mikhail M. *The Dialogic Imagination*. Translated by Caryl Emerson and Michael Holquist. Austin: University of Texas Press, 1981.

Banerjee, Sukanya. *Becoming Imperial Citizens: Indians in the Late-Victorian Empire*. Durham, NC: Duke University Press, 2010.

Barnard, Rita. *Apartheid and Beyond: South African Writers and the Politics of Place*. London: Oxford University Press, 2006.

Barthes, Roland. "The Reality Effect." In *The Rustle of Language*, edited by François Wahl, 141–48. Translated by Richard Howard. Berkeley: University of California Press, 1989.

Behdad, Ali. *Belated Travelers: Orientalism in the Age of Colonial Dissolution*. Durham, NC: Duke University Press, 1994.

Bennett, Herman L. *Africans in Colonial Mexico: Absolutism, Christianity, and Afro-Creole Consciousness, 1570–1640*. Bloomington: Indiana University Press, 2003.

Benton, Lauren A. *Law and Colonial Cultures: Legal Regimes in World History, 1400–1900*. Cambridge: Cambridge University Press, 2004.

Berlant, Lauren. "Intuitionists: History and the Affective Event." *American Literary History* 20, no. 4 (Winter 2008): 845–60.

Best, Stephen M. *The Fugitive's Properties: Law and the Poetics of Possession*. Chicago: University of Chicago Press, 2013.

Best, Stephen M. *None Like Us: Blackness, Belonging, Aesthetic Life*. Durham, NC: Duke University Press, 2018.

Bhana, Surendra. *Indentured Indians in Natal, 1860–1902: A Study Based on Ships' Lists*. New Delhi: Promilla & Co., 1991.

Bhana, Surendra, and Bridglal Pachai, eds. "Charge of Assault against an Estate Manager." In *A Documentary History of Indian South Africans*. Cape Town, South Africa: New Africa Books, 1984.

Bhana, Surendra, and Bridglal Pachai, eds. "Complaint of Ill-Treatment on an Estate." In *A Documentary History of Indian South Africans*. Cape Town, South Africa: New Africa Books, 1984.

Bindman, David. "Blake's Vision of Slavery Revisited." *Huntington Library Quarterly* 58, no. 3/4 (1995): 373–82.

Blake, David, and Elliott Gruner. "Redeeming Captivity: The Negative Revolution in William Blake's Visions of the Daughters of Albion." *Symbiosis: A Journal of Anglo-American Relations* 1, no. 1 (1997): 21–34.

Blake, William. *The Complete Poetry and Prose of William Blake*, edited by David Erdman. Berkeley: University of California Press, 2008.

Boer, Nienke. "The Briny South: Transoceanic Subalternities at the Intersection of Global South and Ocean Studies." *Comparative Literature Studies* 58, no. 3 (2021): 582–603.

Böeseken, Anna J. *Slaves and Free Blacks at the Cape*. Cape Town, South Africa: Tafelberg Publishers, 1977.

Böeseken, Anna J., ed. *Uit die Raad van Justisie, 1652–1672*. Pretoria, South Africa: Die Staatsdrukker, 1986.

Bose, Sugata. *A Hundred Horizons: The Indian Ocean in the Age of Global Empire*. Cambridge, MA: Harvard University Press, 2006.

Bradlow, Edna. "Mental Illness or a Form of Resistance? The Case of Soera Brotto." *African Historical Review* 23 no. 1 (1991): 4–16.

Bragard, Véronique. *Transoceanic Dialogues: Coolitude in Caribbean and Indian Ocean Literatures*. Bern, Switzerland: Peter Lang, 2008.

Brink, André P. *A Chain of Voices*. London: Faber and Faber Limited, 1982.

Brink, J. N. *Ceylon en de Bannelingen*. Amsterdam: H. A. U. M., 1904.

Brink, J. N. *Oorlog en Ballingskap*. Cape Town, South Africa: Nationale Pers, 1940.

Brink, J. N. *Recollections of a Boer Prisoner-of-War in Ceylon*. Amsterdam: H. A. U. M, 1904.

Brown, Christopher Leslie. *Moral Capital: Foundations of British Abolitionism*. Chapel Hill: University of North Carolina Press, 2006.

Burger, A. P. *Worsteljare: Herinneringe van Ds. A.P. Burger, Veldprediker by die Republikeinse Magte tydens die Tweede Vryheidsoorlog*, edited by A. J. V. Burger. Cape Town, South Africa: Nationale Pers, 1936.

Burke, Edmund. "Essay on the Sublime and Beautiful (Complete)." In *Essays*, 49–154. London: Ward, Lock, and Tyler, 1876. *The Making of Modern Law: Legal Treatises, 1800–1926* (accessed August 27, 2022). https://link.gale.com/apps/doc/F0100595359/MOML?u=nuslib&sid=bookmark-MOML&xid=ec3447a6&pg=1.

Burton, Antoinette. "Amitav Ghosh's World Histories from Below." *History of the Present* 2, no. 1 (Spring 2012): 71–77.

Burton, Antoinette. "'Every Secret Thing'? Racial Politics in Ansuyah R. Singh's *Behold the Earth Mourns*." *Journal of Commonwealth Literature* 46, no. 1 (March 2011): 63–81.

Bystrom, Kerry, and Isabel Hofmeyr, eds. "Oceanic Routes: An ACLA Forum." *Comparative Literature* 69, no. 1 (March 2017).

Campbell, Gwyn, ed. *Structure of Slavery in Indian Ocean Africa and Asia*. London: Frank Cass, 2004.

Campbell, Gwyn, and Alessando Stanziani, eds. *Bonded Labour and Debt in the Indian Ocean World*. London: Pickering & Chatto Publishers, 2013.

Carey, Brycchan, and Peter J. Kitson, eds. *Slavery and the Cultures of Abolition: Essays Marking the Bicentennial of the British Abolition Act of 1807*. Woodbridge, UK: D.S. Brewer, 2007.

Carlson, Nancy Naomi, transl. "[Coolitude: petites mains des colonies]." By Khal Torabully. *The Southern Review* 54, no. 2 (2018): 286–87.

Carter, Marina. *Servants, Sirdars and Settlers: Indians in Mauritius, 1834–1874*. Oxford: Oxford University Press, 1995.

Carter, Marina, and Khal Torabully. *Coolitude: An Anthology of the Indian Labour Diaspora*. London: Anthem Press, 2002.

Carter, Marina, and Nira Wickramasinghe. "Forcing the Archive: Involuntary Migrants 'of Ceylon' in the Indian Ocean World of the 18–19th Centuries." *South Asian History and Culture* 9, no. 2 (2018): 194–206.

"Chagos Islanders v Attorney General Her Majesty's British Indian Ocean Territory Commissioner." EWHC 2222 (QB) (October 9, 2003) in *British and Irish Legal Information Institute*. Accessed July 23, 2020. http://www.bailii.org/ew/cases/EWHC/QB/2003/2222.html.

Chanock, Martin. *The Making of South African Legal Culture, 1902–1936: Fear, Favour and Prejudice*. Cambridge: Cambridge University Press, 2001.

Chatterjee, Indrani, and Richard M. Eaton, eds. *Slavery and South Asian History*. Bloomington: Indiana University Press, 2006.

Chaudhuri, Kirti N. *Asia before Europe: Economy and Civilization of the Indian Ocean from the Rise of Islam to 1750*. Cambridge: Cambridge University Press, 1990.

Christiansë, Yvette. "'Heartsore': The Melancholy Archive of Cape Colony Slavery." *The Scholar and Feminist Online* 7, no. 2 (Spring 2009). https://sfonline.barnard.edu/africana/christianse_01.htm.

Coetzee, J. M. *Foe*. New York: Penguin Books, 1987.

Coetzee, J. M. "The Mind of Apartheid: Geoffrey Cronjé (1907–)." *Social Dynamics* 17, no. 1 (1991): 1–35.

Coetzee, J. M. "The Poems of Thomas Pringle." In *Stranger Shores: Essays 1986–99*. London: Vintage, 2001.

Coetzee, J. M. "Realism." In *Elizabeth Costello: Eight Lessons*, 1–34. London: Vintage, 2004.

Coetzee, J. M. "Review: African Poems of Thomas Pringle by Ernest Pereira, Michael Chapman and Thomas Pringle." *Research in African Literatures* 21, no. 3 (Autumn, 1990): 179–82.

Coetzee, J. M. *White Writing: On the Culture of Letters in South Africa*. New Haven, CT: Yale University Press, 1988.

Cohen, Ashley L. "The Global Indies: Historicizing Oceanic Metageographies." *Comparative Literature* 69, no. 1 (March 2017): 7–15.

Correspondence (1901–1903) Relating to Boer Prisoners of War. Colonial Office, 1904. CO 879/75. The National Archives, Kew, Richmond, UK.

Council of Justice Records (CJ), 1652–1843. Western Cape Archives and Records Services, Cape Town, South Africa.
Crais, Clifton, and Thomas V. McClendon, eds. "The Necessity of Slavery: W.S. van Ryneveld." In *The South African Reader: History, Culture, Politics*, 46–48. Durham, NC: Duke University Press, 2014.
Cronjé, Geoffrey. *Afrika sonder die Asiaat: Die Blywende Oplossing van Suid-Afrika se Asiatevraagstuk*. Johannesburg: Publicite Handelsreklamediens (EDMS) Bpk., 1946.
Datta, Pradip Kumar. "The Interlocking Worlds of the Anglo-Boer War in South Africa and India." In *South Africa and India: Shaping the Global South*, edited by Isabel Hofmeyr and Michele Williams, 56–81. Johannesburg: Wits University Press, 2011.
Davids, Achmat. *The Afrikaans of the Cape Muslims*. Pretoria, South Africa: Protea Boekhuis, 2012.
Davis, Natalie Zemon. *Fiction in the Archives: Pardon Tales and Their Tellers in Sixteenth Century France*. Stanford, CA: Stanford University Press, 1987.
Davis, Natalie Zemon. "Judges, Masters, Diviners: Slaves' Experience of Criminal Justice in Colonial Suriname." *Law and History Review* 29, no. 4 (November 2011): 925–84.
Defoe, Daniel. *Robinson Crusoe*, edited by Michael Shinagle. New York: W. W. Norton, 1994.
DeLombard, Jeanine Marie. *Slavery on Trial: Law, Abolitionism, and Print Culture*. Chapel Hill: University of North Carolina Press, 2007.
De Prikkeldraad: Orgaan van de Krijgsgevangenen te Diyatalawa 1, no. 1 (September 10, 1900). Koerant 33. Anglo-Boer War Museum, Bloemfontein, South Africa.
De Prikkeldraad: Orgaan van de Krijgsgevangenen te Diyatalawa 1, no. 2 (September 19, 1900) Koerant 33. Anglo-Boer War Museum, Bloemfontein, South Africa.
De Prikkeldraad: Orgaan van de Krijgsgevangenen te Diyatalawa 1, no. 3 (September 26, 1900). Koerant 33. Anglo-Boer War Museum, Bloemfontein, South Africa.
Desai, Ashwin, and Goolam Vahed. *Inside Indian Indenture: A South African Story 1860–1914*. Cape Town, South Africa: HSRC Press, 2010.
Desai, Ashwin, and Goolam Vahed. *The South African Gandhi: Stretcher-Bearer of Empire*. Stanford, CA: Stanford University Press, 2016.
Desai, Gaurav. "Asian African Literatures: Genealogies in the Making." *Research in African Literatures* 42, no. 3 (Fall 2011): 5–30.
Desai, Gaurav. *Commerce with the Universe: Africa, India and the Afrasian Imagination*. New York: Columbia University Press, 2013.
Desai, Gaurav. "The Novelist as Linkister." *American Historical Review* 121, no. 5 (December 2016): 1531–36.
De Villiers, J. L. *Hoe Ik Ontsnapte: Verhaal van een Merkwaardige Ontsnapping van een Boer uit Engelsch-Indie*. Amsterdam: Hoveker & Wormser, 1904.
De Wet, Con. "Bestuurstinstellinge." In *Die VOC aan die Kaap 1652–1795*, edited by Con de Wet, Leon Hattingh, and Jan Visagie, 113–31. Pretoria, South Africa: Protea Boekhuis, 2017.
De Wet, Con, Leon Hattingh, and Jan Visagie, eds. "Bylae 3: Fiskale aan die Kaap, 1652–1795." In *Die VOC aan die Kaap 1652–1795*, 487–88. Pretoria, South Africa: Protea Boekhuis, 2017.

Dhupelia-Mesthrie, Uma. "The Passenger Indian as Worker: Indian Immigrants in Cape Town in the Early Twentieth Century." *African Studies* 68, no. 1 (2009): 111–34.

Doyle, Laura. *Inter-Imperiality: Vying Empires, Gendered Labor, and the Literary Arts of Alliance*. Durham, NC: Duke University Press, 2020.

Elphick, Richard, and Hermann Giliomee. *The Shaping of South African Society, 1652–1840*. Middletown, CT: Wesleyan University Press, 1988.

Elphick, Richard, and V. C. Malherbe. "The Khoisan to 1828." In *The Shaping of South African Society, 1652–1840*, edited by Richard Elphick and Hermann Giliomee, 3–65. Middletown, CT: Wesleyan University Press, 1988.

Erdman, David V. "Blake's Vision of Slavery." *Journal of the Warburg and Courtauld Institutes* 15, no. 2 (1952): 242–52.

Fabian, Ann. *The Unvarnished Truth: Personal Narratives in Nineteenth-Century America*. Oakland: University of California Press, 2002.

Ferguson, Moira. *Subject to Others: British Women Writers and Colonial Slavery, 1670–1834*. London: Routledge, 1992.

Ferreira, O. J. O. "Boeregeïnterneerdes in Portugal Tydens die Anglo-Boereoorlog (1899–1902) en Hulle Tydverdrywe." *Historia* 42, no. 2 (1997): 33–56.

Festa, Lynn. *Sentimental Figures of Empire in Eighteenth Century Britain and France*. Baltimore, MD: Johns Hopkins Press, 2006.

Finley, Cheryl. *Committed to Memory: The Art of the Slave Ship Icon*. Princeton, NJ: Princeton University Press, 2018.

Forter, Greg. *Critique and Utopia in Postcolonial Historical Fiction: Atlantic and Other Worlds*. Oxford: Oxford University Press, 2019.

Foucault, Michel. *Wrong-doing, Truth-telling: The Function of Avowal in Justice*, edited by Fabienne Bron and Bernard E. Harcourt. Translated by Stephen W. Sawyer. Chicago: University of Chicago Press, 2014.

Frank, Katherine. *Crusoe: Daniel Defoe, Robert Knox, and the Creation of a Myth*. New York: Pegasus Books, 2012.

Franken, J. L. M. *Taalhistoriese Bydraes*. Amsterdam: Balkema, 1953.

Freeburg, Christopher. *Counterlife: Slavery after Resistance and Social Death*. Durham, NC: Duke University Press, 2021.

Frost, Mark R. "Amitav Ghosh and the Art of Thick Description: History in the Ibis Trilogy." *American Historical Review* 121, no. 5 (December 2016): 1537–44.

Fuentes, Marisa J. *Dispossessed Lives: Enslaved Women, Violence, and the Archive*. Philadelphia: University of Pennsylvania Press, 2016.

Gandhi, Mohandas K. *An Autobiography, or the Story of My Experiments with Truth*, edited by Tridip Suhrud. Translated by Mahadev Desai. New Haven, CT: Yale University Press, 2018.

Gandhi, Mohandas K. *The Grievances of the British Indians in South Africa: An Appeal to the Indian Public* (1896). In *Collected Works of Mahatma Gandhi*, vol. 1, 359–93. New Delhi: Publications Division Government of India, 1999.

Gandhi, Mohandas K. "Letter to the *Transvaal Advertiser*, September 5, 1893." In *The Collected Works of Mahatma Gandhi*, supplementary volume 1, reprinted in *The South African Gandhi. An Abstract of the Speeches and Writings of M. K. Gandhi,*

1893–1914, edited by Fatima Meer, 113–14. Durban, South Africa: Madiba Publishers, 1996.

Ghosh, Amitav. *Flood of Fire*. New York: Farrar, Straus and Giroux, 2015.

Ghosh, Amitav. *River of Smoke*. New York: Farrar, Straus and Giroux, 2011.

Ghosh, Amitav. *Sea of Poppies*. New York: Picador, 2009.

Gikandi, Simon. "Rethinking the Archive of Enslavement." *Early American Literature* 50, no. 1 (2015): 81–102.

Gikandi, Simon. *Slavery and the Culture of Taste*. Princeton, NJ: Princeton University Press, 2011.

Giliomee, Hermann. *The Afrikaners: Biography of a People*. Charlottesville: University of Virginia Press, 2010.

Glenn, Ian. "Eighteenth-Century Natural History, Travel Writing and South African Literary Historiography." In *The Cambridge History of South African Literature*, edited by David Attwell and Derek Attridge, 158–80. Cambridge: Cambridge University Press, 2012.

Goonam, Kesaveloo. *Coolie Doctor: An Autobiography*. Durban, South Africa: Madiba Publishers for Institute for Black Research, 1991.

Gosine, Andil. "After Indenture." *Small Axe* 21, no. 2 (July 2017): 63–67.

Goswami, Manu. "Rethinking the Modular Nation Form: Toward a Sociohistorical Conception of Nationalism." *Comparative Studies in Society and History* 44, no. 4 (2002): 770–99.

Govinden, Devarakshanam. *Sister Outsiders: The Representation of Identity and Difference in Selected Writings by South African Indian Women*. Leiden, The Netherlands: Brill, 2008.

Gqola, Pumla Dineo. *What Is Slavery to Me? Postcolonial/Slave Memory in Post-apartheid South Africa*. Johannesburg: Wits University Press, 2010.

Groenewald, Coen. *Bannelinge oor die Oseaan: Boerekrygsgevangenes 1899–1902*. Pretoria, South Africa: J. P. Van der Walt, 1992.

Harries, Patrick. "Slavery, Indenture and Migrant Labour: Maritime Immigration from Mozambique to the Cape, c.1780–1880." *African Studies* 73, no. 3 (2014): 323–40.

Hartman, Saidiya V. *Scenes of Subjection: Terror, Slavery, and Self-Making in Nineteenth-Century America*. Oxford: Oxford University Press, 1997.

Hartman, Saidiya V. "Venus in Two Acts." *Small Axe* 12, no. 2 (June 2008): 1–14.

Heese, H. F. *Reg en Onreg: Kaapse Regspraak in die Agtiende Eeu*. Cape Town, South Africa: University of the Western Cape, 1994.

"HMG Floats Proposal for Marine Reserve Covering the Chagos Archipelago (British Indian Ocean Territory)." Telegram (cable), May 15, 2009. *Wikileaks*. Accessed March 1, 2016. https://wikileaks.org/plusd/cables/09LONDON1156_a.html.

Hofmeyr, Isabel. "The Black Atlantic Meets the Indian Ocean: Forging New Paradigms of Transnationalism for the Global South—Literary and Cultural Perspectives." *Social Dynamics* 33, no. 2 (2007): 3–32.

Hofmeyr, Isabel. "Building a Nation from Words: Afrikaans Language, Literature and Ethnic Identity, 1902–1924." In *The Politics of Race, Class, and Nationalism in*

Twentieth-Century South Africa, edited by Shula Marks and Stanley Trapido, 95–123. London: Longman Group UK Limited, 1987.

Hofmeyr, Isabel. *Gandhi's Printing Press: Experiments in Slow Reading*. Cambridge, MA: Harvard University Press, 2013.

Hofmeyr, Isabel. "Popularizing History: The Case of Gustav Preller." *Journal of African History* 29, no. 3 (1988): 521–35.

Hofmeyr, Isabel. "South Africa's Indian Ocean: Boer Prisoners of War in India." *Social Dynamics* 38, no. 3 (2012): 363–80.

Hontanilla, Ana. "Sentiment and the Law: Inventing the Category of the Wretched Slave in the *Real Audiencia* of Santo Domingo, 1783–1812." *Eighteenth-Century Studies* 48, no. 2 (Winter 2015): 181–200.

Hoogervorst, Tom. "'Kanala, Tamaaf, Tramkassie, en Stuur Krieslam': Lexical and Phonological Echoes of Malay in Cape Town." *Wacana* 22, no. 1 (2021): 22–57.

Howard, Veena R. *Gandhi's Ascetic Activism: Renunciation and Social Action*. Albany: SUNY Press, 2013.

Hunter, J. Paul. *Before Novels: The Cultural Contexts of Eighteenth Century English Fiction*. London: W.W. Norton and Company, 1990.

Huttenback, R. A. "The British Empire as a 'White Man's Country'–Racial Attitudes and Immigration Legislation in the Colonies of White Settlement." *Journal of British Studies* 13, no. 1 (November 1973): 108–37.

"Introduction." *American Historical Review* 121, no. 5 (December 2016): 1521–22.

Jappie, Saarah. "'Many Makassars': Tracing an African-Southeast Asian Narrative of Shaykh Yusuf of Makassar." In *Migration and Agency in a Globalizing World*, edited by S. Cornelissen and Y. Mine, 47–66. London: Palgrave Macmillan, 2018.

Jewell, James Robbins. "Using Barbaric Methods in South Africa: The British Concentration Camp Policy during the Anglo-Boer War." *Scientia Militaria: South African Journal of Military Studies* 3, no. 1 (2003): 1–18.

Johnson, David. "Representing Cape Slavery: Literature, Law, and History." *Journal of Postcolonial Writing* 46, no. 5 (2010): 504–16.

Johnson, David. "Representing the Cape 'Hottentots,' from the French Enlightenment to Post-Apartheid South Africa." *Eighteenth Century Studies* 40, no. 4 (2007): 525–52.

Johnson, Walter. "On Agency." *Journal of Social History* 37, no. 1 (2003): 113–24.

Jones, Stephanie, and Stewart Motha. "A New Nomos Offshore and Bodies as Their Own Signs." *Law & Literature* 27, no. 2 (2015): 253–78.

Joshi, P. S. "Literature of South African Indians." In *Handbook on Race Relations in South Africa*, edited by Ellen Hellman and Leah Abrahams, 612–14. London: Oxford University Press, 1949.

Jung, Moon-Ho. *Coolies and Cane: Race, Labor and Sugar in the Age of Emancipation*. Baltimore, MD: Johns Hopkins University Press, 2006.

Kale, Madhavi. "'Capital Spectacles in British Frames': Capital, Empire and Indian Indentured Migration to the British Caribbean." *International Review of Social History* 41 (1996): 109–33.

Kale, Madhavi. *Fragments of Empire: Capital, Slavery, and Indian Indentured Labor Migration in the British Caribbean*. Philadelphia: University of Pennsylvania Press, 1998.

Kazanjian, David. "Freedom's Surprise: Two Paths through Slavery's Archives." *History of the Present* 6, no. 2 (September 2016): 133–45.

Keck, Stephen. "Involuntary Sightseeing: Soldiers as Travel Writers and the Construction of Colonial Burma." *Victorian Literature and Culture* 43, no. 2 (2015): 389–407.

Kent, Eddy. "'Ship-Siblings': Globalisation, Neo-Liberal Aesthetics, and Neo-Victorian Form in Amitav Ghosh's *Sea of Poppies*." *Neo-Victorian Studies* 8, no. 1 (2015): 107–30.

Khan, Munshi Rahman. *Jeevan Prakash: Autobiography of an Indian Indentured Labourer*. Translated by Kathinka Sinha-Kerkhoff, Ellen Bal, and Alok Deo Singh. New Delhi: Shipra Publications, 2005.

Kindersley, Jemima. *Letters from the Island of Teneriffe, Brazil, the Cape of Good Hope, and the East Indies*. London: J. Nourse, 1777.

Knox, Robert. *An Historical Relation of Ceylon, An Island in the East Indies*. In A. M. Philalethes, *The History of Ceylon, from the Earliest Period to the Year MDCCCXV with Characteristic Details of the Religion, Laws, and Manners of the People, and a Collection of Their Moral Maxims, and Ancient Proverbs to Which Is Subjoined, Robert Knox's Historical Relation of the Island with an Account of His Captivity during a Period of Near Twenty Years*. London: Printed for Joseph Mawman, 1817.

Kotze, C. R. *My Ballingskap*. Bloemfontein, South Africa: Nationale Museum, 1942.

Krebs, Paula M. *Gender, Race, and the Writing of Empire: Public Discourse and the Boer War*. Cambridge: Cambridge University Press, 1999.

Krog, Antjie. "A Hundred Years of Attitude." *Mail & Guardian* (October 8–14, 1999): 28–29.

Kumar, Ashutosh. *Coolies of the Empire: Indentured Indians in the Sugar Colonies, 1830–1920*. Cambridge: Cambridge University Press, 2018.

Kynoch, G. "Controlling the Coolies: Chinese Mineworkers and the Struggle for Labor in South Africa, 1904–1910." *International Journal of African Historical Studies* 36, no. 2 (2003): 309–29.

"L. Sewgolam of Ladysmith: Transfer Documents (1906–1910)." 1270/194–218. Gandhi-Luthuli Documentation Centre, University of KwaZulu-Natal, Westville, Durban, South Africa.

Lal, Vinay. "Nakedness, Nonviolence, and Brahmacharya: Gandhi's Experiments in Celibate Sexuality." *Journal of the History of Sexuality* 9, no. 1/2 (2000): 105–36.

Larson, Pier M. *History and Memory in the Age of Enslavement: Becoming Merina in Highland Madagascar, 1770–1822*. Portsmouth, NH: Heinemann, 2000.

Lee, Debbie. *Slavery and the Romantic Imagination*. Philadelphia: University of Pennsylvania Press, 2002.

"Legal Consequences of the Separation of the Chagos Archipelago from Mauritius in 1965: Summary of the Advisory Opinion." International Court of Justice. February 25, 2019. https://www.icj-cij.org/files/case-related/169/169-20190225-SUM-01-00-EN.pdf.

Lelyveld, Joseph. *Great Soul: Mahatma Gandhi and His Struggle with India*. New York: Vintage Books, 2012.

Lionnet, Françoise. "Shipwrecks, Slavery, and the Challenge of Global Comparison: From Fiction to Archive in the Colonial Indian Ocean." *Comparative Literature* 64, no. 4 (2012): 446–61.

Lionnet, Françoise, and Shu-Mei Shih, eds. *Minor Transnationalism*. Durham, NC: Duke University Press, 2005.

Lively, Adam. *Masks: Blackness, Race, and the Imagination*. Oxford: Oxford University Press, 2000.

Loos, Jackie. *Echoes of Slavery: Voices from South Africa's Past*. Cape Town, South Africa: David Philip Publishers, 2004.

Lowe, Lisa. *The Intimacies of Four Continents*. Durham, NC: Duke University Press, 2015.

Lowry, Donal. *The South African War Reappraised*. Manchester, UK: Manchester University Press, 2000.

Mahler, Anne Garland. "Global South." In *Oxford Bibliographies in Literary and Critical Theory*, edited by Eugene O'Brien, n.p. Oxford: Oxford University Press, 2017. Accessed July 23, 2022. DOI: 10.1093/OBO/9780190221911-0055.

Mangalo, B. E., and Kobus du Pisani. "Victims of a White Man's War: Blacks in Concentration Camps during the South African War (1899–1902)." *Historia* 44, no. 1 (May 1999): 148–82.

Manjapra, Kris. *Colonialism in Global Perspective*. Cambridge: Cambridge University Press, 2020.

Masemola, Michael Kgomotso. "The Memory of Pringle as Prospero, or the Cannibal that Faked Caliban: Issues of Authority and Representation in Thomas Pringle's Ethnographic Poetry." *African Identities* 13, no. 4 (2015): 310–22.

Mason, John Edwin. *Social Death and Resurrection: Slavery and Emancipation in South Africa*. Charlottesville: University of Virginia Press, 2003.

Mbeki, Linda, and Matthias van Rossum. "Private Slave Trade in the Dutch Indian Ocean World: A Study into the Networks and Backgrounds of the Slavers and the Enslaved in South Asia and South Africa." *Slavery & Abolition* 38, no. 1 (2017): 95–116.

Mbembe, Achille. "The Power of the Archive and Its Limits." In *Refiguring the Archive*, edited by Carolyn Hamilton, Verne Harris, Jane Taylor, Michele Pickover, Graeme Reid, and Razia Saleh, 19–26. Dordrecht, South Africa: Kluwer Academic Publishers, 2002.

McKittrick, Katherine. *Dear Science and Other Stories*. Durham, NC: Duke University Press, 2021.

McKittrick, Katherine. "Mathematics Black Life." *The Black Scholar* 44, no. 2 (2014): 16–28.

McMartin, A. "The Early Days of the Natal Sugar Industry, with Special Reference to the Introduction of Varieties." *Proceedings of the 22nd Annual Congress of the South African Sugar Technologists Association*. Durban, South Africa: 1949.

Menon, Tara. "Keeping Count: Direct Speech in the Nineteenth-Century British Novel." *Narrative* 27, no. 2 (May 2019): 160–81.

Mesthrie, Rajend. "New Lights from Old Languages: Indian Languages and the Experience of Indentureship in South Africa." In *Essays on Indentured Indians in South Africa*, edited by Surendra Bhana, 189–206. Leeds, UK: Peepal Tree, 1991.

Metcalf, Thomas R. *Imperial Connections: India in the Indian Ocean Arena, 1860–1920*. Berkeley: University of California Press, 2007.

Mills, Sara. *Discourses of Difference: An Analysis of Women's Travel Writing and Colonialism*. London: Routledge, 1991.

Mishra, Vijay. *The Literature of the Indian Diaspora: Theorizing the Diasporic Imaginary*. New York: Routledge, 2007.

Mohabir, Rajiv. "Translating as a Practice of Transformation." In *I Even Regret Night: Holi Songs of Demerara*, 190–203. Translated by Rajiv Mohabir. Los Angeles: Kaya Press, 2019.

Mohanty, Sachidananda, ed. *Travel Writing and the Empire*. New Delhi: Katha, 2003.

Moodie, T. Dunbar, and Vivienne Ndatshe. *Going for Gold: Men, Mines, and Migration*. Berkeley: University of California Press, 1994.

Morris, Thomas D. "Slaves and the Rules of Evidence in Criminal Trials–Symposium on the Law of Slavery: Criminal and Civil Law of Slavery." *Chicago-Kent Law Review* 68, no. 3 (1993): 1209–40.

Murray, Jessica. "Gender and Violence in Cape Slave Narratives and Post-Narratives." *South African Historical Journal* 62, no. 3 (2010): 444–62.

Natal Ordinances, Laws and Proclamations. Vol. 1 (1843–1870). Compiled by Charles Fitzwilliam Cadiz and Robert Lyon. Pietermaritzburg, South Africa: Vause, Slatter & Co., Government Printers, 1879.

"Negro." *Encyclopædia Britannica; Or A Dictionary of Arts, Sciences, and Miscellaneous Literature*, 6th ed. Vol. 14 (Edinburgh, UK: Archibald Constable and Company, 1823): 750–54. Google Books. Accessed June 18, 2021. https://books.google.com/books?id=3JwrAAAAMAAJ&pg.

Newton-King, Susan. "Family, Friendship, and Survival among Freed Slaves." In *Cape Town Between East and West*, edited by Nigel Worden, 153–75. Pretoria, South Africa: Jacana Media, 2012.

Ngai, Mae. *The Chinese Question: The Gold Rushes and Global Politics*. New York: W. W. Norton, 2021.

Ngai, Sianne. *Ugly Feelings*. Cambridge, MA: Harvard University Press, 2005.

Niehaus, Michael. *Mord, Geständnis, Widerruf: Verhören und Verhörtwerden um 1800*. Bochum, Germany: Posth Verlag, 2006.

Nienaber, P. J. *Nag op St Helena*. Bloemfontein, South Africa: Nationale Pers, 1944.

Northrup, David. *Indentured Labor in the Age of Imperialism: 1834–1922*. Cambridge: Cambridge University Press, 1995.

Ogborn, Miles. "The Power of Speech: Orality, Oaths and Evidence in the British Atlantic World, 1650–1800." *Transactions of the Institute of British Geographers* 36 (2011): 109–25.

P. M. R. "Die Ontsnapping." *Die Huisgenoot* (May 23, 1941): 69.

Page, Norman. *Speech in the English Novel*. London: Palgrave Macmillan, 1988.

Pandiri, Ananda M. *A Comprehensive, Annotated Bibliography on Mahatma Gandhi*. Westport, CT: Greenwood Press, 1995.

Parekh, Bhikhu C. *Colonialism, Tradition, and Reform: An Analysis of Gandhi's Political Discourse*. New Delhi: Sage, 1989.

Paton, Diana. "Punishment, Crime, and the Bodies of Slaves in Eighteenth Century Jamaica." *Journal of Social History* 34, no. 1 (2001): 923–54.

Pearson, Michael N. *The Indian Ocean*. New York: Routledge, 2003.

Penn, Nigel. *Murderers, Miscreants and Mutineers: Early Colonial Cape Lives*. Pretoria, South Africa: Jacana Media, 2015.

Penn, Nigel. *Rogues, Rebels and Runaways: Eighteenth Century Cape Characters*. Cape Town, South Africa: David Philip Publishers, 1999.

Philip, NourbeSe M. *Zong!* Middleport, CT: Wesleyan University Press, 2008.

Pillay, Kathryn. "'The Coolies Here': Exploring the Construction of an Indian 'Race' in South Africa." *Journal of Global South Studies* 34, no. 1 (Spring 2017): 22–49.

Pirbhai, Mariam. *Mythologies of Migration, Vocabularies of Indenture: Novels of the South Asian Diaspora in Africa, the Caribbean, and Asia-Pacific*. Toronto: University of Toronto Press, 2009.

Pratt, Mary Louise. *Imperial Eyes: Travel Writing and Transculturation*. 2nd ed. New York: Routledge, 2008.

Preller, G. S. *Ons Parool: Dae uit die Dagboek van 'n Krygsgevangene*. Cape Town, South Africa: Nationale Pers, 1938.

Prince, Mary. *The History of Mary Prince: A West Indian Slave*, edited by Sara Salih. New York: Penguin Books, 2004.

Pringle, Thomas. "Slavery at the Cape of Good Hope." *Anti-Slavery Monthly Reporter*, January 31, 1827. Reprinted in Mary Prince, *The History of Mary Prince: A West Indian Slave*, edited by Sara Salih, 104–15. New York: Penguin Books, 2004.

Pringle, Thomas. *The South African Letters of Thomas Pringle*, edited by Randolphe Vigne. Cape Town, South Africa: Van Riebeeck Society for the Publication of Southern African Historical Documents, 2011.

"Questionnaire Relative to Slaves, with Translation into French." *Documents Pertaining to the Cape of Good Hope*. KAB A148. Western Cape Archives and Records Services, Cape Town, South Africa, 1–4.

"R (on the application of Bancoult No 2) (Appellant) v Secretary of State for Foreign and Commonwealth Affairs (Respondent)." *The Supreme Court: Case Details*. Case ID: UKSC 2015/0021. Accessed July 23, 2022. https://www.supremecourt.uk/cases/uksc-2015-0021.html.

Rastogi, Pallavi. *Afrindian Fictions: Diaspora, Race, and National Desire in South Africa*. Columbus: The Ohio State University Press, 2008.

Rauwerda, A. M. "Naming, Agency, and 'A Tissue of Falsehoods' in *The History of Mary Prince*." *Victorian Literature and Culture* 29, no. 2 (2001): 397–411.

Reid, Anthony, ed. *Slavery, Bondage & Dependency in Southeast Asia*. Brisbane, Australia: University of Queensland Press, 1983.

Report of Coolie Commission, Appointed to Inquire into the Condition of the Indian Immigrants in the Colony Of Natal; The Mode in Which They Are Employed; And

Also to Inquire into the Complaints Made by Returned Immigrants to the Protector of Emigrants at Calcutta. Pietermaritzburg, South Africa: Keith & Co., Printers to the Legislative Council, 1872.

"Report on Boer Prisoners-of-War (Gov. 31258)." Colonial Office. Ref. CO 537/453 (1901). The National Archives, Kew, Richmond, UK.

Richardson, Peter. "Chinese Indentured Labour in the Transvaal Gold Mining Industry, 1904–1910." In *Indentured Labour in the British Empire 1834–1920*, edited by Kay Saunders, 260–90. London: Routledge, 2018.

Richardson, Peter. "The Natal Sugar Industry, 1849–1905: An Interpretative Essay." *Journal of African History* 23, no. 4 (1982): 515–27.

Rörich, Eric. "Onstnapping uit Diyatalawa-Kamp." *Die Huisgenoot* (October 3, 1941): 31.

Ross, Robert. *Cape of Torments: Slavery and Resistance in South Africa*. London: Routledge, 1983.

S. Bhana Collection. Acc. No. 957/641–655 (1875–1887). Gandhi-Luthuli Documentation Centre, University of Kwazulu-Natal (Westville), Durban, South Africa.

Samuelson, Meg. "'Lose Your Mother, Kill Your Child': The Passage of Slavery and Its Afterlife in Narratives by Yvette Christiansë and Saidiya Hartman." *English Studies in Africa* 51, no. 2 (2009): 38–48.

Sanadhya, Totaram. *My Twenty-One Years in the Fiji Islands and the Story of the Haunted Line*. Translated by John Dunham Kelly and Uttra Kumari Singh. Suva: Fiji Museum, 1991.

Schoeman, Chris. *Vegter en Balling: Boereoorlog-ervarings van Veldkornet Charles von Maltitz*. Cape Town, South Africa: Tafelberg, 2013.

Scholtemeijer, H. *Balling oor die See: Uit die Dagboek van 'n Krygsgevangene*. Bloemfontein, South Africa: Nationale Pers, 1949.

Schrikker, Alicia, and Nira Wickramasinghe. *Being a Slave: Histories and Legacies of European Slavery in the Indian Ocean*. Leiden, The Netherlands: Leiden University Press, 2020.

Scoble, John. *British Guiana: Facts! Facts!! Facts!!!* London: Johnston & Barrett, Printers, 1840.

Sen, Simonti. *Travels to Europe: Self and Other in Bengali Travel Narratives 1870–1910*. New Delhi: Orient Longman, 2005.

Sexton, Jared. "Afropessimism: The Unclear Word." *Rhizomes: Cultural Studies in Emerging Knowledge* 29 (2016). https://doi.org/10.20415/rhiz/029.e02.

Sharma, Lalbihari. *I Even Regret Night: Holi Songs of Demerara*. Translated by Rajiv Mohabir. Los Angeles: Kaya Press, 2019.

Sharpe, Christina. *In the Wake: On Blackness and Being*. Durham, NC: Duke University Press, 2016.

Sharpe, Jenny. *Immaterial Archives: An African Diaspora Poetics of Loss*. Chicago: Northwestern University Press, 2020.

Sharpe, Jenny. "'Something Akin to Freedom': The Case of Mary Prince." *Differences* 8, no. 1 (1996): 31–56.

Shaw, D. J. "Thomas Pringle's Plantation." *Environment and History* 5, no. 3 (1999): 309–23.

Sheik, Ayub. "B D Lalla's *The Black Coolie*: A Struggle for a Voice." *Current Writing: Text and Reception in Southern Africa* 27, no. 1 (2015): 50–60.
Shell, Robert C.-H. *Children of Bondage: A Social History of the Slave Society at the Cape of Good Hope, 1652–1838*. Middletown, CT: Wesleyan University Press, 1994.
Shell, Robert C.-H. "The Short Life and Personal Belongings of One Slave, Rangton of Bali, 1673–1720." *Kronos* 18 (1991): 1–6.
Shell, Robert C.-H., and Archie Dick. "Jan Smiesing: Slave Lodge Schoolmaster and Healer, 1697–1734." In *Cape Town Between East and West*, edited by Nigel Worden, 128–52. Pretoria, South Africa: Jacana Media, 2012.
Shell, Robert C-.H., and S. E. Hudson. "Introduction to S. E. Hudson's 'Slaves.'" *Kronos* 9 (1984): 44–70.
Shimpo, Mitsuru, Ong Jin Hui, Steven Vertovec, Ravinder K. Thiara, Darshan Singh Tatla, and Michael Twaddle. "Asian Indentured and Colonial Migration." In *The Cambridge Survey of World Migration*, edited by Robin Cohen, 45–76. Cambridge: Cambridge University Press, 1995.
Shirer, William L. *Gandhi: A Memoir*. New York: Simon and Schuster, 2012.
Shockley, Evie. "Going Overboard: African American Poetic Innovation and the Middle Passage." *Contemporary Literature* 52, no. 4 (Winter 2011): 791–817.
Singh, Ansuyah R. *Behold the Earth Mourns*. Cape Town, South Africa: Cape Times Limited, 1960.
Sinha, Mrinalini. "The Strange Death of an Imperial Idea: The Case of *Civis Britannicus*." In *Oxford Handbook of Modernity in South Asia*, edited by Saurabh Dube, 29–42. Oxford: Oxford University Press, 2011.
Skaria, Ajay. "What Gandhi's Racism Tells Us about Anti-Racist Politics Today." *The Wire*, July 14, 2020. https://thewire.in/history/gandhi-racism-blacks-satyagraha-blm.
Smallwood, Stephanie E. "The Politics of the Archive and History's Accountability to the Enslaved." *History of the Present* 6, no. 2 (Fall 2016): 117–32.
Smallwood, Stephanie E. *Saltwater Slavery: A Middle Passage from Africa to American Diaspora*. Cambridge, MA: Harvard University Press, 2007.
Smethurst, Paul. "Introduction." In *Travel Writing, Form, and Empire: The Poetics and Politics of Mobility*, edited by Julia Kuehn and Paul Smethurst. London: Routledge, 2008.
Smith, Iain R., and Andreas Stucki. "The Colonial Development of Concentration Camps (1868–1902)." *Journal of Imperial and Commonwealth History* 39, no. 3 (2011): 417–37.
Soske, Jon. *Internal Frontiers: African Nationalism and the Indian Diaspora in Twentieth-Century South Africa*. Athens: Ohio University Press, 2017.
Sparrman, Anders. *A Voyage to the Cape of Good Hope, towards the Antarctic Polar Circle, and Round the World: But Chiefly into the Country of the Hottentots and Caffres, from the Year 1772, to 1776*. Vol. 2. 2nd ed. London: G.G.J. & J. Robinson, 1786.
Spivak, Gayatri Chakravorty. "Can the Subaltern Speak?" In *Marxism and the Interpretation of Culture*, edited by Cary Nelson and Lawrence Grossberg, 271–313. Champaign: University of Illinois Press, 1988.
Stoler, Ann Laura. *Along the Archival Grain: Epistemic Anxieties and Colonial Common Sense*. Princeton, NJ: Princeton University Press, 2009.

Stoler, Ann Laura. "Colonial Archives and the Arts of Governance." *Archival Science* 2 (2002): 87–109.

Subrahmanyam, Sanjay. "Connected Histories: Notes towards a Reconfiguration of Early Modern Eurasia." *Modern Asian Studies* 31, no. 3 (1997): 735–62.

Tannen, Deborah. *Talking Voices: Repetition, Dialogue, and Imagery in Conversational Discourse*. 2nd ed. Cambridge: Cambridge University Press, 2007.

Theal, G. M., ed. *Records of the Cape Colony: Copied for the Cape Government, from the Manuscript Records in the Public Record Office, London*. London: William Clowes and Sons, Limited, 1905.

Thomas, Helen. *Romanticism and the Slave Narratives: Transatlantic Testimonies*. Cambridge: Cambridge University Press, 2000.

Thomas, Sarah. *Witnessing Slavery: Art and Travel in the Age of Abolition*. New Haven, CT: Yale University Press, 2019.

Tinker, Hugh. *A New System of Slavery: The Export of Indian Labour Overseas, 1830–1920*. Oxford: Oxford University Press, 1974.

"Trial of the Naidoos and Others for Picketing." *Indian Opinion*, December 26, 1908. Reprinted in *The South African Gandhi. An Abstract of the Speeches and Writings of M.K. Gandhi, 1893–1914*, edited by Fatima Meer, 718–19. Durban, South Africa: Madiba Publishers, 1996.

Trollope, Anthony. *Australia and New Zealand*. Vol. 2. Cambridge: Cambridge University Press, 2013.

"UK Apology over Rendition Flights." BBC *News*, February 21, 2008. http://news.bbc.co.uk/2/hi/uk_news/politics/7256587.stm.

Ulrich, Nicole. "'Journeying into Freedom': Traditions of Desertion at the Cape of Good Hope, 1652–1795." In *A Global History of Runaways: Workers, Mobility and Capitalism, 1600–1850*, edited by Marcus Rediker, Titas Chakraborty, and Matthias van Rossum, 115–34. Berkeley: University of California Press, 2019.

Upham, Mansell George. "*Groote Catrijn*: Earliest Recorded Female *Bandiet* at the Cape of Good Hope: A Study in Upwards Mobility." *Capensis* 3, no. 97 (1994): 8–33.

Vahed, Goolam. "'An Evil Thing': Gandhi and Indian Indentured Labour in South Africa, 1893–1914." *South Asia: Journal of South Asian Studies* 42, no. 4 (2019): 654–74.

Van Blerk, J. A. *Op die Bermudas Beland: My herinneringe uit die Tweede Vryheidsoorlog*. Cape Town, South Africa: A.A. Balkema, 1949.

Van der Hoeven, T. *Gevangen op Ceylon*. Utrecht, The Netherlands: Bosch, 1901.

Van der Watt, J. S. *Leven der Boeren-krijgsgevangenen op Ceylon*. Pretoria, South Africa: ZA Boekhandel, 1905.

Van Hartesveldt, Fred R. *The Boer War: Historiography and Annotated Bibliography*. Westport, CT: Greenwood Publishing Group, 2000.

Van Rossum, Matthias, Alexander Geelen, Bram van den Hout, and Merve Tosun, eds. *Testimonies of Enslavement: Sources on Slavery from the Indian Ocean World*. New York: Bloomsbury Academic, 2020.

"Various Slave Returns, 1816–1834." Slave Office (SO) 7/36. Western Cape Archives and Records Service, Cape Town, South Africa.

Vaughan, Megan. *Creating the Creole Island: Slavery in Eighteenth-Century Mauritius*. Durham, NC: Duke University Press, 2005.

Vergès, Françoise. *Monsters and Revolutionaries: Colonial Family Romance and Metissage*. Durham, NC: Duke University Press, 1999.

Vigne, Randolph. *Thomas Pringle: South African Pioneer, Poet & Abolitionist*. Woodbridge, UK: Boydell & Brewer/James Currey, 2012.

Vine, David. *Island of Shame: The Secret History of the U.S. Military Base on Diego Garcia*. Princeton, NJ: Princeton University Press, 2009.

Vink, Markus. "'The World's Oldest Trade': Dutch Slavery and Slave Trade in the Indian Ocean in the Seventeenth Century." *Journal of World History* 14, no. 2 (2003): 131–77.

Visagie, L. A. *Terug na Kommando: Die Avonture van Willie Steyn en Vier Ander Krygsgevangenes*. Cape Town, South Africa: Nasionale Pers Beperk, 1932.

Von Braun, C. J. A. E. *Taktische Eindrucke Wahrend des Sudafrikanischen Krieges in Natal 1899–1900 Erganzt Wahrend der Kriegsgefangenschaft in St Helena 1901–1902*. Berlin: Eisenschmidt, 1903.

Voss, A. E. "The Personalities of Thomas Pringle." *English in Africa* 18, no. 1 (1991): 81–96.

Voss, A. E. "'The Slaves Must Be Heard:' Thomas Pringle and the Dialogue of South African Servitude." *English in Africa* 17, no. 1 (May 1990): 61–81.

Walker, Christine. *Jamaica Ladies: Female Slaveholders and the Creation of Britain's Atlantic Empire*. Chapel Hill: University of North Carolina Press, 2020.

Ward, Kerry. *Networks of Empire: Forced Migration in the Dutch East India Company*. Cambridge: Cambridge University Press, 2009.

War Office. *General Questions Relating to Boer & Foreign Prisoners of War Taken during the South African War, 1899–1902*. London: Harrison and Sons, 1905.

Welch, Dennis M. "Essence, Gender, Race: William Blake's Visions of the Daughters of Albion." *Studies in Romanticism* 49, no. 1 (2010): 105–31.

Wessels, A. *A Century of Postgraduate Anglo-Boer War (1899–1902) Studies: Masters' and Doctoral Studies Completed at Universities in South Africa, in English-speaking Countries and on the European Continent, 1908–2008*. Bloemfontein, South Africa: Sun Press, 2009.

Wessels, A. "Die Anglo-Boereoorlog (1899–1902) in die Afrikaanse Letterkunde: 'n Geheelperspektief." *Td Die Joernaal vir Transdissiplinêre Navorsing in Suider-Afrika* 7, no. 2 (December 2011): 185–204.

Wessels, Elria, ed. *Bannelinge in die Vreemde: Die Krygsgevangene van die Anglo-Boereoorlog, 1899–1902*. Pretoria, South Africa: Kraal Uitgewers, 2010.

Wheeler, Roxann. *The Complexion of Race: Categories of Difference in Eighteenth-Century British Culture*. Philadelphia: University of Pennsylvania Press, 2000.

White, Sophie. *Voices of the Enslaved: Love, Labor, and Longing in French Louisiana*. Chapel Hill: University of North Carolina Press, 2019.

Wickramasinghe, Nira. *Slave in a Palanquin: Colonial Servitude and Resistance in Sri Lanka*. New York: Columbia University Press, 2020.

Wicomb, Zoë. "South African Short Fiction and Orality." In *Telling Stories: Postcolonial Short Fiction in English*, edited by Jacqualine Bardolph, 157–70. Amsterdam: Rodopi, 2001.

Wicomb, Zoë. *Still Life*. New York: The New Press, 2020.
Wilderson, Frank B. *Afropessimism*. New York: Liveright, 2020.
Winslow, Miron. *Winslow's: A Comprehensive Tamil and English Dictionary*. Madras, India: Asian Educational Services, 1991 (1862).
Wood, Marcus. *Blind Memory: Visual Representations of Slavery in England and America, 1780–1865*. Manchester, UK: Manchester University Press, 2000.
Worden, Nigel. "Cape Slaves in the Paper Empire of the VOC." *Kronos*, no. 40 (2014): 23–44.
Worden, Nigel. "Indian Ocean Slaves in Cape Town, 1695–1807." *Journal of Southern African Studies* 42, no. 3 (2016): 389–408.
Worden, Nigel. *Slavery in Dutch South Africa*. Cambridge: Cambridge University Press, 2010.
Worden, Nigel, and Gerald Groenewald, eds. *Trials of Slavery: Selected Documents Concerning Slaves from the Criminal Records of the Council of Justice at the Cape of Good Hope, 1705–1794*. Cape Town, South Africa: Van Riebeeck Society for the Publication of South African Historical Documents, 2005.
Yang, Anand A. *Empire of Coolies: Indian Penal Labor in Colonial Southeast Asia*. Berkeley: University of California Press, 2021.
Yang, Anand A., Kamal Sheel, and Ranjana Sheel, eds. *Thirteen Months in China: A Subaltern Indian and the Colonial World: An Annotated Translation of Thakur Gadadhar Singh's Chīn Me Terah Mās*. Oxford: Oxford University Press, 2017.
Young, Hershini Bhana. *Illegible Will: Coercive Spectacles of Labor in South Africa and the Diaspora*. Durham, NC: Duke University Press, 2017.

INDEX

Note: page numbers followed by *f* refer to figures.

abolitionism, 66, 71; aesthetics of, 57
abolitionist discourse, 12, 22, 57, 92; American, 170n8
abolitionist movement (Cape), 22, 50, 52, 171n22
abolitionists, 12, 50, 58, 66, 81, 83, 93, 172n56; language of sentiment and, 4, 64, 70, 172n58; mimetic function of painting and, 76; writings by, 3, 49, 63, 98. *See also* Pringle, Thomas
affect, 3, 161n5
Afrikaner nationalism, 14, 112, 127–29
Afrikaner nationalists, 5, 14, 165n22
Afrikaners, 5, 124, 127, 129, 131, 139–41, 178n3
Allen, Richard B., 104, 162n15
ambiguity, 12, 42, 45, 99
amok, 26–28, 167n39
Andaman Islands, 85, 178n8
Anderson, Clare, 84–85, 103, 161n4, 178n8
antislavery: activism, 170n9; activists, 4, 12, 18, 49–50, 98; discourse, 49, 107; movement, 71, 101, 176n24; propaganda, 110; writings, 22, 27, 52, 101
apartheid, 14–15, 107, 128, 133; discourse of separateness of, 183n39; ideology, 16, 183n34; legal theory, 159; regime, 112; resettlement schemes of, 140; resistance writing under, 182n10; slavery as allegory for, 163n30; South African Indian fiction writing and, 134–35, 144, 153; state, 1, 184n45; theorists, 5, 9–10, 14, 131–32 (*see also* Cronjé, Geoffrey)
archive, 11, 43, 81; of enslavement, 12, 18, 22, 42; heartsore and, 68; imperial, 15; of

imperial control, 1, 10; legal, 3; official, 44, 74; silences of, 67; slave, 12, 44, 79; of slavery, 42, 76
archives, 5, 145; Caribbean, 169n2; contemporary art and, 81; enslaved speech and, 42, 44; enslaved voices in, 12; of enslavement, 19, 36, 43, 79; ledgers and, 73; legal, 1, 18, 20, 28, 32–33, 35, 83, 164n13, 165n18; of power, 11; slave, 36, 47; of slavery, 165n17; violence of, 43, 46
Arya, Usharbudh, 98, 177n64
Australia, 84, 144, 176n22

Bakhtin, Mikhail, 41, 168n77. *See also* heteroglossia
Bannerjee, Sukanya, 88, 175n8
Barnard, Rita, 140, 183n34
Barthes, Roland, 30–31
Batavia: slavery and, 6, 7f, 18, 24–25, 162n15; slaves returned to, 23
Bencoolen, 85, 178n8
Bengal, 7, 23f
Best, Stephen, 11, 15, 43–45, 168n80, 169n2
bhajan, 99–100, 107, 176n38
bittereinders, 112, 130
Black Atlantic, 18, 52, 161n2; abolitionists, 83; archive of enslavement in, 42; cultural imaginary of, 58; historiography of slavery in, 163n5, 168n80; imaginative sphere of, 84
Blackness, 15, 174n96
Black studies, 42, 76
Blake, William, 58, 61, 171n42, 171n44

Boer Republics, 9, 85, 110, 115, 133; Brink and, 123–24; De Villiers and, 125; sentiment and, 13, 112, 131. *See also* Orange Free State (Oranje Vrijstaat)

Boer war: concentration camps, 10, 112; suffering of, 5, 14

Boer war prisoners, 9–10, 111–12, 121, 116, 126, 129; imperial gaze of, 121; memoirs by, 10, 107, 123, 181n49; sentiment and, 3, 116; writings of, 107. *See also* Brink, J. N.

Brink, J. N., 9, 108–10, 121, 126; *Recollections of a Boer Prisoner of War in Ceylon*, 119–20, 122–24, 127

British Cape Colony, 3, 27, 47–53, 83–85, 111, 169n86; abolitionism and, 22, 67; colonial art from, 78; slavery in, 4, 8, 170n14. *See also* Council of Justice; Council of Policy; Pringle, Thomas; Sparrman, Anders

British Empire, 93, 100, 154, 179n15; anti-immigration laws in, 183n36; Brink and, 109; emancipation of the enslaved of, 8, 49, 78, 82; prisoner-of-war memoirs and, 110; sentiment and, 13, 112; war internment camps of, 116, 179n15, 180n25, 180n27 (*see also* Diyatawala)

British Guiana, 8, 84, 101–2

British India, 100, 103; *bittereinders* and, 112; indentured laborers from, 8, 85, 140; laborers from, 84; South Asian inhabitants of, 111; war prisoners in, 2, 9, 107, 125

British Indian Ocean Territory (BIOT), 154–56

British Romanticism, 58, 171n42. *See also* Blake, William; Wordsworth, William

Burger, A. P., 128–29

Burma, 84–85, 121, 178n8

Calcutta, 7*f*, 84, 87, 102, 122; in *Sea of Poppies* (Ghosh), 103, 105

Cape Colony. *See* British Cape Colony

Cape of Good Hope (Cabo de Goede Hoop), 7, 17, 22–25, 120; abolitionism in, 71 (*see also* Pringle, Thomas); British takeover of, 50–51; colonial writings in, 49; Dutch, 4, 44; slavery and, 2, 6, 17–18, 20, 52–53, 67–68, 71, 165n20, 166n27. *See also* Council of Justice; Council of Policy; Dutch East India Company

Ceylon, 15, 20, 157; indenture and, 84; slavery and, 6–7, 18, 23*f*, 45, 52, 161n4, 163n4, 170n20; war prisoners in, 2, 9, 109, 111–13, 116–26, 130, 181n61. *See also* Brink, J. N.; Dutch East India Company; Knox, Robert

Chagos Archipelago, 15, 154–58. *See also* British Indian Ocean Territory (BIOT)

Chamberlain, Joseph, 88, 92–93

Chanock, Martin, 137–38

children, 127, 132–33; Boer War concentration camps for, 10, 111–12, 179n12; enslavement and, 19, 39, 53–54, 56–57, 76; of indentured laborers, 83; Khoisan, 84

Christiansë, Yvette, 46, 67–68, 165n17. *See also* heartsore

civil servants, 12, 49

Coetzee, J. M., 29, 78, 134, 136, 138; *Foe*, 186n15; *White Writing*, 58, 129

colonialism, 11, 50, 60, 73, 101, 136, 184n45

complaints (legal), 93–97, 110

coolie, 85–88, 98–100, 106–7, 147–49, 175n12, 175n14, 176n36

coolitude, 105, 107

Coromandel: slavery and, 6–7, 23*f*

Council of Justice, 1, 17–20, 25–26, 32–33; delegates of, 37; documents, 25, 45; enslaved speech in, 22–24; records, 22, 26, 35, 45, 67

Council of Policy, 23, 25

Cronjé, Geoffrey, 10, 14, 131–32, 137–42, 144–45, 152–53; politics of, 183n39; rhetoric of, 183n34

Cugoano, Quobna, 18, 36, 50

Davis, Natalie Zemon, 36, 40, 164n13, 165n18

Defoe, Daniel, 181n46; *The Life and Strange Surprising Adventures of Robinson Crusoe*, 29–30, 122, 155–59. *See also* Knox, Robert

Desai, Ashwin, 147, 174n2

Desai, Gaurav, 103–4, 152, 184n45

De Villiers, J. L., 124–27

Diego Garcia, 156, 185n5

direct speech, 26, 32–34, 163n1, 167n44, 172n62; of the enslaved, 12, 18–22, 25, 28–31, 35, 37, 40, 42–46, 48–49, 57–59, 67, 69, 80; of Khoisan people, 24

displacement, 3, 9–11, 79, 101, 108, 148, 159; *Behold the Earth Mourns* (Singh), 135; forced, 2, 16; imperial, 16, 121, 155–56;

Indian Ocean and, 107, 161n4; involuntary, 6; legal narratives about, 15; oceanic, 5, 156
Diyatalawa camp, 13, 109, 112–13, 115–17, 126, 179n15, 179n19
Dutch East India Company (Vereenigde Oostindische Compagnie, VOC), 2, 6, 18, 31, 120; capital punishment and, 51, 164n11; Dutch legal system and, 164n13; settlements, 8; ships, 7; slavery and, 20, 22–25, 121, 165n21; territories, 50
Dutch Guiana, 8, 84
Dutch Timor, 7, 23f, 27
Dutch West India Company (WIC), 20, 22, 164n13, 165n21

East Africa, 184n45; indenture and, 8, 84; slavery and, 2, 7–8, 22–23, 51, 84, 155, 165n20. *See also* modernity: East African
emotion, 3, 12, 44, 78, 142, 161n5
enslaved persons, 2, 8, 22, 37, 51, 74, 79, 102, 120, 162n15, 166n27; direct speech by, 12; formerly, 50; imagined sentiments of, 18; sale of, 71
enslavement, 10, 15, 61, 68, 86; archives of, 12, 18–19, 22, 36, 42–43, 79; Atlantic Ocean history of, 103; conjugal love as alternative to, 60; indenture and, 107; racial dynamics of, 6; violence of, 79
Equiano, Olaudah, 18, 36, 50

Festa, Lynn, 22, 76, 78, 163n7, 172n53, 172n58, 176n24
Fiji, 8, 84, 105
Finley, Cheryl, 79–81
fiscals, 19, 35, 37, 48, 52, 69, 167n44
Foucault, Michel, 36, 168n70
Freeburg, Christopher, 15, 163n5
French Caribbean, 8, 84
Fuentes, Marisa J., 42, 164n10, 170n8

Gandhi, Mohandas K., 4, 9, 13, 83–85, 107–8, 133, 139, 161n8, 175n8, 182n3, 185n55; *Autobiography*, 10, 14, 98, 107, 132, 146–52, 182n3, 185n63, 185n65; celibacy of, 150, 185n64; on coolie, 86–88, 100, 102; *The Grievances of the British Indians in South Africa (Green Pamphlet)*, 4, 12, 87–94, 96, 98, 147, 152; *Indian Opinion*, 127. *See also* grievances; Lelyveld, Joseph

Ghosh, Amitav: *River of Smoke*, 102, 104; *Sea of Poppies*, 102–5, 107
Gikandi, Simon, 18, 74, 76, 161n2, 184n45
Global South, 6, 22, 162n10, 162n12; solidarities, 103; studies, 5
Goonam, Kesaveloo, 144–47
Gqola, Pumla Dineo, 15, 163n31, 166n27
Great Trek, 9, 111, 128
grievances, 50, 96, 107; material, 4, 9, 12–13, 83, 88–89, 92, 98, 100, 102; sentimental, 4, 12, 83, 88–89, 92–93, 132, 152, 176n22
Group Areas Act, 133, 135

Hartman, Saidiya, 15, 18, 41–44, 56, 78
heartsore, 46, 67–68
heteroglossia, 12, 41, 46
Hofmeyr, Isabel, 111–12, 128, 130, 162n10, 181n62, 184n44
Hudson, Samuel E., 12, 63–66, 74, 79, 81
Die Huisgenoot, 129–30, 181n60

immigrants: indentured, 99–100; nonindentured Indian, 137; permissible, 141; undesirable, 139; would-be, 152
Immigration Regulation Amendment Act, 135, 141, 147–48
imperialism, 16, 155; British, 140–41; European, 2; high, 124
indenture, 4–5, 8, 13, 82–86, 90, 98–102, 104–7, 133, 152–53, 175n14, 177n59; *Behold the Earth Mourns* (Singh) and, 144–45; Chagos Archipelago and, 155–56; Gandhi's writings on, 147, 151; *The Heart Knows No Colour* (Moodley) and, 146; in Kumar, 177n41; literatures of, 177n60; in Mauritius, 161n4; nineteenth-century, 162n17, 174n2, 176n24; in South Africa, 10, 145, 185n53. *See also* Ghosh, Amitav: *Sea of Poppies*
indenture contracts, 8, 10, 14, 82–87, 97, 100, 104, 137, 140, 145–46, 152, 183n34; *Coolie Doctor* (Goonam) and, 145; legal language of, 107, 133, 141; South African Indian writing and, 144. *See also* Cronjé, Geoffrey
indentured labor, 101, 103–4, 143; abolition of, 100; Cronjé on, 140; Gandhi on, 132, 175n8; in Natal, 87, 96, 174n7; representation of, 83; South Asian diaspora of, 84; sugar and, 182n17

Index · 207

indentured laborers, 2–3, 7f, 8, 12–13, 83–88, 90–91, 93–94, 97, 102–7, 132–33, 137, 140, 145–46, 177n58; Chagos Archipelago and, 155, 157; descendants of, 5, 14; Gandhi and, 147–49, 151–52; grievances of, 9; in Natal, 2, 13, 83–85, 87–88, 96, 98, 100, 174n7; legal complaints by, 83, 93, 98; sentiment and, 21

Indian Ocean, 1–3, 5–11, 13, 21, 157, 159, 170n21; British colonies in, 52, 178n8; communities, 51; displacement and, 2, 5–6, 107, 161n4; empire and, 9, 84, 154; indenture and, 13, 21, 104, 174n2; sentiment and, 5, 98; slavery and, 13, 18, 21, 162nn14–15; world, 1, 6, 14, 18, 82, 84, 86, 162n14. *See also* Chagos Archipelago; Dutch East India Company

indigeneity, 139, 156–57

Jamaica: indentured labor and, 84; slavery and, 164n10, 164n12
Java, 7, 23f, 27, 162n15
Johnson, David, 163n30, 166n28
Johnson, Walter, 42, 168n80

Kale, Madhavi, 101–2, 176n24
Khoisan people, 8, 24, 51, 66, 84, 164n11, 166nn27–29, 169n95
Kindersley, Jemima, 26–29
Knox, Robert, 15, 122–23, 157, 181n46, 186n10

labor, 2, 6, 10, 50, 60, 102, 145, 156; Black, 136, 174n96; coerced, 86; coolie, 100; forced, 7, 22; hard, 1, 46; migrant, 143, 174n7, 184n42; migration, 83–84; slave, 102–3, 158, 165n21. *See also* indenture; indentured labor
law, 10–11, 21, 25, 32, 43, 91, 98, 137–39; common, 136; coolie and, 87; indentured speech and, 94; language of, 97, 100, 141–42; material grievances and, 13; rhetoric of, 14, 133; speech in, 41; statute, 146
ledgers, 10; imperial, 11; slave, 12, 50, 71, 73–74, 76, 79–81
Lee, Debbie, 58, 171n42, 172n45
legal verisimilitude, 31, 37, 40, 45, 159; slave speech and, 12, 21–22, 29, 33, 35
Lelyveld, Joseph, 145, 148
Lionnet, Françoise, 10, 177n59
Lowe, Lisa, 3, 86

McKittrick, Katherine, 76, 81
Madagascar: slavery and, 6–8, 22, 23f, 51, 155, 161n4, 165n20
Madras, 7f, 9, 84, 87, 112
Malabar: slavery and, 6–7, 18, 23f, 163n4
Malacca, 7–8, 23f, 27, 85, 178n8
Malaya, 84, 112
Marossi, Hinza, 53, 60–64, 78, 172n48, 172n53
Mascarene Islands, 6, 52, 84, 165n20; literature of, 177n59
Mauritius, 32, 105, 144, 177n59; Chagos Archipelago and, 154–56; French, 18; indentured labor and, 84–85, 102–4, 107, 155, 161n4, 178n8; slavery and, 45, 155, 161n4, 163n4
Melayu language, 23, 26
memoirs, 119, 121; by Boer war prisoners, 10, 13–14, 107, 110, 112, 118, 123–24, 127–30, 152, 181n49 (*see also* Brink, J. N.)
Mesthrie, Rajend, 98–99, 176n36
migration: Chinese indentured, 84; forced, 21, 103, 155; labor, 13, 83–84, 100; from Mozambique, 174n7
Mishra, Vijay, 105, 107
modernity: East African, 152; European, 2
Mozambique: Boer war prisoners and, 112; migration from, 174n7; slavery and, 8, 22, 23f, 165n20

Natal, 8, 84, 107, 111, 133–34; Colonial-born Indians and, 184n50; coolie and, 86–87, 98–99, 106, 175n14, 176n36; hills, 144; Immigration Restriction Act, 137, 139; indentured laborers in, 2, 13, 83–85, 87–88, 96, 98, 100, 174n7; legislative assembly/council, 89, 93; sugarcane plantations in, 174n6. *See also* Gandhi, Mohandas K.; Singh, Ansuyah R.
nationalism, 124, 183n39. *See also* Afrikaner nationalism; Afrikaner nationalists
National Party, 112, 128, 133, 135, 181n59
nostalgia, 14, 17, 21, 49, 110, 117, 125

ocean studies, 5, 162n10, 162n12
Office of the Registrar and Guardian of Slaves, 12, 49, 52, 68, 70
Orange Free State (Oranje Vrijstaat), 9, 85, 109, 111, 115, 133

Page, Norman, 30–31
pamphlets, 31, 100; abolitionist, 36, 58, 83; Gandhi's, 4, 10–12, 83; on indenture, 101; political, 1, 3, 110; war prisoners and, 116, 118. *See also* Gandhi, Mohandas K.: *The Grievances of the British Indians in South Africa* (*Green Pamphlet*); Pringle, Thomas
Passenger Indians, 86, 88, 92, 184n50
Paton, Alan, 134; *Cry the Beloved Country*, 144
Paton, Diana, 164n10, 164n12
penal transportation, 84–85, 103
Philip, M. NourbeSe, 79, 174n97
Pratt, Mary Louise, 60–61, 110, 121, 126, 166n28, 169n95
Preller, Gustav S., 128, 181n62
De Prikkeldraad, 113, 114f, 118, 180n25
Prince, Mary, 50, 61; *The History of Mary Prince*, 53–54, 56–58, 66, 171n35
Pringle, Thomas, 4, 50, 52–53, 64–66, 70, 74, 93, 101, 107–8, 158, 161n9, 171n24; "The Bechuana Boy," 59–62, 78, 81; poetry of, 10, 12, 58–60, 71, 76; polemical writings of, 171n22; "The Slave Dealer," 61–62; "Slavery at the Cape of Good Hope," 53–58, 83; *South African Letters*, 171n32. *See also* Marossi, Hinza; Prince, Mary: *The History of Mary Prince*; Wicomb, Zoë: *Still Life*
prisoners of war. *See* Boer war prisoners; war prisoners

racialization, 3, 26, 29; of the enslaved, 4, 50, 66; sentiment and, 161n7
Rastogi, Pallavi, 135, 182n7, 184n44, 185n53
Robben Island, 1, 37
Roberts, Colin, 155–56, 158–59
Roberts, G. J., 68–69, 71

Scoble, John, 101–2
sentiment, 1, 3–5, 9–11, 19, 29, 33, 42, 49, 70, 78, 98, 100, 159, 161n7; abolitionist writings and, 4, 51, 54, 56–57, 59, 64, 107; anti-British, 116–18; Boer Republics and, 110; Cronjé and, 132, 141; displacement and, 15; the enslaved and, 13, 21; erasure of, 95; filial, 39; indenture and, 152; political discourse and, 89; race and, 27; slave, 34, 67; South African Indian writers and, 132; war prisoners and, 112–13, 123, 131

Seychelles, 154–56
Sharma, Lalbihari, 98, 105–6
Shell, Robert, 63, 66, 161n4, 165n20, 165n24
Singh, Ansuyah R., 132, 134; *Behold the Earth Mourns*, 10, 14, 132–36, 141–47, 150, 153, 182n17
slaveholders, 1–2, 4, 12, 17, 19, 27, 30, 37, 40, 62, 162n15, 170n4; coolie-money and, 86; diaries and letters of, 43; female, 38, 65, 166n32; powers of, 42; the sentimental and, 79; slaves testifying against, 21, 48–49, 52, 56, 68; speech of, 58, 65–66. *See also* Hudson, Samuel E.
slavery, 5–6, 8, 11, 13, 18–22, 28–29, 40, 51–52, 56–60, 62–63, 70–71, 78–79, 93, 105, 159, 161n4, 164n13, 166n27, 166n32, 170n8, 170n14; aesthetics of, 74, 76, 79, 171n38; as allegory for apartheid, 163n30; amelioration of, 49, 67; archives of, 42, 76, 165n17; Chagos Archipelago and, 155–56, 158; coolie and, 86; Dutch East India Company and, 165n21; end of, 82; filial relationships under, 37; forced migration networks of, 103; heteroglossic textual inscriptions of, 69; historiography of, 163n5, 168n80; indenture and, 102, 107; indenture as new system of, 83, 100–101, 104; Indian Ocean, 10, 162nn14–15; law and, 25; role of women in perpetuating system of, 38; Romantic aesthetic of, 50, 171n44; violence of, 53, 74, 78–79, 83; violence of research on, 15. *See also* abolitionism; abolitionists; Hudson, Samuel E.; Pringle, Thomas
slaves, 20–31, 37, 50–51, 55, 62, 64–66, 84, 93, 102, 158, 169n95; Chagos Archipelago and, 155, 157; coolie-money and, 86; Khoisan people and, 164n11, 166n27; legal complaints and, 52, 68; marriage between, 19; sentiment and, 3, 58, 63; silent, 71; speech/speaking and, 18, 39, 49, 59, 67, 74 (*see also* speech: enslaved; speech: slave). *See also* enslaved persons
slave trade, 81, 174n96; art and, 76; Atlantic, 6, 73, 104; British, 49; Dutch East India Company and, 165n21; end of, 8, 56, 68; public agitation against, 50; Robinson Crusoe and, 158; transatlantic, 6
Smallwood, Stephanie E., 11, 43, 73, 168n80

Index · 209

solidarity, 6; Indian Ocean and, 159; subaltern, 22
South Africa, 9–10, 133–36; apartheid-era, 4, 14; concentration camps in, 111–12; coolie and, 147; indenture in, 10, 145, 185n53; indentured labor in, 175n8; indentured laborers in, 8, 14, 84–85, 87, 137, 145; South Asians (British Indians) in, 5, 12, 14, 83, 85–86, 89, 92–93, 107, 127, 131–32, 135, 137–44, 146–47, 152, 183n39 (*see also* South African Indians); sugarcane plantations in, 182n17; war prisoners from, 180n25. *See also bittereinders*; Boer Republics; Brink, J. N.; Gandhi, Mohandas K.; Great Trek; National Party; Pringle, Thomas; *volk*
South African Indians, 137, 139, 142, 152; apartheid and, 135; Cronjé and, 153; indenture and, 183n34; writing by, 14, 107, 134–35, 144, 146, 153, 182n7, 184n44 (*see also* Gandhi, Mohandas K.; Goonam, Kesaveloo; Singh, Ansuyah R.)
South African Republic (Zuid-Afrikaansche Republiek), 9, 85, 111, 130, 133, 149
South African War, 112, 125; first, 9; second, 2, 9, 85, 107, 110–11, 122, 127, 130, 162n18, 178n4
South Asia, 9–10, 98–99; indenture and, 8, 84, 155; prisoner-of-war camps in, 129; slavery and, 6–7, 22, 51, 121, 165n20
Southeast Asia, 9, 24; Dutch, 27; penal settlements in, 178n8; slavery and, 2, 6–7, 22, 51, 121, 165n20
Sparrman, Anders, 27, 55, 167n41, 170n22
speech, 1–3, 9, 11–13, 25, 28, 41, 61, 79, 91, 159; acts, 35, 51; collective, 39; enslaved, 19, 22, 26, 30–32, 41–45, 49, 66–67, 80; impossible, 11, 46; indentured laborers and, 83, 90, 94–95, 103; instances of, 29; legal, 6; sentimental, 50; slave, 21, 40, 42, 49, 59; subaltern, 2, 13, 46, 82, 158. *See also* direct speech
Spivak, Gayatri C., 13, 46
Stoler, Ann Laura, 11, 87, 161n7, 165n18
Stowe, Harriet Beecher: *Dred*, 170n8; *Uncle Tom's Cabin*, 51
Straits Settlements, 85, 178n8
subaltern, the, 5, 13, 15, 46
subjectivity in bondage, 1, 7, 15; black, 18, 161n2

sugar, 144–45; plantations, 8, 104, 106, 136, 182n17
Sulawesi, 7, 27
Suriname, 20, 98, 105, 107, 177n64; Dutch, 164n13

Tannen, Deborah, 25–26, 30, 46
testimony, 30–32, 35; slave, 49, 74, 166n32
Tinker, Hugh, 100, 175n12
Torabully, Khal, 105–7, 161n4, 177n59
travel literature, 14, 107
travel narratives, 121, 123–24, 166n28, 169n95
travelogues, 36, 73, 122–23; imperial, 107, 110
Trinidad, 8, 84, 101, 105
Turner, J. M. W., 76, 78–79

untranslatability, 12, 42

Vahed, Goolam, 147, 174n2
Van Batavia, Jephta, 31, 33–35, 44–46, 171n49
Van Madagascar, Caesar, 1–3, 16, 159
Van Madagascar, Reijnier, 35–40, 46
Van Mallebar, Cupido, 17–20, 28, 46, 171n29
Vaughan, Megan, 32, 161n4, 163n4
violence, 11, 38; amok and, 26; of the archives, 43, 46; against the enslaved, 44, 168n73; imperial, 1; Indian Ocean and, 6; libidinal investment in, 43; research on slavery and, 15; of slavery, 53, 74, 78–79, 83; of slaves, 27, 29, 40, 49; speech and, 2
volk, 128–30, 140; Afrikaans, 127; Afrikaner, 131

war prisoners, 2, 7f, 9, 21, 110–12, 115, 118, 121, 124, 126–27; memoirs by former, 14, 110, 125; South African, 122. *See also bittereinders*; Boer war prisoners
Wicomb, Zoë: *Still Life*, 61, 171n24, 172n48
women, 40, 117, 127; Boer, 111; Boer War concentration camps for, 10, 112, 179n12; cruel, 65; enslaved, 25, 66, 170n8; indentured labor and, 93; role of, 37–38
Wordsworth, William, 58, 171n42

Young, Hershini Bhana, 100, 164–65n17, 166n32

www.ingramcontent.com/pod-product-compliance
Lightning Source LLC
Chambersburg PA
CBHW050243170426
43202CB00015B/2897